Policing

Development & Contemporary Practice

Peter Joyce

SAGE

Los Angeles | London | New Delhi
Singapore | Washington DC

First published 2011

Reprinted 2013

SAGE Publications Ltd
1 Oliver's Yard
55 City Road
London EC1Y 1SP

SAGE Publications Inc.
2455 Teller Road
Thousand Oaks, California 91320

SAGE Publications India Pvt Ltd
B 1/I 1 Mohan Cooperative Industrial Area
Mathura Road
New Delhi 110 044

SAGE Publications Asia-Pacific Pte Ltd
3 Church Street
#10-04 Samsung Hub
Singapore 049483

Library of Congress Control Number: 2009938436

British Library Cataloguing in Publication data

A catalogue record for this book is available from
the British Library

ISBN 978-1-84787-459-7
ISBN 978-1-84787-460-3 (pbk)

Typeset by C&M Digitals (P) Ltd, Chennai, India
Printed by Ashford Colour Press Ltd., Gosport, Hampshire.

MIX
Paper from
responsible sources
FSC® C011748

Policing

Contemporary Practice

1847874606

Sage

-

2011

To my wife Julie and my daughters Emmeline and Eleanor

Contents

List of acronyms

ACAS	Advisory, Conciliation and Arbitration Service
ACPO	Association of Chief Police Officers
AFO	Authorised Firearms Officer
APA	Association of Police Authorities
APACS	Assessment of Policing and Community Safety
BCU	Basic Command Unit
BME	Black and Minority Ethnic
BVPI	Best Value Performance Indicator
CAA	Comprehensive Area Assessment
CDRP	Crime and Disorder Reduction Partnership
CID	Criminal Investigation Department
CJPOA	Criminal Justice and Public Order Act
CPS	Crown Prosecution Service
CRE	Commission for Racial Equality
CSP	Community Safety Partnership
CSR	Comprehensive Spending Review
DPP	District Policing Partnership; also Director of Public Prosecution
DSSO	Diversity Staff Support Organisations
DVU	Domestic Violence Unit
DAW	European Arrest Warrant
EU	European Union
HMIC	Her Majesty's Inspectorate of Constabulary
HMCIC	Her Majesty's Chief Inspector of Constabulary
IOM	Integrated Offender Management
INI	Impact Nominal Index
IPCC	Independent Police Complaints Commission
LAA	Local Area Agreement
LCJB	Local Criminal Justice Board
LEN	Legal Enforcement Network
LGA	Local Government Association
LSCB	Local Safeguarding Children Board
LSP	Local Strategic Partnership
MACC	Mutual Aid Coordination Centre
MAPPA	Multi-Agency Public Protection Arrangements

MARAC	Multi-Agency Risk Assessment Conference
MPA	Metropolitan Police Authority
MPS	Metropolitan Police Service
NETCU	National Extremism Tactical Coordination Unit
NIC	National Information Centre
NCJB	National Criminal Justice Board
NDNAD	National DNA Database
NIM	National Intelligence Model
NPIA	National Policing Improvement Agency
NRC	National Reporting Centre
OCJR	Office for Criminal Justice Reform
PACE	Police and Criminal Evidence Act
PCT	Partnership and Communities Together
PAT	Problem Analysis Triangle
PCA	Police Complaints Authority
PCB	Police Complaints Board
PCSO	Police Community Support Officer
PDA	Personal Digital Assistant
PNC	Police National Computer
PND	Police National Database; also Penalty Notice for Disorder
PNICC	Police National Information and Coordination Centre
POP	Problem Oriented Policing
PPAF	Policing Performance Assessment Framework
PPO	Prolific and other Priority Offenders
PSA	Police Superintendents' Association
PSAs	Public Service Agreements
PSU	Police Support Unit
SARA	Scanning, Analysis, Response, Assessment
SIA	Security Industry Authority
SIS	Schengen Information System
SLA	Service Level Agreement
SOCA	Serious Organised Crime Agency
SPG	Special Patrol Group
YISP	Youth Inclusion and Support Panel
YOT	Youth Offending Team
ZT	Zero Tolerance

Key dates in the development of policing in the UK

The Statute of Winchester (1285)

The 1285 Statute of Winchester developed the Anglo-Saxon principle of local self-policing. It required all towns (initially in the summer months) to appoint a night watch to guard the entrances to the town and arrest suspicious strangers. This new system was referred to as 'watch and ward'. It also introduced the procedure of the hue and cry whereby all able-bodied citizens were required to help arrest a criminal.

The Dublin Police Act (1786)

The Dublin Police Act established the Dublin Metropolitan Police. This force was the first 'new' (or professional) police force, consisting of officers who were paid a wage, in the United Kingdom. The Dublin Metropolitan Police District was divided into four districts, each headed by a chief constable. A salaried magistrate was appointed to each of these districts, appointed by the Lord Lieutenant. The force was abolished as a separate organisation in 1925 when policing throughout the Irish Republic became the responsibility of the *Garda Siochana*.

The Glasgow Police Act (1800)

The 1800 Glasgow Police Act provided a professional police force for that city. It was financed by a rate levied on houses and businesses by the City Council and was under the control of the Lord Provost, three baillies (magistrates) and nine commissioners, who were elected each year from the traders and merchants of the city. The measure was the forerunner of similar Acts of Parliament affecting other cities and burghs throughout Scotland. A general power to establish professional police forces in the burghs was provided by the 1833 Burghs and Police (Scotland) Act and the Policing of Towns (Scotland) Act 1850. The General

Police and Improvement (Scotland) Act 1862 extended these powers to other urban areas.

The Irish Constabulary Act (1822)

This Act created a professional police force across Ireland. The barony (a Tudor unit of local government operating below the county) was the basic unit of police organisation. The Lord Lieutenant appointed a chief constable to each barony, which were in turn grouped into four provincial areas, and in each the Lord Lieutenant appointed an Inspector General (sometimes referred to as a General Superintendent). County rate-payers met half of the costs. The style of policing provided by the Irish Constabulary was paramilitary. Constables were armed and housed in barracks and police stations throughout Ireland. The Irish Constabulary was renamed the Royal Irish Constabulary in 1867 and provided the model for the Royal Ulster Constabulary when this force was set up after the partition of Ireland in 1922.

The Metropolitan Police Act (1829)

This Act established the first 'new' police force on mainland Britain, the Metropolitan Police Force. It covered all of London (with the exception of the City of London) and parts of the neighbouring counties of Middlesex, Surrey and Kent. The force was funded by a Police Rate, levied in each parish on those eligible to pay the Poor Rate. It was initially under the day-to-day control of two commissioners (since reduced to one) who were accountable to the Home Secretary.

The Municipal Corporations Act (1835)

This measure was concerned with the reform of local government. It established locally elected councils in urban Britain which were required to set up police forces. These were controlled by a committee of the council termed the Watch Committee and paid for by rates levied on local property owners. The Watch Committee initially exerted a considerable degree of control over local policing arrangements, including the appointment of the chief constable.

The Rural Constabulary Act (1839)

This Act gave magistrates at Quarter Sessions the *discretionary* power to establish professional police forces throughout the county, paid for out of the rates and controlled by a chief constable whom the magistrates appointed. Although subject to considerable control by the magistrates, county forces established by this Act were subject to a greater degree of supervision by the Home Secretary than their urban counterparts. This measure was not widely adopted for reasons that included cost and the concern that adopting the measure would entail the loss of the traditional ability of rural elites to retain control over the conduct of their own affairs.

The County and Borough Police Act (1856)

This legislation imposed a requirement on Watch Committees in towns and magistrates in rural areas to establish professional police forces in their locality. As an inducement to do this, central government offered a financial contribution towards the costs incurred by local forces (initially equivalent to one-quarter of the costs of pay and clothing). However, this money would be paid only if forces obtained a certificate to vouch that the force was conducted efficiently. This certificate was issued by an inspector who visited each force and reported back to the Home Office – the origins Her Majesty's Inspectorate of Constabulary.

The Police Act (1919)

Police strikes occurred in 1918 and 1919 that were organised by the National Union of Police and Prison Officers. The resultant 1919 Police Act forbade police officers to join trade unions or to go on strike but set up the Police Federation as a statutory advisory body to represent the views of police officers (now up to the rank of chief inspector) on all matters related to their welfare and efficiency. The Act also introduced a number of centralising measures into policing by enabling the Home Secretary to issue regulations concerning the conditions of work of police officers in areas that included government, pay and allowances.

The Police Act (1964)

The measure provided for a tripartite (or three-way) division of control whereby responsibility for the conduct of police affairs was shared between the Home Office, chief constables and police authorities. The latter were newly created by this legislation and were initially composed of two-thirds councillors and one-third magistrates for the area embraced by the police force. The 1964 Act sought to determine the precise responsibilities to be undertaken by each of these three partners and to define the relationships between them. The Act also enabled the Home Secretary to compel police force amalgamations, the first of which occurred in 1965.

The Local Government (Scotland) Act (1973)

This Act built upon the 1967 Police (Scotland) Act and reduced the number of police forces in Scotland to eight – six cover areas controlled by one regional authority and two cover more than one regional authority. These forces are maintained either by a police authority or a joint police board. Since 1999, policing has been a devolved responsibility to the Scottish government and comes under the overall jurisdiction of the Cabinet Secretary for Justice.

The Police and Criminal Evidence Act (1984)

The legislation gave the police a number of key powers, which included the ability to stop and search a person or a vehicle in a public place, enter private property, search the premises and seize material found there (with or without a warrant), arrest, take fingerprints and other non-intimate samples and detain a person in custody. The Act rationalised these powers across England and Wales, thus providing a national raft of police powers. The legislation introduced a number of safeguards to regulate the manner in which these powers were exercised, which were contained in the Act itself or in detailed Codes of Practice. The 1984 legislation abolished the Police Complaints Board and replaced it with the Police Complaints Authority.

The Prosecution of Offences Act (1985)

This measure established an independent service to prosecute persons charged with criminal offences. This task had formerly been carried out by the police. The Crown Prosecution Service (CPS) has undergone a number of changes since its formation, including the introduction of statutory charging by the 2003 Criminal Justice Act, which resulted in charging decisions for some offences being transferred from the police to the CPS.

The Convention on the Establishment of a European Police Office (1995)

The Convention on the Establishment of a European Police Office (Europol) was drawn up by the European Council in July 1995 and it was created in 1998. Europol is funded by EU member states and its work is conducted by liaison officers seconded to Europol headquarters from police organisations of member countries. Europol is not responsible for conducting criminal investigations, but serves as an intelligence agency to facilitate the exchange of information between police organisations of member states and to analyse information received from them in connection with transnational crime.

The Police and Magistrates' Courts Act (1994)

This legislation significantly increased the powers of the Home Office over policing. The main provisions of this Act were to enable the Home Secretary to set national objectives (later termed 'ministerial priorities' and now 'ministerial objectives') for the police service and to devise performance targets to assess their attainment. The Act also introduced cash-limited budgets, thereby enhancing the government's control over expenditure. Police authorities became free-standing bodies whose key role was to draw up an annual, costed, local policing plan, which contained a statement of national and local objectives, performance indicators and finances available. The composition of police authorities was also amended by the introduction of independent members alongside councillors and magistrates.

The Police Act (1996)

This measure consolidated a number of reforms that had been previously made to the governance of policing and, additionally, developed earlier legislation by making incremental adjustments to changes that had already been introduced. The powers of the Home Secretary were further enhanced to include responsibility for promoting the efficiency and effectiveness of the service, to determine objectives for police authorities, to issue codes of practice for police authorities, to set minimum budgets and to give directions to police authorities where inspection had found them to be inefficient or ineffective.

The Crime and Disorder Act (1998)

The 1998 Act required the police service to engage in multi-agency (or partnership) arrangements. These included crime and disorder reduction partnerships (CDRPs) (termed community safety partnerships (CSUs) in Wales) whose role was to develop and implement a strategy for reducing crime and disorder in each district and unitary local authority in England and Wales. The Act also provided for the establishment of multi-agency Youth Offending Teams drawn from local authority education and social services departments, the probation and health services and the police, which perform a number of functions relating to youth offending.

The Local Government Act (1999)

This Act introduced the principle of best value as a mechanism to improve the performance of police forces. Best value required local authorities, police authorities and fire and rescue service authorities (termed Best Value Authorities) to secure continuous improvement in the delivery of its services in order to achieve the objectives specified in the legislation of economy, efficiency and effectiveness.

The Human Rights Act (1998)

The 1998 Human Rights Act incorporated the provisions of the European Declaration of Human Rights into UK domestic law. The practical impact of this was that complaints by UK citizens alleging that their human rights had been flouted by public authorities, which included the police service, could now be determined by domestic courts rather than requiring the citizen to approach the European Court of Human Rights.

The Greater London Assembly Act (1999)

The Home Secretary had exercised the role of the police authority for the Metropolitan Police Service since its creation in 1829. This situation was ended by the 1999 legislation which established the Greater London Assembly and an independent Metropolitan Police Authority (MPA) to oversee policing in London. The role of the MPA is similar to that performed by police authorities elsewhere in England and Wales and includes approving the police budget set by the Mayor of London.

The Regulation of Investigatory Powers Act (2000)

The 2000 legislation lays down circumstances under which an individual's right to privacy (guaranteed by the European Declaration of Human Rights) can be infringed by the state when investigating serious crime. This Act developed existing safeguards related to *intrusive surveillance* (surveillance conducted in a private location where a presumption of privacy would normally apply), enabling a range of agencies that included the police to obtain warrants from a Secretary of State to intercept telephone calls and other forms of electronic communication such as emails and internet usage. Covert intelligence-gathering (or *directed surveillance*), including the use of informants, was also subject to the Act. This typically takes place in a public place and is authorised by police officers, whose actions are subject to a Code of Practice.

The Police (Northern Ireland) Act (2000)

This legislation created a new police force for Northern Ireland to replace the Royal Ulster Constabulary. It is supervised by the Northern Ireland Policing Board, composed of 19 political and independent members. The features of the Police Service of Northern Ireland include the recruitment of new members on the basis of 50% Catholics and 50% non-Catholics from April 2002 until a target figure of 30% Catholic membership has been attained. Responsibility for policing and criminal justice was devolved to the Northern Irish Assembly in April 2010.

The Police Reform Act (2002)

The 2002 Police Reform Act focused on the performance culture of the service. It enhanced the power of central government through mechanisms that included the production of a national policing plan and the issuance of codes of practice for chief constables to promote the efficiency and effectiveness of police forces. The Home Secretary could require Her Majesty's Inspectorate of Constabulary (HMIC) to inspect a force and direct police authorities to institute remedial measures where the inspection indicated the force was not effective or efficient. The minister was also empowered to direct the police authority to submit an action plan as to how deficiencies of this nature would be addressed. The 2002 Act also replaced the Police Complaints Authority with the Independent Police Complaints Commission, which could appoint non-police personnel to investigate some complaints made against the police.

The Serious Organised Crime and Police Act (2005)

The 2005 Act created a Serious Organised Crime Agency (SOCA). It is headed by a Director-General and the organisation is accountable to the Home Secretary, who is responsible to Parliament for its performance. The main advantage of SOCA was that it brought together under one organisational roof a number of bodies that were concerned with combating serious crime. These included the National Criminal Intelligence Service, the National Crime Squad and aspects of work performed by HM Customs and Excise and the Home Office. The agency was given a number of important powers with which to tackle serious crime, including compulsory powers to compel individuals to cooperate with investigations by answering questions, providing information or producing documents.

The Police and Justice Act (2006)

This legislation amended the composition of police authorities whereby magistrates ceased to be a specific membership category. The Act also removed the requirement for police authorities to conduct best value reviews and prepare best value plans, although it is still required to operate according to best value criteria. The Act also removed the requirement on the Home Secretary to publish a national policing plan, but the minister was alternatively given the power to determine the strategic priorities for police authorities following consultation with the Association of Police Authorities (APA) and Association of Chief Police Officers (ACPO).

Preface

This book is concerned with the development and contemporary practice of policing in England and Wales. It aims to place contemporary policing within its historical context and to consider current and future developments within the framework of previous practice.

Chapter 1 provides a brief historical account of the development of a professional system of policing in the early decades of the nineteenth century. It examines the factors that caused the breakdown of the old parish constable system and considers the nature and philosophy of the new system that replaced it. Particular attention is devoted to the methods that were adopted to secure the concept of policing by consent that characterises policing in England and Wales, and the extent to which this principle had been achieved by the end of the nineteenth century.

A key function of the reformed system of policing was to combat crime. Chapter 2 considers the methods that were adopted to achieve this and particularly focuses on the period since 1945 when key changes affecting the scale and nature of crime have underpinned a number of developments affecting the methods, structure, organisation and weaponry of the police service and the appliance of technological developments to police work.

In order to combat crime the police may require powers that are additional to those possessed by ordinary members of the general public under common law. The topic of police powers is the focus of Chapter 3. Initially, police powers developed on a piecemeal, and frequently localised, basis but they were rationalised in the 1984 Police and Criminal Evidence Act, which provided a standardised raft of police powers across England and Wales. The significance of this Act in terms of policing and in connection with safeguarding the rights of the general public in their dealings with the police is considered in this part of the book, which also includes a discussion of the police complaints machinery.

The issue of police powers is closely allied to methods of policing. Chapter 4 considers the ways in which policing has been delivered since 1829 and the rationale for changes that have resulted in the development of new styles of policing. Preventive, reactive and proactive police methods are analysed and there is a full discussion of new approaches that include problem-oriented policing, zero tolerance policing and neighbourhood policing.

The discussion in Chapter 4 regarding the delivery of policing is extended in Chapter 5, which considers the role played by the police within the criminal justice system. It examines the relationship between the police and other agencies such as the Crown Prosecution Service and considers the role of the police service in contemporary developments that have sought to produce a 'joined-up' system of criminal justice.

Chapter 6 is concerned with the governance of policing. It examines chrono-logically the key changes that have affected the control and accountability of the police service in England and Wales and seeks to provide an understanding of the forces, such as the new public management agenda, that have promoted change. The chapter also seeks to consider the significance of developments associated with the empowerment agenda on the future governance of the service.

The relationship between police and public is an important aspect of police control and accountability. Chapter 7 examines this issue with specific reference to diversity. It examines the extent to which the police service has affectively responded to the challenges posed by race and gender issues and places particular emphasis on the extent to which the police service has successfully applied the recommendations put forward by Sir William Macpherson in his 1999 report. It also evaluates what further steps are required to enable the police service to truly represent the society that it polices.

Chapter 8 examines the political orientation of police work. It examines two main areas – the development of processes and procedures that were put forward in the latter decades of the twentieth century to enable the service to respond to manifestations of protest and dissent, and the significance of these developments in connection with political rights and civil liberties. It also considers the role of agencies that include the Security Service (MI5) in tackling subversion. This chap-ter examines the way in which various organisations within the police service (such as the Association of Chief Police Officers and the Police Federation) seek to influence the police policy agenda.

Crime has developed considerably since the formation of professional policing in the nineteenth century and increasingly assumes an international dimension. Chapter 9 considers the global dimension of crime and how supranational bodies such as the European Union have developed policing and criminal justice initia-tives to counter it.

The final chapter focuses on the issue of financing the police service, and is especially concerned with the impact that financial restraints may exert over the future operations of the service.

I would like to thank Peter Shipley (formerly editor of the ACPO journal, *Policing Today*), Neil Wain (Chief Superintendent in the Greater Manchester Police Force) and my colleague at MMU, Graham Smyth, who have contributed ideas or material for this book. A number of extremely helpful comments were also received from two reviewers (both anonymous). I would also like to pay tribute to Sarah-Jayne Boyd and Caroline Porter for commissioning this work and for their considerable patience relating to its preparation.

Peter Joyce
January 2010

1

The emergence and development of professional policing

CHAPTER AIMS

The aims of this chapter are:

- To discuss the historical development and the key characteristics of the old policing system and methods of law enforcement;
- To consider the factors that resulted in the breakdown of this system during the course of the eighteenth century and to analyse reasons for the reluctance to embark upon a root-and-branch reform of policing at that time;
- To examine the progress of police reform from 1829 until the end of the nineteenth century;
- To provide an understanding of the principle and practice of the concept of policing by consent and to evaluate the extent to which this ideal had been attained in England and Wales by the end of the nineteenth century;
- To briefly identify the current structure and organisation of policing in England and Wales, Northern Ireland and Scotland.

The old policing system – key developments

The origins of the English system of policing are to be found in the Anglo-Saxon period (400–1066), in which the onus on preventing wrongdoings and initiating against those who had broken the law was placed on the local community and those who were victims of crime (Rawlings, 2008: 47). This system emphasised the mutual responsibility of all inhabitants for law enforcement, in which all became responsible for each other's conduct.

The basis of this Anglo-Saxon system was that small groupings of people were organised into tythings, which consisted of ten households and were headed by a tythingman, who was the forerunner of the office of constable, which emerged during the reign of Edward III during the fourteenth century. In addition to detaining suspected criminals, one of the constable's key functions in that period was to summon the militia. Later, in the Tudor period, functions that related to administering the poor law and enforcing action against vagrants were added to the constables' duties. Tythings were grouped into hundreds, a subdivision of the county (the larger ones of which were divided into units, frequently termed divisions). The hundred was headed by a hundred-man, who exercised a number of functions that included the administration of justice and organising the supply of troops. The office was held by local notables. The hundred-man was responsible to the shire-reeve (or sheriff) who was in charge of the county whose rule was enforced through the sherriff's courts.

The Norman Conquest (1066) developed this Anglo-Saxon system in a number of important ways. The system of frankpledge built upon the existing principle that households grouped in tythings should exercise joint responsibility for each other's conduct by requiring all adult males to be members of a tything and to swear an oath that they would conduct themselves in a lawful manner. The 1166 Assize at Clarendon required the tything to denounce to the sheriff those of its members suspected of having committed a crime, and the accusation was initially investigated by the tythingman and a jury of 12 members and took place at the tything frankpledge hearings.

The 1285 Statute of Winchester, passed in the reign of Edward I, was an important development in the history of policing in England. It provided for the appointment of two high constables in each hundred, below which were the petty constables in each tything. It also established the principle of local responsibility for police-related matters by introducing the procedure of the hue and cry, whereby all able-bodied citizens were required to help arrest a criminal and required the hundred to compensate the victim of a robbery when the hue and cry had been raised but the offender had escaped.

It also compelled all towns (initially in the summer months) to establish a night watch to guard the entrances to the town and to arrest suspicious strangers. The constable was responsible for supervising these arrangements, which also included improved arrangements for day policing. This new system was referred to as 'watch and ward' (watch by night and ward by day). The duty to participate in the watch was placed on all householders and its role was subsequently developed to that of keeping good order in the town at night.

Law enforcement

The early system of law enforcement reflected the power relationships that were characteristic of feudalism – the absence of strong central authority and the dominance of the aristocracy. However, attempts were made to enhance the degree of central control over the system of policing and law enforcement following the

Norman Conquest. Officials termed 'Keepers of the Peace' were appointed by Richard I in 1195 to preserve the peace in disturbed areas, and in 1327 Conservators of the Peace were appointed in each county to help preserve law and order. In 1361, Edward III subsequently appointed 'a good and lawful man' in each county, whose role was to maintain the peace and whose functions subsequently expanded into more general forms of law enforcement. These adopted the title given to them in the 1361 legislation as 'justices of the peace', who later assumed the title of 'magistrate' in the sixteenth century. These developments were at the expense of traditional feudal power relationships, one feature of which was the declining role performed by the sheriff towards the end of the twelfth century. By the end of the eleventh century this office tended to be filled by powerful members of the aristocracy, whose power became viewed as a threat to the monarch.

Justices were appointed by the monarch and owed their allegiance to him. The 1361 Act required that the Justices should meet four times a year to transact business, providing the origins of the Quarter Sessions. Subsequently, in 1605, provision was made for the holding of local sessions, where no jury was required, to conduct minor affairs. This was the origin of Petty Sessions, although this procedure was not given statutory recognition until 1828.

This measure helped to erode the feudal power structure, since those who were appointed as Justices tended to be landowning gentry rather than the feudal elite whose power rested on the ownership of large estates (or 'manors') and were termed the 'lords of the manor' (or court baron). Matters pertaining to the administration of manorial affairs (such as manorial lord–tenant relationships) were dispensed through the manorial court, which was presided over the lord of the manor's steward. Above the manorial court stood the hundred court, whose role extended to the administration of law and order. Some manors were given the judicial powers of hundred courts by the Crown and were termed 'courts leet'.

The appointment of constables was technically a matter for the manorial courts or the courts leet, a procedure that helped to assert the pre-eminence of the Justices over the constables and provided the backbone for the 'old' policing system that was in place until the early decades of the nineteenth century. However, as the role of parishes as a unit of local administration increased during the Tudor period, appointments were sometimes made at this level. This trend was accelerated following the restoration of the monarchy in 1660, although manorial courts continued to appoint parish constables in some areas until their role was formally ended by the 1842 Parish Constables Act, when it was transferred to the Justices at Quarter Session.

Policing during the eighteenth century

By the eighteenth century a system of policing had evolved that was based on constables appointed in each locality (which was often the 'parish' although other jurisdictions such as 'township' were also used), whose role was ultimately supervised by magistrates (although intermediaries such as Head of High Constables appointed by the magistrates at Quarter Session might exercise a more detailed element of supervision). The constables were generally unpaid (although there were some rare local exceptions to this) but they were able to obtain income from fees derived from the administration of justice. They typically served in office for one year.

This system of policing was faced with a number of problems during the eighteenth century. The role of constables expanded beyond the enforcement of law and order into a wide range of additional functions that included the inspection of alehouses and exercising supervision over the night watch. The duties that the office entailed often resulted in a reluctance to serve by those who were selected, and this problem became more acute as the industrial revolution progressed. The industrial revolution created a new class of urban middle-class property-owners with businesses to run and little time to devote to civic affairs.

In some areas, those who were chosen to act as constables were able to appoint deputies. This procedure was formalised by legislation affecting Westminster in 1756 (Rawlings, 2008: 51) but was not universally permitted. Where it was sanctioned, concern was sometimes expressed by contemporaries concerning the calibre of those who stepped into the office, some of whom were 'scarcely removed from idiotism' (Critchley, 1978: 18). Additionally, by the end of the seventeenth century, a person who apprehended a felon received exemption from a judge (in the form of a certificate commonly called a 'Tyburn Ticket') from serving as a parish constable. These could be sold to persons appointed to this role, who thus had to be replaced by an alternative whose dedication in performing the tasks required of a constable might be lacking.

Voluntarism was also a feature of the night watch, whose functions expanded into that of providing a system of night police in urban areas. In 1735 legislation affecting two London parishes was passed whereby householders substituted the duty to serve in the watch for the ability to pay a rate to employ watchmen (often referred to as 'Old Charlies') to discharge this responsibility, whose role extended to maintaining social order by taking action against drunkenness and prostitution and targeting persons who were acting suspiciously. Rawlings (2008: 53) observed that by the end of the eighteenth century ventures of this nature (the Watch Acts) extended to other areas of London and beyond.

A further problem affected the magistrates. Although in rural areas these tended to be landowners, shortages of these officials in the towns required selection from other social groupings whose commitment to civic duty was sometimes surpassed by an enthusiasm to use the office as a source of personal gain. This was a particular problem in London, where 'trading justices', who were styled 'a byword for corruption' (Landau and Beattie, 2002: 46), brought considerable disrepute on the office of magistrate by exploiting it in ways that included exacting fees for performing their duties, retaining fines they levied from criminals and colluding with informants. This led to the replacement of unpaid magistrates in London with salaried stipendiaries who operated from Bow Street and latterly from a further seven police offices established by the 1792 Middlesex Justices Act. This reform is discussed in more detail below.

The need for fundamental reform

A key difficulty with the old system of policing was that its organisational base (the parish or township) was too small and the numbers of constables supplemented by watchmen too low to counter contemporary crime and public disorder problems or to curb manifestations of immoral behaviour. Although it was impossible to gauge 'real' levels of crime, contemporary observations suggested that 'from the last quarter of the eighteenth century through to the 1820s problems of crime and order maintenance were regarded as particularly acute (Rawlings, 2002: 106).

This issue became a crisis in urban areas where the growth of towns that accompanied the agricultural and industrial revolutions made for transient populations which the historic system could not police effectively. Features of the old system of policing, such as raising the hue and cry, fell into disuse in this changed social setting. It led to the conclusion that 'the breakdown in law and order marched in step with the industrial revolution' (Critchley, 1978: 21). Many contemporaries viewed crime as spiralling out of control while the only solution to outbreaks of disorder was to deploy the military. However, the time taken to move troops from their barracks on to the streets and the cumbersome procedure through which they could be deployed (requiring a magistrate to 'read the Riot Act') often provided time for a riot to take a firm hold. The likely response of the troops was to shoot protesters, which smacked of tyrannical government. These problems were evidenced in the 1780 anti-Catholic Gordon riots, which took place on 2–9 June and entailed the use of cavalry and infantry. Almost 300 people died in this event and around 200 were severely injured.

Attempts to substitute the military with volunteer organisations, which included the yeomanry, failed to offer an effective remedy, as was revealed in the Peterloo massacre that took place in St Peter's Fields, Manchester, in 1819. Here the death of 11 people and the wounding of over 400 people attending a political demonstration emphasised the need for a non-military force to maintain public order.

Police reform during the eighteenth century

Although the old policing system was failing to cope with contemporary crime and law and order problems in English towns, there was a considerable degree of reluctance to institute a root-and-branch reform of the old system. There were several reasons for this, including the sporadic character of crime and disorder, which failed to exert a constant pressure to bring about reform (Critchley, 1978: 41). However, the key explanation for this situation was the desire of local elites to retain control over their own localities. Their concern rested on a perception that a reformed system of policing would be under the control of central government (as was the case in France). It was presented in a manner that went beyond the selfish defence of vested interests to argue that centralised control would lead to abuses, in particular undermining the 'rights and liberties' of English people. This view was shared by 'aristocratic Tories and working class radicals alike' (Reiner, 1985: 13), and was encapsulated in a petition presented to Parliament by Sir Robert Wilson MP in 1830, who argued that the police force could be used 'to crush the liberties of the people' (Sir Robert Wilson, quoted in Rawlings, 2002: 123).

Objections to the creation of a French-style 'Bourbon police force' were especially evident when, in the wake of the 1780 Gordon Riots, William Pitt's government brought forward a Bill in 1785 to provide for a unified policing system across London to be controlled by three salaried commissioners. Criticism was voiced concerning the powers given to those who would be appointed as police officers under the new arrangements, and also to the nature of control exerted over the new force. On this occasion, opposition from the City of London (which was unhappy about being incorporated into the rest of London under these proposals, thus undermining its self-governing status) succeeded in blocking it. Consequently, a number of initiatives were put forward which sought to prop up rather than replace the old system of policing. The key measures to secure this more limited objective are discussed below.

Thief-takers

One development to remedy weakness in the historic system of policing was through the use of private detectives. The role of private detectives, or what has been termed 'freelance thief takers' (Rawlings, 2008: 65), was to secure the return of stolen good and/or bring criminals to justice. Thief-takers were paid either by the victim of a crime or from a reward offered by the government in connection with a serious crime such as highway robbery. It was a practice that accelerated in the late eighteenth century. They thus filled a void in the system of policing as the role of constables did not extend to the investigation and prosecution of crime.

However, this system was subject to abuse. Thief-takers might organise the theft of goods and then secure payment for their return or they might extort money from a thief as the price of not handing them over to the authorities. A particular abuse was to act as a go-between between thief and victim to secure the return of stolen property in return for a fee (Morton, 2002: 39–41). This situation was catered for in legislation enacted in 1717 termed the Jonathan Wild Act. This measure, which was named after the infamous thief-taker Jonathan Wild, made it a capital offence to receive a reward under the pretext of helping an owner to secure the return of goods in cases where no thief was prosecuted.

Although the system of private thief-takers was prone to serious abuse (and in this sense can be regarded as an undesirable aspect of the old system of policing), it was not totally ineffective in dealing with criminal activities. Contemporary accounts observed that following Jonathan Wild's execution in 1725 far fewer criminals were brought to justice (Morton, 2002: 43). The role of thief-takers was adversely affected by powers given to magistrates during the 1830s to deny thief-takers a reward. However, they were the forerunners of informants, whose role is discussed in Chapter 2.

The system of privately-employed thief-takers was supplemented in the eighteenth century by those who were financed through public funds. This system originated with the employment by individual magistrates of their own constables to supplement parish constables. An important example of this was the Bow Street Runners, organised by the Fielding brothers who were the Chief Magistrates at Bow Street, London, between 1748 and 1780. The role of the runner was to detect crimes reported to the magistrates' office.

The force was initially paid for by rewards obtained from apprehending criminals (which might be provided by government in order to secure a conviction) and later by a central government grant. Its key significance in the development of policing was that it was outside the control of the parishes within which it operated (Rawlings, 2008: 56). This model was more widely adopted throughout London (with the exception of the City of London) under the provisions of the 1792 Middlesex Justices Act, whereby seven police offices were set up, staffed by stipendiary magistrates who supervised a small number of paid police officers.

Private police forces

The formation of private police forces was designed to protect the interests of those who paid for them. An important example of this was the Marine Police, instigated at the suggestion of the London magistrate Patrick Colquhoun in 1798 and initially paid for by merchants operating on the River Thames. This was given official status under the 1800 Thames River Police Act, whose superintending magistrates were under the direct control of the Home Secretary.

Policing arrangements associated with Improvement Acts

The employment of paid police officers by ratepayers to supplement the parish constables was a development that occurred in some of the larger urban areas in the late eighteenth and early years of the nineteenth century. It secured Parliamentary approval in the form of Improvement Acts. This legislation authorised rates to be collected to pay for a wide range of municipal services whose actions were supervised by an elected body of ratepayers. An important example of this was the 1792 Manchester and Salford Police Act, which permitted rates to be levied on householders to pay for a range of services that included 'the cleansing, lighting watching and regulation (of) the streets, lanes, passages and places within the towns of Manchester and Salford'. These functions were superintended by an elected body of ratepayers termed 'commissioners'.

The policing arrangements provided for by legislation of this nature were typically a night watch that operated alongside a day police controlled by the parish constables, whose appointment remained governed by the historic feudal arrangements. The constables could be aided in their work by paid officials such as Beadles.

Legislation of this nature could prove costly and was an option usually adopted by large and wealthy towns, although the 1847 Town Police Clauses Act provided a *pro forma* for local acts of this nature which could be adopted in areas not included in the 1835 Municipal Corporations Act (Steedman, 1984: 15). Additionally, the 1833 Lighting and Watching Act provided a general power for localities to appoint a small number of paid constables. These were controlled and directed by a small committee of 'inspectors' who were elected by ratepayers. The importance of this legislation to the policing of small towns is discussed by Davey (1983).

Back-up forces to aid in an emergency

Civil emergencies typically took the form of public disorder. The military could be summoned by the civil authority (a magistrate) to deal with the situation but, as has been noted above, this course of action was often inappropriate.

The 1831 Special Constables Act permitted magistrates to enrol special constables in times of emergency. This Act built upon earlier measures in 1673 and 1820, providing for the temporary (but compulsory) enrolment of citizens to deal with specific emergencies. The 1831 Act retained the element of compulsion but this was abandoned in 1835 when legislation made membership of the Special Constabulary a voluntary choice. It was observed, however, that the Special Constabulary was hardest to recruit in the areas where it was most needed, a problem arising from the lack of a substantial middle class in the manufacturing districts (Mather, 1959: 83).

Accordingly, the 1843 Enrolled Pensioners Act provided for the compulsory enrolment of out-pensioners of Chelsea hospital as special constables as a response to public order emergencies, and a further Act of 1846 made similar provisions for out-pensioners of Greenwich hospital (Mather, 1959: 87).

The reinvigoration of the parish constable system

Crime and disorder were not confined to urban areas, and episodes that included the swing riots and anti-poor law disturbances during the 1830s affected rural areas in the early decades of the nineteenth century. Although the formation of a professional police force was one option available to rural areas following the passage of the 1839 Rural Constabulary Act, as is discussed below, there was a reluctance to do this. As a result, attempts were made to revitalise the operations of the old parish constable system.

The 1842 Parish Constables Act provided for the supervision of parish constables (who could be voluntary or paid) by a superintending constable who was paid for from the county rate and was under the exclusive control of the local Justices. Some areas continued to appoint parish constables even after the creation of a professional policing force under the provisions of the 1856 County and Borough Police Act. Their appointment remained possible under the 1872 Parish Constables Act if the Quarter Sessions felt the appointment justified or where the parish requested the magistrates to do so.

The development of the new system of policing

The attempts discussed in the previous section to prop up the old system of policing rather than introduce root-and-branch reform met with varying degrees of success. Night watches provided for under Improvement Acts, for example, sometimes offered a relatively effective form of policing (Joyce, 1993: 199–201), some features of which (such as the use of beat patrols) became a subsequent feature of 'new' police forces when these were introduced. Other reforms were, however, less effective. The 1842 Parish Constables Act, for example, was branded a 'complete failure' (Brown, 1998: 178), and there was no consistency in the way in which policing was delivered throughout England and Wales.

These deficiencies justified the establishment of a new, professional, system of policing, in which those who performed the office were paid a wage. This developed slowly during the early decades of the nineteenth century and the main developments to bring it about are referred to below.

The 1829 Metropolitan Police Act

The 1829 Act provided for a police force across London and the surrounding area, with the exception of the City of London, which developed its own 'new' policing arrangements in the 1839 City of London Police Act. It was initially controlled by two commissioners (Charles Rowan and Richard Mayne) and was under the ultimate control of the Home Secretary.

The 1835 Municipal Corporations Act

This measure was mainly concerned with establishing locally elected councils in urban Britain. It also provided for the creation of police forces that were controlled by a committee of the council termed the Watch Committee and paid for by rates levied on local property owners. The Watch Committee initially exerted a considerable degree of control over local policing arrangements.

Political opposition, which centred on the validity of the Charter of Incorporation creating the new system of urban government, resulted in temporary arrangements being provided for Birmingham, Manchester and Bolton, in which a borough-wide force was placed under the control of a government-appointed commissioner until the courts had determined the legality of the Charter of Incorporation. (The background to the 1839 Manchester Police Act is discussed in Joyce, 1993.)

The 1839 Rural Constabulary Act

This Act gave magistrates at Quarter Sessions the *discretionary* power to establish 'new' police forces throughout the county, paid for out of the rates and controlled by a chief constable whom the magistrates appointed. Although subject to considerable control by the magistrates, county forces established by this Act were subject to a greater degree of control by the Home Secretary than their urban counterparts.

This measure was not widely adopted for reasons that included the cost of the new policing arrangements, the belief that an increased number of police officers did not necessary result in a reduction in crime and the ability of magistrates to swear in special constables to cope with public disorder (Emsley, 1983: 77). The 1842 Parish Constables Act was seen in many rural areas as an alternative to the implementation of the 1839 measure. The Act was also perceived to smack of centralisation, which would entail the loss of the traditional ability of rural elites to retain control over the conduct of their own affairs. Adoption of the measure was also flavoured by political considerations, the Tories being against reform and the Whigs supportive of it. Thus by the end of 1841 the legislation had been adopted in 22 English counties in whole or in part (Eastwood, 1994: 240).

The 1856 County and Borough Police Act

This legislation made it compulsory for 'new' police forces to be established in both towns and counties. A key reason for this rested on the contemporary concern of the threat of vagrant crime, associated with unemployed soldiers returning from the Crimean War, which required a uniformity in the provision of policing across England and Wales that was lacking under existing arrangements (Steedman, 1984: 26). The fear of vagrancy built upon the concern felt by the rural gentry arising from opposition to the 1834 Poor Law Amendment Act and encouraged them to accept a reformed policing system (Rawlings, 2002: 125–126).

As an inducement to the degree of compulsion, central government funding, initially equivalent to one-quarter of the costs of pay and clothing (increased to one-half in 1874), was given to forces certified as efficient by the newly-created Inspectorate. Additionally, in most counties, the Petty Sessions divisions (rather than Quarter Sessions) were at the apex of police organisation, thereby retaining the geographic and administrative power of individual magistrates (Steedman, 1984: 47).

Late nineteenth-century legislation

The development of policing was affected by two Acts enacted in the 1880s. The 1882 Municipal Corporations Act sought to limit the existence of small police forces by providing that newly incorporated boroughs could only have their own police forces if they had a population in excess of 20,000. The 1888 Local Government Act provided that control over county police forces would be discharged by a standing joint committee consisting of 50% elected councillors and 50% magistrates.

Policing by consent

The above section has referred to the progress and nature of police reform being influenced by a desire not to create a police force under the central direction of central government. This intention also influenced the philosophy of policing, which is the focus of this section.

Reforms to policing in England and Wales during the nineteenth century sought to establish the principle of policing by consent. This approach was embodied in the 'General Instructions' issued to members of the newly-formed Metropolitan Police in 1829, which were echoed in the 'Nine Principles of Police' (Reith, 1956: 287–288). These declarations emphasised the importance of the police service operating with the support of those they policed, and the concern to secure a system of policing by consent influenced a number of developments affecting the manner in which the delivery of policing was constructed in its formative years.

Local organisation and control

As has been argued above, outside London (where the Home Secretary served as the police authority between 1829 until 1999) policing was organised locally and controlled by local people who were initially drawn from the property-owning classes. Watch Committees in the towns and magistrates in rural areas exercised considerable authority over policing in its formative years in the nineteenth century in an attempt to dispel the impression that the reformed system would be the agent of the government, trampling roughshod over the rights of the people.

The preventive style of policing

One of the main objectives of policing was to prevent crime and this was performed by the home beat method, whereby police officers patrolled small geographic areas on foot. Their task was essentially passive, based on the belief that their physical presence would deter the commission of crime. They were not encouraged to pursue a more active role within the community since actions regarded as an unnecessary intrusion in people's lives would have had an adverse impact on popular support for the reformed system of policing.

The emphasis that was placed on preventive policing was at the expense of detective work, which was given a relatively low profile in early nineteenth-century police forces. One reason for this was that detectives were popularly equated with spies, and this would have provided the new system of policing with a direct link to the reviled French system of policing. The Metropolitan Police did not establish a detective branch until 1842, which was reorganised as the Criminal Investigation Department (CID) in 1878.

The rule of law and police powers

From its outset, the performance of professional police officers in England and Wales was subject to constraints imposed by the rule of law. Police officers were required to use formalised procedures against those who had broken the law, and to apply those procedures without fear or favour to those who had transgressed.

Additionally, at the outset of professional policing, officers were given no special powers with which to discharge their duties. The spectre of police officers equipped with an array of powers that might be used in an arbitrary manner was thought to be inconsistent with the citizens' exercise of civil and political liberties. Accordingly, the police were initially able to exercise only common law powers. This emphasised their image as 'citizens in uniform' (Royal Commission on Police Powers and Procedure, 1929), who were 'paid to give full-time attention to duties which are incumbent on every citizen in the interests of community welfare and existence' (Reith, 1956: 288).

Minimum force

The desire to dispel the image of the reformed police service as arbitrary and overbearing extended beyond the powers given to police officers and affected the weaponry with which they were provided. It was assumed that there was an inverse correlation between the resort to physical force and obtaining the cooperation of the public for the task of policing. As a result, police officers were not routinely armed and merely carried a truncheon which was designed for their personal protection. The absence of weaponry that could be used in an offensive posture was designed to ensure that when the police were required to intervene to uphold law and order, they would initially rely on 'persuasion, advice and warning' (Reith, 1956: 287) and only if this failed would they use physical force, which should be the minimum that was required to achieve their objective. This concern was also evident in the choice of colour for police uniforms, which were frequently blue or brown but never red, the colour associated with the military.

The service role of policing

Although a reformed policing system that more effectively protected life and property would appeal to all law-abiding persons, the latter role was clearly of most benefit to the wealthy, who owned property that required protecting. Thus in order to 'sell' policing to a wider audience (and in particular to the working classes), its task extended beyond law enforcement. This was the origin of the 'social service function of the police' (Fielding, 1991: 126), in which a diverse range of activities (some of which were designed to tackle the social causes of crime and others which were not crime-related) were pursued by officers seeking to befriend the community and to dispel the image that police work was exclusively concerned with the exercise of coercive authority against the lower social classes. Several studies (Cumming et al., 1965 and Punch and Naylor, 1973) attest to the continued importance of this area of police work in post-war Britain.

Recruitment

Initially, police forces deliberately recruited their personnel from the working class (save for the most senior ranks of the service who in the formative years of the reformed system were frequently ex-army officers). A study of the City of Manchester Police Force revealed that between 1859 and 1900 unskilled workers (the bulk of whom described themselves as 'labourers') constituted over 50% of the total intake of officers (Joyce, 1991: 142). This situation meant that police work had the status of a job, the performance of which required little training.

This policy of recruiting 'fools dressed in blue' (Steedman, 1984: 7) was partly pursued for economic reasons (since working-class recruits could be paid less than members of higher social groups) but was also a means through which members of the working class could be incorporated into the machinery of the newly emerging capitalist state. The tendency for officers below the rank of chief constable to be selected from serving policemen offered the possibility that police work could be an avenue of social mobility for working-class people.

Working-class recruitment also ensured that police officers would act deferentially to those who were their social superiors and act in accordance with their interests and instructions with a particular objective of providing 'an ordered and supervised system of control'. This was especially directed against the regulation of vagrants (since these were regarded as potential criminals) (Steedman, 1984: 58–59), but also extended towards behaviour such as prostitution and drunkenness since immoral and disorderly behaviour offended the propertied classes. It was an important factor in securing the consent of 'respectable' people to the new system of policing.

Additionally, the recruitment of police officers from the working class might also aid the attainment of consent between the police and the lower classes. Police officers who were drawn from the lower end of the social scale might find it easier to relate to fellow members of the working class with whom they came into contact, and to discharge their duties without displaying a sense of class hatred towards them. Similar sentiments governed suggestions that were put forward in the late twentieth century in connection with the need to recruit police officers from minority ethnic communities.

The attainment of policing by consent: orthodox and revisionist accounts

The extent to which the developments that have been discussed above succeeded in securing the consent of all members of society is the subject of much academic debate. The view of orthodox police historians was that initial opposition to the police culminated in the 1830s. The murder of PC Culley at a political rally in Cold Bath Fields, London, in 1833 and the subsequent public enquiry were viewed as an important watershed. Following this, the success of the police in combating crime and disorder was an important underpinning of consent and enabled them to overcome any serious resistance to their presence on the streets and secure the cooperation (hence the consent) of most sections of society (Reith, 1943: 3; Critchley, 1978: 55–56). However, the extent to which consent was obtained has been challenged by revisionist historians.

Orthodox historians focus on crime as a key problem which professional policing was developed to address in the interests of all members of society. However, revisionists emphasise that the motive for police reform was 'the maintenance of order required by the capitalist class' (Reiner, 1985: 25), whose control over polic-ing (exercised by local urban elites through the mechanism of the Watch Committee) enabled them to ensure that the attention of the police was directed at all actions that threatened to undermine it – 'crime, riot, political dissidence and public morality' (Reiner, 1985: 25). It was in the latter sense that police officers were depicted as 'domestic missionaries' whose purpose was to alter the behav-iour and moral habits of the lower social orders (Storch, 1976).

Revisionist historians emphasised working-class hostility towards the new sys-tem of policing as evidence that the prime role of police work was to enforce discipline over this section of society. Storch drew attention to widespread oppo-sition to the police in the middle decades of the nineteenth century within indus-trious working-class communities, which saw them as 'unproductive parasites' (men who did not work productively for a living) and viewed their presence as 'a plague of blue locusts' (Storch, 1975). Working-class resentment to the police, arising in part from their intrusions into working-class pastimes and leisure activ-ities, has also been documented in a study of the Black Country (Philips, 1977).

Revisionist accounts thus reject the orthodox position that hostility towards the new police was a relatively short-lived phenomenon and instead conclude that consent was heavily determined by a person's position in the social ladder. The level of consent was greatest from the property-owning middle classes (including those who comprised the petty bourgeoisie, such as shop keepers) who stood to gain most from police activities. However, working-class hostility was more endur-ing. Those at the lower end of the social ladder granted tolerance to the police which was, at best, 'passive acquiescence', broken by frequent outbreaks of conflict throughout the nineteenth century (Brogden, 1982: 202–228).

BOX 1.1

POLICE PROPERTY

Revisionist accounts suggest that a key role performed by the police in the nineteenth century was to regulate the behaviour of the lower social orders and to impose on them the moral habits and standards of behaviour of 'respectable' members of society. The elites who controlled policing were willing to give the police a relatively free hand to discharge this function (acting aggressively within the law or perhaps outside it) and this situation gave rise to the concept of 'police property' (Lee, 1981). This term is applied to social groups which possess little or no rights in society and thus are not in a position to formally object to their treatment by the police.

The definition of which groups constitute police property is not stable and changes over time. It may embrace any grouping whose habits or behaviour are deemed to be

(Continued)

(Continued)

unacceptable to those who wield power in society or those who are deemed to pose a threat to their social position. In nineteenth-century Liverpool, 'participants in the street economy' (Brogden, 1982: 232) were accorded this status, which was later imposed on minority ethnic communities in the twentieth century.

Although groups that are treated aggressively by the police lack formal means (or lack the access to these means) to redress their treatment, they may articulate their grievances through alternative methods. In Liverpool, for example, a link has been drawn between the outbreaks of disorder directed at the police by those who were regarded as police property in the nineteenth century and the riots that occurred in Toxteth in 1981 (Brogden, 1982). Outbreaks of disorder may give rise to pressures on the police from political or economic elites to alter their behaviour towards targeted social groups since continued mistreatment can lead to disorder on a scale that poses a threat to the existing social order.

Police–working-class relationships in the early twentieth century

The relationship between the police and the working class showed signs of improvement during the early years of the twentieth century. Legitimacy (that is, an acceptance of the right of the police to function in civil society) became widespread even though specific interventions might be less acceptable, especially by those on the receiving end of them.

The incorporation of the working class into the British political institutions tended to defuse some of the hostility towards the police within working-class communities (Reiner, 1985: 61). One local study suggested that in the decade following the First World War 'the whole pattern of relations between the police and the working class in North London had begun slowly, but subtly, to change from outright physical confrontation to an unwritten system of tacit negotiation' (Cohen, 1979, quoted in Fitzgerald et al., 1981: 119). The generally improved relationship between police and public can be explained by several changes which occurred after the First World War affecting 'the conditions and composition of the ... working class ... the position of youth within the generational division of labour, and ... the changing function of the police force in the developing structure of the capitalist state'. These resulted in changing the relations between the police and working class 'from outright confrontation to an unwritten system of tacit negotiation' (Cohen, 1979, quoted in Fitzgerald et al., 1981: 119).

Subsequent developments included the greater level of working-class affluence after the Second World War, which created a more socially integrated society. These changes underpinned what has been described as 'the golden age of policing', which was 'marked by popular respect and obedience for authority' (Fielding, 1991: 36) and led to the conclusion that:

by the 1950s, 'policing by consent' *was* achieved in Britain to the maximal degree it is ever attainable – the wholehearted approval of the majority of the population who do not experience the coercive exercise of police powers to any significant extent, and *de facto* acceptance of the legitimacy of the institution by those who do. (Reiner, 1985: 51)

The development of new policing in Ireland

The 'old' system of policing in Ireland was performed by high constables (appointed by County Grand Juries) and petty constables (appointed by Court Leets or Sheriffs Tourns, operating at parish level). By the eighteenth century this system was ineffective.

Initial reform sought to shore up the old system. In 1738 County Grand Juries were empowered to appoint a number of sub-constables (initially four and, in 1783, eight) in each barony (a barony being derived from Tudor administration in Ireland and was the unit of administration below the county). These constables were paid and assisted the magistrates and parish constables. In 1749 county magistrates were empowered to appoint constables in places where no local appointments had been made.

Further reform took place in 1787 when, outside Dublin, the Lord Lieutenant was authorised to appoint chief constables for each baronial district. County Grand Juries would appoint sub-constables to these districts. Much of the day-to-day operations of the force was performed by magistrates, thus providing an element of local control. This measure was augmented by a further piece of legislation in 1792. However, neither provided for a system of policing that operated throughout Ireland (in particular because County Grand Juries became increasingly reluctant to appoint constables) and much reliance was placed on the military to counter disturbances that occurred in the late eighteenth and early decades of the nineteenth century.

In order to deal with this problem, a further measure of police reform occurred in 1814 when the Peace Preservation Force (usually referred to as Peelers) was created. This legislation enabled the Lord Lieutenant to declare a county (or a barony or a half barony) to be in a state of disturbance. Having done this, a stipendiary magistrate, who exercised control over all local magistrates in the disturbed area, was appointed. A police force consisting of a chief constable and up to 50 constables would effectively garrison the area until the disturbance had passed. Constables who served in this force were usually from a military background. Initially, local ratepayers footed the bill for this force, but in 1817 an amendment to the legislation permitted central government to contribute up to two-thirds of the cost. By 1822 the force numbered around 2,300 and operated in about half of Ireland's counties. Its effectiveness was adversely affected by factors that included the small size of the force, hostility from the public and the deployment of constables in small detachments (Palmer, 1988: 231).

The development of new policing in Ireland – the Irish Constabulary

The legislation of 1787 and 1792 was replaced by the 1822 Irish Constabulary Act. The initial intention of the government was to place this new police force under the control of the government, but compromises were made whereby the barony remained the basic unit of police organisation. The Lord Lieutenant appointed a chief constable to each barony and in turn he appointed a number of constables. County magistrates retained the power to also appoint constables and sub-constables, but the use of this power was gradually relinquished. The chief constable was required to submit a report to the Lord Lieutenant every three months.

Baronies were grouped into the four provincial areas, and in each the Lord Lieutenant appointed an Inspector General (sometimes referred to as a General Superintendent). The Inspector Generals' role included drawing up general regulations for the police in their area. At first, the full cost of policing was met by central government, but subsequently county ratepayers met half of the costs.

The style of policing provided by the Irish Constabulary was paramilitary. Constables were armed and housed in barracks and police stations throughout Ireland. The great bulk of constables were from Catholic backgrounds, but the officers tended to be Protestant.

Further reform was provided by the 1836 Irish Constabulary Act. The main effect of this measure was to centralise control over policing. The four provincial areas headed by an Inspector General were replaced by one Inspector General and two deputies, who exercised control throughout Ireland (with the exception of Dublin). A hierarchy was established through the creation of the rank of Head Constable as the highest rank to which those who joined as ordinary constables could aspire. The more senior officers (including chief constables) were usually appointed from out-side the force. After 1846 the government fully funded the Irish Constabulary.

Much of the work of the new force was directed at disturbances that were a frequent feature of Irish political life. The role of the Irish Constabulary in dealing with Fenian violence was recognised by Queen Victoria, who renamed the force the Royal Irish Constabulary (RIC) in 1867. The force was abolished following the introduction of partition in 1922. However, the RIC was the model for the policing arrangements conducted in Northern Ireland by the newly-formed Royal Ulster Constabulary.

Policing in Dublin

Policing in Dublin differed from the system throughout the remainder of Ireland. Initially, the City of Dublin Corporation superintended the parish constables and night watch, although in the early 1720s it devolved some of its powers on to Dublin's parishes. In 1778, the 21 parishes were divided into six units termed 'wards', and constables were appointed by the Ward Mote Courts.

Dublin became the first area in the United Kingdom to be provided with a 'new' policing system. The 1786 Dublin Police Act established the Dublin Metropolitan Police District headed by a High Constable. The Police District was divided into four districts, each headed by a chief constable. A salaried magistrate was appointed to each of these districts, appointed by the Lord Lieutenant. The police force was armed; officers were paid and were mainly Protestant.

A brief period of local control exerted by the Dublin Corporation over policing was initiated in 1795 but abandoned in 1798 when the four districts were restored. The Lord Lieutenant appointed a Superintendent Magistrate for Dublin and he appointed a High Constable for Dublin and the four chief constables who headed each district. A government-appointed magistrate (a divisional justice) was also appointed to each of the four districts. The 1808 Dublin Metropolitan Police Act extended the jurisdiction of the force which now operated over six districts.

Subsequent reform replaced the Superintendent Magistrate and Divisional Justices with 18 divisional justices (three per district), 12 of whom were appointed by the Lord Lieutenant and six by the Dublin Corporation. The 1836 Dublin Police Act removed the last vestiges of local control over the force, which was placed in the hands of the Chief Secretary for Ireland, with day-to-day control being vested in the hands of two magistrates appointed by the Lord Lieutenant.

One of the key roles of the Dublin Metropolitan Police was to control social conduct, and they were frequently accused of doing this in an aggressive manner.

The development of new policing in Scotland

Scottish policing rested on the voluntary principle, the first constables being appointed in 1617. In the cities, the constables were augmented by watchmen to guard the area at night. By the eighteenth century, constables appointed by the Justices performed a range of functions in connection with the maintenance of order and were empowered to summon public aid in order to quell disturbances. Although they were often paid, their tenure in office was of a limited duration.

A professional police force was briefly established in Glasgow in 1779, but collapsed because there was no provision for it to be supported by the levying of a local rate (Donnelly and Scott, 2005: 45–46). The 1800 Glasgow Police Act provided for a professional police force for that city, whose underlying ethos was that of crime prevention. It was financed by a rate levied on houses and businesses by the City Council and was under the control of the Lord Provost, three baillies (magistrates) and nine commissioners who were elected each year from the traders and merchants of the City (Donnelly and Scott, 2005: 47).

Separate Acts of Parliament subsequently established similar policing arrangements for a number of other cities and burghs. A general power to establish professional police forces in the burghs was provided by the 1833 Burghs and Police

(Scotland) Act, which also enabled burghs to adopt powers relating to cleansing, lighting and paving. The Policing of Towns (Scotland) Act 1850 and the General Police and Improvement (Scotland) Act 1862 extended these powers to other urban areas and this resulted in the creation of around 100 burgh police forces.

The 1857 Police (Scotland) Act imposed a compulsory requirement on the commissioners of supply in each county (who performed most of the local government functions in these areas until their replacement by county councils by the 1890 Local Government (Scotland) Act) to establish police forces in the counties and also permitted existing burgh forces to be amalgamated with the county force if the magistrates and town council of the burgh and the commissioners of supply in the county were agreed on this course of action.

These forces were administered by a police committee that consisted of a maximum number of 15 commissioners and the Lord Lieutenant and Sheriff of the county. The commissioners of supply were responsible for levying a 'police assessment' to finance the force and a key role of the police committee was to appoint a chief constable, who was responsible for the day-to-day activities of the force and for appointing and dismissing constables.

The contemporary structure and organisation of policing in the United Kingdom

This section seeks to briefly update the historical material presented above and chart key developments concerned with the current structure and organisation of policing in the United Kingdom.

England and Wales

The structure of policing in England and Wales was provided for by the 1964 Police Act and the 1972 Local Government Act. The 1964 Act enabled the Home Secretary to compel police force amalgamations, the first of which was the creation of the Mid Anglia Constabulary in 1965. The 1972 measure provided for the alignment of police forces with the newly-created structure of local government and eventually resulted in the formation of 43 separate police forces each with its own police authority. Each force is headed by a chief constable (the term 'commissioner' being used in London for the Metropolitan Police Service).

Each force is divided into a number of territorial areas. These were formerly referred to as divisions, although the term Basic Command Unit (BCU) is now commonly used by many forces. Divisions/BCUs are usually under the control of a chief superintendent, although the Metropolitan Police Service utilises the term commander for an officer performing this function.

Basic Command Units (BCUs)

Basic Command Units play an integral role in contemporary policing. They are 'the main operating unit of police forces' (Loveday et al., 2007: 10), are responsible for delivering 'the vast bulk of everyday policing services' (HMIC, 2005: 13) and are central in attaining the objectives put forward by recent Labour governments in reducing both the level and the fear of crime (Home Office, 2001). Their key role is to deliver level-1 services and they also gather criminal intelligence, conduct criminal investigations and provide rapid responses to emergencies (Loveday et al., 2007: 10). They have been described as the key level 'at which there is engagement between the police and local communities' (HMIC, 2001: 15), in particular through BCU involvement with crime and disorder reduction partnerships (CDRPs).

However, BCUs have not developed in a standardised fashion and their structure and organisation are subject to considerable variation across England and Wales. They are not necessarily coterminous with local authorities or CDRPs: in 2007 there were 375 CDRPs and 228 BCUs, which meant that some BCUs had to deal with more than one CDRP (Loveday et al., 2007: 34). It has been noted (HMIC, 2004: 76–77) that they differ in size, some comprising over 1,000 officers whereas others have below 200. This means that the resources, in terms of both finance and personnel, that their commanders have at their disposal to address the wide range of local problems they are required to deal with are subject to considerable variation across the country.

Northern Ireland

During the 1990s, attempts were made to find a political solution to the political violence in Northern Ireland. These culminated in the signing of the 1998 Good Friday Peace Agreement. This created a new structure of devolved government for Northern Ireland, consisting of the Northern Ireland Assembly and an executive headed by a first minister and composed of representatives of Northern Ireland's main political parties, which entered into a power-sharing arrangement.

One aspect of the Belfast (or 'Good Friday') Agreement was the establishment of a commission to examine the future policing arrangements in Northern Ireland. This took the form of an enquiry (Independent Commission on Policing in Northern Ireland, 1999) that was chaired by Chris Patten. This recommended the creation of a Police Service of Northern Ireland, overseen by a Northern Ireland Policing Board that would monitor the efficiency and effectiveness of the force, and act as the equivalent of a police authority that exists in England, Wales and Scotland. This Board and the new police force were created by the 2000 Police (Northern Ireland) Act.

The Board is composed of 19 political and independent members. Sinn Fein initially refused to join the Northern Ireland Policing Board, one of its main objections being that insufficient power over policing had been devolved locally. However, in February 2007 Sinn Fein agreed to join the Northern Ireland Policing Board and to participate in the district policing partnerships. This decision paved the way for the ultimate devolution of police and criminal justice functions to the Northern Ireland Assembly, which was finally achieved in early 2010.

This new police force took over from the RUC on 4 November 2001. Its features included recruiting new members on the basis of 50% Catholics and 50% non-Catholics from April 2002 until a target figure of 30% Catholic membership (as recommended by Patten) had been attained. By early 2008 this target was relatively close to being reached. The force numbers around 7,500 officers and almost 4,000 civilian staff. Its budget in 2008/09 was almost £1.2 billion, which is included in the block grant paid to the Northern Ireland executive.

Scotland

No significant measures affecting the structure of policing were passed following the enactment of the 1890 Local Government (Scotland) Act until 1975, although the process of consolidation derived from the 1967 Police (Scotland) Act reduced the number of forces from 49 in 1945 to 22 in 1968 (Gordon, 1980: 30). The 1973 Local Government (Scotland) Act, when implemented in 1975, further reduced the number of forces to eight – six covered areas controlled by one regional authority and two covered more than one regional authority. These forces are maintained either by a police authority or a joint police board. The universal introduction of a unitary system of local government for Scotland that was created by the 1994 Local Government etc (Scotland) Act did not affect the structure of policing.

Since 1999, policing has been a devolved responsibility to the Scottish government that comes under the overall jurisdiction of the Cabinet Secretary for Justice. In June 2009 there were in excess of 17,000 police officers in Scotland and around 6,500 civilian employees. The overall cost of policing is above £1 billion a year (HMIC Scotland, 2009: para 1.7).

QUESTION

Analyse the measures that were pursued to secure the principle of policing by consent. To what extent had this been achieved by the end of the nineteenth century?

To answer this question you should draw upon the material above and consult some of the material to which reference is made. In particular you should:

- Discuss what you understand by the concept of 'policing by consent';
- Examine the methods that were introduced to secure the implementation of this principle;

- Evaluate the extent to which policing by consent had been achieved, contrasting the orthodox and revisionist accounts;
- Present a conclusion in which the shortcomings in both orthodox and revisionist accounts are considered.

REFERENCES

Brogden, M. (1982) *The Police: Autonomy and Consent*. London: Academic Press.

Brown, A. (1998) *Police Governance in England and Wales*. London: Routledge.

Cohen, P. (1979) 'Capitalism and the Rule of Law', Paper presented at the National Deviancy Conference and Conference of Socialist Economists, London, January, reproduced in M. Fitzgerald, G. McLennan and J. Pawson (eds), (1981), *Crime and Society: Readings in History and Theory*. London: Routledge.

Critchley, T. (1978) *A History of Police in England and Wales* (revised edition). London: Constable.

Cumming, E., Cumming, I. and Edell, L. (1965) 'Police as Philosopher, Friend and Guide', *Social Problems*, 22(3): 276–286.

Davey, B. (1983) *Lawless and Immoral: Policing a Country Town 1838–1857*. Leicester: Leicester University Press.

Donnelly, D. and Scott, K. (eds) (2005) *Policing Scotland*. Cullompton, Devon: Willan Publishing.

Eastwood, D. (1994) *Governing Rural England*. Oxford: Oxford University Press.

Emsley, C. (1983) *Policing and Its Context 1750–1850*. Basingstoke: Macmillan.

Fielding, N. (1991) *The Police and Social Conflict: Rhetoric and Reality*. London: Athlone Press.

Fitzgerald, M., McLennan, G. and Pawson, J. (1981) *Crime and Society: Readings in History and Theory*. London: Routledge

Gordon, P. (1980) *Policing Scotland*. Glasgow: Scottish Council of Civil Liberties.

Her Majesty's Inspectorate of the Constabulary (HMIC) (2001) *Going Local – the BCU Inspection Handbook*. London: HMIC.

Her Majesty's Inspectorate of Constabulary (HMIC) (2004) *Modernising the Police Service: A Thematic Inspection of Workforce Modernisation – the Role, Management and Deployment of Police Staff in England and Wales*. London: Home Office.

Her Majesty's Inspectorate of Constabulary (HMIC) (2005) *Closing the Gap: A Review of the 'Fitness for Purpose' of the Current Structure of Policing in England and Wales*. London: HMIC.

Her Majesty's Inspectorate of Constabulary Scotland (2009) *Independent Review of Policing: A Report for the Cabinet Secretary for Justice*. Edinburgh. HMIC Scotland.

Home Office (2001) *Policing a New Century: A Blueprint for Reform*. Cm 5326. London: TSO.

Independent Commission on Policing in Northern Ireland (1999) *A New Beginning: Policing in Northern Ireland. The Report of the Independent Commission on Policing in Northern Ireland*. London: TSO.

Joyce, P. (1991) 'Recruitment Patterns and Conditions of Work in a Nineteenth-century Urban Police Force: A Case Study of Manchester 1842–1900', *Police Journal*, LXIV (2): 140–150.

Joyce, P. (1993) 'The Transition from "Old" to "New" Policing in Early Nineteenth-century Manchester', *Police Journal*, LXVI (2): 197–210.

Landau, N. and Beattie, J. (2002) *Law, Crime and English Society 1660–1830*. Cambridge: Cambridge University Press.

Lee, J. (1981) 'Some Structural Aspects of Police Deviance in Relation to Minority Groups', in C. Shearing (ed.), *Organisational Police Deviance*. Toronto: Butterworths.

Loveday, B., McClory, J. and Lockhart, G. (2007) *Fitting the Bill: Local Policing for the Twenty-first Century*. London: Policy Exchange.

Mather, F. (1959) *Public Order in the Age of the Chartists*. Manchester: Manchester University Press.

Morton, J. (2002) *Supergrasses & Informers and Bent Coppers Omnibus*. London: Time Warner Paperbacks.

Palmer, S. (1988) *Police and Protest in England and Ireland 1780–1850*. Cambridge: Cambridge University Press.

Philips, D. (1977) *Crime and Authority in Victorian England*. London: Croom Helm.

Punch, M. and Naylor, T. (1973) 'The Police: A Social Service', *New Society*, 17 May, pp. 358–361.

Rawlings, P. (2002) *Policing: A Short History*. Cullompton, Devon: Willan Publishing.

Rawlings, P. (2008) 'Policing before the Police', in T. Newburn (ed.), *Handbook of Policing* (2nd edition). Cullompton, Devon: Willan Publishing.

Reiner, R. (1985) *The Politics of the Police*. Brighton: Wheatsheaf Books.

Reith, C. (1943) *British Police and the Democratic Ideal*. Oxford: Oxford University Press.

Reith, C. (1956) *A New Study of Police History*. London: Oliver and Boyd.

Royal Commission on Police Powers and Procedure (1929) *Report of the Royal Commission on Police Powers and Procedure*. Cmd 3297. London: HMSO.

Steedman, C. (1984) *Policing the Victorian Community: The Formation of English Provincial Forces, 1856–80*. London: Routledge and Kegan Paul.

Storch, R. (1975) 'The Plague of Blue Locusts: Police Reform and Popular Resistance in Northern England 1840–1857', *International Review of Social History*, 20: 61–90.

Storch, R. (1976) 'The Policeman as Domestic Missionary', *Journal of Social History*, IX (4), Summer: 481–509.

2

The police response to crime

CHAPTER AIMS

The aims of this chapter are:

- To evaluate changes in the nature of crime during the twentieth century;
- To analyse how the police service responded to these changes in connection with reforms made to methods of policing;
- To discuss changes made or proposed to the structure and organisation of policing in response to the changing nature of crime;
- To consider developments affecting police weaponry in response to contemporary crime issues;
- To consider the use made by the police of technology in combating contemporary crime.

The changing nature of crime after 1945

Significant changes to both the scale and the nature of crime took place after the outbreak of war in 1939. The war provided new opportunities for criminal enterprise. It has been observed that:

> Before the outbreak of hostilities there is little doubt that the ordinary public eschewed crime. They probably saw their involvement as little more than fending for their families, but now new doors were opened for old and new criminals alike. Now, with bomb-damaged shops and buildings open to looting, all kinds of goods came onto the black market and into receivers' hands. There was a steady trade in stolen ration books. Undercover of blackout the smash-and-grab raid proliferated. (Morton, 2002: 205)

Further developments affecting the nature of crime occurred following the end of the war in 1945. It was conducted by new breed of criminal – 'cunning, ruthless and well-informed … younger, fitter, harder, more resourceful and more energetic than the pre-war criminals' (Morton, 2002: 206).

In this period, the enterprise of individual criminals gave way to more collective forms of activity, such as smash-and-grab raids and armed robbery, the latter constituting a major form of crime during the 1960s. The teams that carried out these crimes were often recruited on an *ad hoc* basis (Morton, 2003: 229–230), although the shift from craft-based forms of crime to project-based enterprises was sometimes characterised by careful planning and organisation (McIntosh, 1971). The latter were organised by professional criminal masterminds who recruited teams specifically for a particular criminal enterprise and were willing to use violence to achieve their aims. This resulted in spectacular crimes involving vast sums of money, the first successful major post-war example of which was the 'Great Mail-bag Robbery' on 21 May 1952, in which £287,000 in cash was stolen (Morton, 2003: 235). Other examples included the 'Great Train Robbery' on 8 August 1963, when an estimated £2.5 million was stolen, which at that time was the biggest theft the world had ever known (Morton, 2003: 242). Activities of this nature were continued into the 1970s when cash in transit became a particular target.

A separate (although related) development was the rise of criminal gangs wielding control within specific geographic areas and whose focus was particularly directed at controlling existing criminal activities. Gangs of this nature were not a new development and had existed in the latter years of the nineteenth century in a number of cities. In many ways, the activities of the Sabinis in London in the inter-war years (which embraced protection rackets centred on gambling and drinking pursuits) provided a model for the development of subsequent criminal gangs, which were characterised by being centred on families for whom crime was important both for profit and also for the power and prestige it bestowed on gang leaders. This form of criminal activity was epitomised by the activities of the Krays in East London and the Richardsons in South London during the 1950s and 1960s and has been argued to have provided the roots of modern professional, organised crime (Carrabine et al., 2004: 188).

New forms of crime emerged after the 1960s, fuelled by factors such as increased affluence, consumerism, changes in moral attitudes and technological developments. This gave rise to activities that included pornography, the counterfeiting of goods, VAT fraud and (especially during the 1980s) drugs. It has been argued that the promotion of materialist values during the Thatcher era helped to fuel crime (Carrabine et al., 2004: 190).

Some of these modern forms of criminal activity embraced new forms of management, which is referred to as 'organised crime'. This term describes activities conducted at national and international levels, characterised by an enhanced degree of organisation than had previously existed. Organised criminals have been defined as 'those involved, normally working with others, in continuing serious criminal activities for substantial profit, whether based in the UK or elsewhere' (NCIS definition, quoted in Home Office, 2004a: 7). This definition highlighted that many organised crime groups 'were, at root, businesses and often sophisticated ones' (Home Office, 2004a: 7), whose scale of operations was vast and included drug trafficking, excise fraud, VAT fraud and organised immigration crime (Home Office, 2004a: 8).

Globalisation and technology have further helped to fuel the growth of organised crime: 'globalisation ... has made it increasingly easy for foreign organised criminals to set up base in major European cities such as London. ... New technologies provide new and more effective means to commit crime ... as well as more secure ways of communicating with criminal groups' (Home Office, 2004a: 11). The international dimension of contemporary crime is growing. In 2003, Europol reported 'a significant growth in the EU of the cross-border activities of organised crime groups in the areas of drug-trafficking, illegal immigration, trafficking in human beings, financial crime and smuggling (House of Lords European Union Committee, 2004: para 25). This situation has given rise to developments based on the principle of mutual recognition of member states' national criminal laws and procedures by the other EU countries and the establishment of new institutions that include Europol and Eurojust.

One further aspect of the international dimension of contemporary criminal enterprise has been crime based on diverse ethnic communities. It has been argued that criminal gangs, whose members derived from London's minority ethnic communities, were engaged in activities that included running protection rackets, importing fake electrical games and trafficking women to use as prostitutes (Cowan and Hyder, 2005). However, it has been argued that 'the extent to which ties into ethnic communities translate into international criminal operations or conspiracies' (such as the Yardies or Triad) is 'complex and debatable' (Carrabine et al., 2004: 192).

The police response to the post-1945 character of crime (1): Methods

Changes affecting the conduct of crime since 1945 have made for significant changes in police methods, structure and organisation. This has had an impact on all aspects of police work, although the work performed by detectives has been especially affected by these developments. This section examines some of these key changes.

Rule-bending

One early development affecting the police response to new forms of post-war crime was rule-bending. This involved police officers, usually detectives, engaging in activities that included planting evidence and physically abusing suspects in order to obtain a confession, which during the 1960s and 1970s was viewed as an indispensable requirement if a conviction was to be secured. On occasions, these confessions were fabricated. Some units, including the West Midlands Serious Crime Squad, secured a degree of notoriety in connection with activities of this nature, where violence became an aspect of organisational culture.

Although the justification for these actions was that methods of this nature were required to deal with the new breed of professional, hardened criminals who emerged in the post-war period, they led to serious miscarriages of justice that were highlighted by the report into the police investigation into the murder of Maxwell Confait (Fisher, 1977). The major problem was the relative lack of rights for suspects, whose treatment at that time was founded on Judges' Rules rather than legislation. As is discussed in Chapter 3, the 1984 Police and Criminal Evidence Act went a long way to remedying abuses of this nature, replacing the old Judges' Rules with codes of practice covering a wide range of police activities and providing for the tape-recording of interviews.

The use of informants

The police gain information regarding crime and criminals from a number of sources. These include members of the general public and other public officials who gain information during the course of their work. Another source of information is gained from informants (sometimes the term *grass* or *supergrass* is used), who have regularly been used by the police to get intelligence on criminals and criminal activities. Much of this type of work was historically conducted on a personal basis between a detective and his/her 'snitch', although some informants were registered on the authority of a senior officer in a police force. In more recent years police forces have established central source handling units to exercise supervision over the use of informants and the information that they provide. Some forces have also developed IT to manage the information obtained from informants. One example of the latter is the Police Informants Management System used by the Hertfordshire Constabulary.

There are several categories of informants (Morton, 2002: xiii), whose motives for doing so are varied. Some informants may be associated with criminals without themselves having carried out criminal activities. Others may be recruited by the police following their arrest or conviction for a serious crime. They then become willing to provide evidence regarding their associates for this crime and sometimes for others that have been committed earlier. This process is also known as 'turning Queen's evidence', in return for which the informant will either receive a much reduced sentence or total immunity from prosecution. Self-preservation is the main motive in these circumstances.

Those who have taken this path include the bank robber Bertie Smalls in 1971. He was given immunity from prosecution in return for information that led to the arrest of 27 of his former criminal colleagues (Morton, 2002: 56). Informants (or supergrasses) were also used in Northern Ireland in the early 1980s to combat politically motivated violence. One estimate suggested that between 1981 (when Christopher Black turned supergrass) and 1984 at least 446 people were charged on the basis of supergrass information (Gifford, 1984: 10). The use of informants was aided by reforms to the judicial process in Northern Ireland, especially the removal of juries hearing 'scheduled offences' – the so-called Diplock Courts that were introduced following the 1973 Northern Ireland (Emergency Powers) Act.

Informants may be the only available source of evidence against some forms of criminal activity, including gang-related crime. In these cases, the capacity to conduct crime may be crippled by the informant's testimony. For this reason, the courts have on occasions upheld the practice of informants being given lenient sentences (Morton, 2002: 76–77). However, there have also been a number of problems traditionally associated with the use of informants.

These include the spectre of serious, hardened criminals not being adequately brought to justice for the crimes they have committed, and perhaps being rewarded for the information they have provided. Concerns of this nature might persuade juries not to convict those named by informants. The evidence they provide may not always be reliable and they may only provide partial information in order to preserve their credibility with the criminal fraternity. It has also been alleged that police officers may turn a blind eye (or be asked to turn a blind eye by the informant's detective 'minder') to other crimes committed by an informant in order to keep the informant 'onside'. This situation may mean that informants are able to act as powerful criminals in their own right, furnished with a degree of police protection.

Informants will require protection by the police, which may entail them not being arrested when apprehended at the scene of a crime. It is highly unlikely that the court will be made aware of this situation in order to preserve the integrity of the informant. If they are required to provide evidence in court, it may be given in a manner (the witness being able to use a pseudonym, appear in court behind screens with a voice distorter and be immune from any form of effective cross-examination) that undermines the fairness of the judicial process.

A final difficulty is that the system of informants may abet police corruption. Informants construct a close working relationship between a police officer and a criminal. Corruption may arise when informants enjoy immunity from arrest for criminal acts they have carried out, in return for which police officers may demand some of the proceeds of the crime. A system whereby payment by criminals is made to police officers may then extend further into bribes, for example where criminals who are not informants pay money to avoid arrest for their crimes.

Informants played a major role in police work during the 1970s (Morton, 2002: 304). Their use subsequently declined, although they have been viewed as one way of improving detection rates (alongside other methods that included crime pattern analysis) (Audit Commission, 1993). Technology (in the form of telephone tapping, bugging and other forms of surveillance) provides alternative ways to obtain information regarding criminal activities. However, although technology avoids some of the problems associated with the use of informants, it carries its own problems, especially in connection with the invasion of civil liberties.

In 1994, the Association of Chief Police Officers (ACPO) sought to provide guidance to police forces concerning the procedures to be adopted in connection with the use of informants. However, questions remain as to the extent to which it was followed (Morton, 2002: 303). The 2000 Regulation of Investigatory Powers Act provided a statutory basis for the authorisation and use of covert surveillance, informants and undercover officers.

Infiltrators

Infiltrators typically pose as a member of a gang and provide information to the police regarding its criminal activities or they may be persons who seek to construct a relationship with an individual criminal in an attempt to secure evidence regarding his or her crimes. This role may be performed by police officers working under cover, or it may be carried out by civilians who act in a manner similar to that of informants.

A key problem posed by infiltrators is whether they merely report on criminal activities or whether they act as an *agent provocateur* and organise criminal acts that might not otherwise have been committed. This raises the issue of entrapment, which, as a defence relating to the actions of a person charged with a criminal offence, has operated less effectively in the UK than in the USA (Morton, 2002: 237–238). The use of evidence obtained through infiltration was initially regulated by the 1984 Police and Criminal Evidence Act, which gave the trial judge discretion to refuse to admit evidence which might undermine the fairness of the proceedings. The use of infiltrators is now governed by the 2000 Regulation of Investigatory Powers Act.

Surveillance

There are two main types of surveillance – mass surveillance and targeted surveillance. The former is not directed at any specific target and the latter involves the use of a wide range of techniques that include interception of telephone calls and bugging. Key developments included the 1985 Interception of Communications Act, which placed a warrant system to 'tap' telephones on a statutory footing, and the 1997 Police Act, which gave the police service powers to 'bug and burgle' in order to gather intelligence in connection with combating serious crime.

The 1998 Human Rights Act established the right to privacy and family life, and the freedoms of expression and peaceful assembly and association with others. Article 8 (concerned with privacy) required policing methods that infringed privacy to be founded on statute. This requirement was fulfilled in the 2000 Regulation of Investigatory Powers Act. The 2000 legislation developed existing safeguards provided through warrants in relation to telephone tapping to other forms of electronic communication (such as emails and the internet). Covert intelligence was also regulated by the Act, including the use of informants. The safeguards established by the Act included a tribunal to hear complaints from members of the public.

Intelligence-led policing

The need to amass information on criminals and criminal activity using devices which include informants, surveillance and technological, and academic applications such as crime mapping and offender profiling that enable specific groups of offenders (especially prolific offenders) or particular patterns of behaviour to be targeted, have become key components of a method of policing known as intelligence-led policing. A particular aim of this approach is to improve the standard of police performance by raising the level of detected crimes. Intelligence-led policing is based upon a belief that the police service was failing to address 'the systemic sources of crime and crime patterns' (Tilley, 2003: 313). This method is discussed in more detail in Chapter 4.

The police response to the post-1945 character of crime (2): Structure and organisation

The changed pattern of crime after 1945 was matched by a reorganisation of the police service, including the establishment of specialist crime-fighting units operating at any location within individual forces (such as the Metropolitan Police's Ghost Squad, which existed between 1945 and 1949). A similar development in this force was the establishment of a squad of detectives whose main roles included conducting surveillance and undercover work in connection with crime. This unit became known as the 'flying squad' and it was given independent status in 1948. In the late 1970s, the flying squad was incorporated into an enlarged central robbery squad whose role was primarily to deal with armed robbery and other forms of serious organised crime.

Other developments occurred elsewhere in England and Wales to counter new post-war criminal activities. One of these was the formation, during the 1960s, of regional crime squads. They operated across police force boundaries and their work was integrated by a national coordinator. A danger common to elite units of the kind referred to above is the autonomy they possess and their potential to develop as a 'firm within a firm'.

Developments connected with the national and international organisation of crime tended to question traditional organisational structures and gave rise to a number of further developments that are considered below.

Police force amalgamations

The present structure of policing in England and Wales is based upon 43 forces. However, there is considerable disparity in their size (19 forces currently have fewer than 2,000 officers) and this situation has prompted successive Home Secretaries to consider organisational reform in order to secure enhanced efficiency and improved service delivery.

In 1993 a White Paper suggested that the present structure of police forces in England and Wales did not make the most effective use of resources available for policing, and section 14 of the 1994 Police and Magistrates' Courts Act provided the Home Secretary with the ability to amalgamate forces. No progress was made with this reform, but it was resurrected in the Labour government's 2003 Green Paper, which floated the idea of creating larger 'strategic' forces at regional level and 'lead' forces (Home Office, 2003: paras 6.6 and 6.10). This issue was subsequently taken up by Her Majesty's Inspectorate of Constabulary (HMIC) in a report published on 16 September 2005 that suggested a fundamental reform of the structure of police forces in England and Wales.

The key justification for amalgamation was the need to deliver a better level of performance in what are termed the 'protective services' (activities designated as level 2 services by the National Intelligence Model, which is discussed on page 77). These embrace activities that extend beyond the boundaries of either Basic Command Units or individual police forces and are grouped under seven headings:

- Counter terrorism and extremism;
- Serious organised (including that committed by criminal gangs) and cross-border crime;
- Civil contingencies and emergency planning;
- Critical incident handling;
- Major crime (homicide);
- Public order;
- Strategic roads policing.

An eighth heading – protecting vulnerable people under the categories of domestic abuse, missing persons, child abuse and the management of violent and sexual offenders – was subsequently identified (HMIC, 2009: 8).

These tasks involved activities that were conducted beyond the boundaries of Basic Command Units (BCUs) and entailed a force-level response (and sometimes operations involving more than one force). However, it was argued that these functions were not performed to a consistently high standard across the board. It was pointed out, for example, that not all forces had Major Investigation Teams to counter serious crimes (HMIC, 2005: 7). Further, only 13 of the 43 forces had fully resourced specialist murder units that allowed for the better use of skilled specialist teams for serious crime and that minimised the disruption to the everyday aspects of BCU work (HMIC, 2005: 11). Intelligence was singled out as an area of work that required particular improvement since this was essential to combat serious crime.

The thrust of the report was that 'size mattered' when it came to making improvements in police performance to enable all forces to deliver the 'protective services' to an acceptable standard (HMIC, 2005: 7). The aim of the reform was to create organisations 'that are large enough to provide a full suite of sustainable services, yet small enough to be able to relate to local communities' (HMIC, 2005: 13). It was argued that the minimum size of a force should be 4,000 officers (HMIC, 2005: 14), which suggested a drastic pruning of the existing number of police forces into a smaller number of larger forces. The total number could be as low as 13 (Loveday, 2006: 10).

Impediments to police force reform

The then Home Secretary, Charles Clarke, supported reform along the lines proposed in the HMIC report. There were, however, difficulties with the proposed changes, including the possibility that reform could be achieved by alternative methods. These included the development of improved collaborative arrangements between forces, the adoption of a 'lead force' concept (which could entail either a lead force taking charge of specific aspects of work or the designation of a lead force covering all aspects of work at regional level) and the federation of forces (whereby local forces would retain their autonomy but would contract together to provide a common set of protective services). The 'lead force' concept had received a limited form of endorsement by the Home Affairs Select Committee (Home Affairs Committee, 2005: 24). Proposals to compel police forces to merge were abandoned when John Reid replaced Charles Clarke as Home Secretary in May 2006. However, as is argued in the concluding chapter, this issue remains on the future policing agenda.

The formation of the NCIS and the NCS

During the 1970s a number of national squads were formed to gather intelligence on activities that included the drugs trade, illegal immigration and football hooliganism. These units were brought together in 1992 under the organisational umbrella of the National Criminal Intelligence Service (NCIS) to perform 'a supply and support role in relation to agencies which ... have enforcement and investigative functions' (Walker, 2000: 202). It was controlled by the Home Office and additional functions (such as the formation, in 1995, of a special unit to focus on groups involved in the theft of vehicles and mobile building equipment) were subsequently added to its responsibilities. The NCIS had no executive arm, although its regional organisation matched that of the regional crime squads which were themselves subject to a loose form of national coordination based in London.

In 1996, the Home Secretary announced his intention to form a new national crime unit to tackle drug traffickers and other organised crime. It would be composed of two sections. One would be concerned with intelligence gathering, based on the existing NCIS supplemented by some MI5 officers. The other unit, with which it would closely cooperate, was the National Crime Squad (NCS). This would be an operational unit, consisting of the regional crime squads amalgamated into a national unit. These reforms were subsequently incorporated into the 1997 Police Act.

The Security Service (MI5) and serious crime

MI5 was formed in 1909 to thwart the spying activities conducted in Britain by the nation's enemies. It was primarily an intelligence-gathering body. The end of the cold war resulted in MI5 straying from its initial brief, and in 1992 it was assigned the lead role in countering terrorism on mainland Britain. Approximately one half of its resources were devoted to combating Northern Irish terrorism (Rimington, 1994).

The IRA ceasefire necessitated the development of yet new areas of responsibility, and the 1996 Security Service Act allocated MI5 the responsibility for dealing with 'serious crime' in addition to its existing functions. This theoretically gave MI5 a broad remit since 'serious crime' was defined as an offence that carried a sentence of three years or more on first conviction, or any offence involving conduct by a large number of persons in pursuit of a common purpose. This raised the possibility of demarcation disputes (or 'turf wars') arising between the police and MI5, although the relatively small size of MI5 (which then had fewer than 2,000 staff) made it unlikely that this agency would seek to usurp mainstream policing roles.

The role given to MI5 by the 1996 Security Services Act was contentious. A former chief constable, John Alderson, argued that it was fatal to involve MI5 with ordinary crime because of its lack of accountability. He stated that this organisation worked by infiltrating organisations, jobs and lives, operating 'almost like a cancer ... destroying trust and security between people'. He accused the Home Secretary of seeking to turn Britain into a police state, with MI5 becoming an East German-style Stasi force with half the population spying on the other half (Alderson, 1996).

The police service was also concerned about this development, in particular that MI5 would become the lead agency in dealing with matters such as drugs and organised crime, and become a *de facto* national police organisation, the British equivalent of the American FBI (Federal Bureau of Investigation). This led ACPO to view favourably the suggestion to set up a national police squad to deal with serious crime, which would act as the operational arm of the NCIS.

The Serious Organised Crime Agency

It has been argued that the social and economic costs of serious organised crime, including the costs of combating it, are £20 billion (Bassett et al., 2009: 21).

The Labour government's concern with the extent of organised crime was evidenced by the formation, in September 2003, of a Cabinet Subcommittee on Organised Crime. It was tasked with advancing a national and international strategy to combat organised crime and its initial role was to set the priorities towards which the relevant law enforcement agencies should work (Home Office, 2004a: 3).

In order to further pursue the campaign against organised crime, the government enacted the 2005 Serious Organised Crime and Police Act, which created a Serious Organised Crime Agency (SOCA). SOCA is headed by a Director-General and its work is guided by a small board. The organisation is accountable to the Home Secretary, who is responsible to Parliament for its performance.

The personnel of SOCA are not police officers, although they possess the powers, responsibilities and roles associated with those employed within the police service. The agency may also utilise a number of important powers with which to tackle serious crime. These include compulsory powers (broadly similar to those given to the Serious Fraud Office in the 1987 Criminal Justice Act) whereby individuals are compelled (through the mechanism of a disclosure notice) to cooperate with investigations by answering questions, providing information or producing documents (Owen et al., 2005: 20–23). The 2005 legislation also introduced statutory procedures to foster the more widespread use of 'Queen's evidence' to encourage defendants to testify against co-defendants.

The main advantage of SOCA was that it brought together under one organisational roof a number of bodies that were concerned with combating serious crime. These were the National Criminal Intelligence Service, the National Crime Squad, the investigative and intelligence work performed by HM Customs and Excise in relation to serious drug trafficking and the recovery of criminal assets and the responsibilities exercised by the Home Office for organised immigration crime.

This reform was designed to remedy existing defects that included overlapping responsibilities in areas such as combating drug trafficking (Home Office, 2004a: 22). It was concluded that this new body would 'lead to a greater consistency of approach' and provide 'a critical mass in key skill areas, address current problems of duplication and coordination, limit bureaucracy, provide opportunities for economies of scale, and represent a "one stop shop" for our international partners'. High-quality intelligence was argued to be of utmost importance in the fight against organised crime, and SOCA was designed to address some of the key weaknesses in the generation, dissemination and use of intelligence material' (Home Office, 2004a: 22 and 29).

There were, however, difficulties associated with the government's proposals. Particular concern was voiced over the powers of the new agency. These included the requirement to cooperate with investigations by answering questions, which was viewed as a fundamental change in the relationship between the state and its citizens, who had historically enjoyed the right that they were not compelled to cooperate with the authorities. It was also argued that this power was subject to insufficient safeguards as to who could authorise these procedures, in what circumstances they should be used and to whom they should apply (Justice, 2004: 4–5).

The police response to the post-1945 changing nature of crime (3): Weaponry

Violence has become a major aspect of contemporary crime and a problem faced by police officers performing routine duties. This has arisen from two key developments: (1) changes affecting the context within which policing operates (especially the decline in respect for those in positions of authority and the consequent problems faced by the police when seeking to impose their will); and (2) the increased willingness of those engaged in crime to utilise violence to pursue their criminal ends. Between 1 April 2007 and 31 March 2008 the number of police operations in which firearms were authorised was 21,181, an increase of 17.5% on the previous year (although officers rarely need to fire their weapons in such episodes) (Coaker, 2009). The willingness of criminals to use violence has resulted in a number of important developments affecting the weaponry and equipment available to police officers.

One development arising from the increased use of violence has been the introduction of tasers (sometimes, and perhaps erroneously, referred to as stun guns). These are 'an alternative to lethal force or used just below the point at which you would deploy lethal force' (Sprague, 2009). These were trialled in five forces in April 2003 and in September 2004 the Home Secretary approved their discretionary use by all chief officers. Authorised Firearms Officers (AFOs) deploy them when a firearms authority had been granted in accordance with guidance provided by ACPO (2003). Since 20 July 2007, AFOs in England and Wales have been permitted to use tasers in operations or incidents where the use of firearms had not been authorised but where they were facing violence or threats of violence of a severity to warrant the use of force to protect themselves or the public. On 1 September 2007 trials were initiated into the use of tasers by police units which were not AFOs when facing similar threats of violence (McNulty, 2007).

Lethal force

The actions of police officers are governed by the constraints imposed by the 1967 Criminal Law Act. This legislation covers the use of reasonable force – a police officer (or a member of the general public exercising the power of citizens' arrest) is permitted to use only force that is reasonable in the circumstances in self-defence or in the defence of another, to defend property, to prevent crime or lawfully arrest an offender. The 1984 Police and Criminal Evidence Act (PACE) also conferred on a police constable the authority to use reasonable force to exercise the powers under that Act unless this power could be exercised only with the consent of some person other than a police officer.

A particular problem arises with the use of lethal force by police officers, especially when an innocent person is injured or killed. There have been several examples of this. These include the killings by police officers of James Ashley in 1998, Harry Stanley and Roger Sylvester in 1999 and Jean Charles de Menezes in 2005. In the latter case it was openly admitted that the Metropolitan Police Service (MPS) was operating a 'shoot to kill' policy with regard to terrorists. However, there is a marked reluctance by the Crown Prosecution Service (CPS) to prosecute officers whose use of force may be viewed as unreasonable or inappropriate and in none of these cases was an officer prosecuted for criminal actions.

The key criteria used by the CPS in determining whether to prosecute a police officer are whether the degree of force used was justified in the circumstances and whether it was excessive in the circumstances. When force is used in connection with preventing a crime or effecting an arrest, 'necessity may not equate with reasonableness', and the nature and degree of force used, the seriousness of the offence which is being prevented or in respect of which an arrest is being made, and the nature and degree of force used against an officer by a person resisting arrest must be considered (Crown Prosecution Service, 2008: 13–14).

Although police officers who are required to deal with armed criminals perhaps deserve the benefit of the doubt when they make an honest mistake, the image of the police suffers when it appears that officers are above the law and able to escape any sanction for serious errors of judgement.

The police response to the post-1945 changing nature of crime (4): Technology

A number of technological developments have been pursued to enable the police to combat crime and, in particular, to stay one step ahead of criminals. The Police Science and Technology Strategy Group (created in 2002) became the driving force behind developments of this nature, which are embraced within the framework of a Police Science and Technology Strategy, the first of which was published in 2003. The role of this Group is 'to ensure the police service is equipped to exploit the opportunities in science and technology to deliver effective policing as part of a modern and respected criminal justice system', in particular by identifying gaps between police requirements and existing capabilities (Home Office, 2004b: 3–4).

Technology has a number of practical applications, which include crime mapping, whereby information on criminal offences is linked to geographic data to produce maps that identify 'hot spots' which then guide the deployment of resources. Some of the key applications of technology in contemporary policing are discussed below.

Storage and dissemination of crime information

The ability of police officers anywhere in the country to access certain basic information from anywhere in the country, such as lists of known criminals, wanted or missing persons, stolen property and registered vehicles, was enhanced by the introduction of the Police National Computer (PNC) into police work in 1974 (the latest version of which entered service in 1991). Information stored on the PNC was by an additional application called Phoenix, an intelligence information system that provides the police with instant information regarding a suspect's criminal record, last known address, car details, accomplices and aliases. The PNC stores around 97 million records on its databases. The nationwide availability of the PNC required all police forces to report information in a standardised fashion. This was developed by the Crime and Incident Reporting application of the National Strategy for Police Information Systems launched in 1994.

The ability of the police to respond to major incidents involving criminal activity in several parts of the country – and thus necessitating cooperation by different police forces – was enhanced by the Home Office Large Major Enquiry System. It enables actions taken by officers in one forces to be recorded and accessed by colleagues working on the same investigation in another force. HOLMES 2 enables incidents in different forces to be linked by cross-matching details of a person, vehicle, address or telephone number in one investigation's database with details held in another. This capability has advanced police computer usage from information storage and retrieval into the area of crime investigation.

A number of national computer facilities have been developed to enable the police to cope with serious crime. These include the Violent and Sex Offender Register (ViSOR) and the National Video Identification Database. The National Automated Fingerprint Identification System (NAFIS) initially provided the police service with a national fingerprint database. This has since been replaced by the National Automated Fingerprint Identification System (IDENT1). On 31 October 2007, 7.3 million persons in England, Wales and Scotland had fingerprint records stored on the national fingerprint system, IDENT1 (Hillier, 2008a).

There are, nonetheless, weaknesses in the use made by police forces of computer technology. Officers may lack the training to use it to its optimum efficiency (a shortcoming that affected the Stephen Lawrence murder investigation (Home Office, 1999: para 14.5). The Bichard Inquiry (Bichard, 2004) that followed the Soham murders drew particular attention to the deficiencies affecting information-sharing within the police service. This gave rise to a number of developments that included the IMPACT Nominal Index (INI). This enables individual police forces to share information they have gathered locally. The INI provides pointers as to the location where those looking for information can find it. It was intended that INI would provide direct access to such material through the mechanism of a Police National Database. However, problems with the nature of data stored by individual forces have impeded the progress of this reform. An additional problem is that forces remain highly insular in their adoption of such technology. The National Policing Improvement Agency has been given a remit to remedy such problems.

The National DNA Database

The application of technological advances to detecting crime has been enhanced by the establishment in 1995 of the National DNA Database (NDNAD) for the police. The custodian of this database is the National Policing Improvement Agency (NPIA).

The 1994 Criminal Justice and Public Order Act amended PACE to allow the collection of DNA samples. 'DNA samples' refer to biological material either taken from individuals of left at crime scenes. These samples are analysed to produce code numbers (called 'profiles') that are stored on the National DNA Database. Samples may be taken if a person is charged with, or is reported for summons, or is convicted of a recordable offence. The samples, and the DNA profiles that are obtained from them, are retained and can be speculatively searched against other samples and profiles held by, or on behalf of, the police.

If a person is not prosecuted, or is acquitted, the samples and profiles are to be destroyed. The 2001 Criminal Justice and Police Act further amended PACE to remove the requirement to destroy samples following an acquittal or prosecution, although the samples thus retained can only be used for the purposes of preventing and detecting crime, investigating an offence or conducting a prosecution. The 2003 Criminal Justice Act further amended PACE to allow the police to take DNA and fingerprints without consent from anyone who is arrested for a recordable offence and who is subsequently detained in a police station (Hillier, 2008a).

DNA is a key weapon in the war against crimes that entail some form of physical contact between the criminal and his or her target, and is a good defence against miscarriages of justice arising from a person being found guilty of a crime that he or she did not commit. The capabilities of DNA as a method of detecting crime have been enhanced in the early years of the twenty-first century by the development by the Forensic Science Service of 'DNAboost', which can help to distinguish between samples taken from a surface that a number of people have touched or when only a small DNA sample has been collected.

The availability of DNA samples has further benefits in solving old, serious crimes for which no person was apprehended at the time, but for which DNA samples existed and which are now capable of analysis. This process is referred to as cold case review.

By 2000 there were 775,000 DNA samples in the database (Barnett, 2000). That year the government announced that it intended to include the genetic fingerprints of all arrested persons in this database, and these could then be matched against evidence gathered from crimes which remained unsolved. Around 3.7% of the population are represented on the NDNAD and 'a typical month has seen suspects identified for 15 murders, 31 rapes and 770 car crimes' (Flint, 2004: 1). It was later estimated that on 31 October 2007 there were 4,188,033 persons whose DNA profile was retained in the National DNA Database (which included the UK and other forces such as the Channel Islands). Of these, 4,165,300 consisted of samples provided after arrest and 22,700 were voluntary samples. For England alone, the figures were 3,916,500 samples provided following arrest and 21,600 provided voluntarily (Hillier, 2007).

However, although it is argued that DNA is more or less foolproof, it is not completely infallible and may still result in innocent people being convicted. Samples can be mixed up and, additionally, the decision as to whether a match has been discovered is made by human beings whose work can be subject to error.

There are also civil liberties considerations that especially arise from the retention on the NDNAD of the DNA samples of those who had either not been charged with a crime or who had been acquitted by a court. The government was very keen that these DNA samples should be retained. These numbered approximately 200,000 people, whose samples were collected between May 2001 and December 2005. It was stated that from these 200,000 records, around 8,500 were linked with crime scene profiles involving 1,400 offences including 114 murders, 116 rapes and 68 sexual offences (Hillier, 2008b). However, in late 2008, the European Court of Human Rights declared this practice to be unlawful and in response to this judgment, the 2010 Crime and Security Act established new time limits for the retention of DNA samples.

National Ballistics Intelligence Service (NABIS)

This was set up in 2009 in response to the illegal possession and use of firearms which are used to commit gun crime. It provides a national database of all recovered firearms and ballistic material coming into the possession of the police. This includes items such as rounds of ammunition, cartridge cases and projectiles. The database further links these ballistics items to tactical intelligence recorded by police forces and other UK law enforcement agencies. NABIS also provides a police-governed forensic capability to link firearms incidents. It can test fire, analyse and link firearms and ballistic material to items submitted from other incidents across the UK. The role it performs is intelligence-based and evidential material required as evidence in court is delivered by independent forensic science providers (NABIS, 2009).

Surveillance techniques

Crime may be prevented or detected by the use of surveillance devices. Contemporary police work employs a wide range of these.

CCTV

Close-circuit television (CCTV) constitutes a form of mass surveillance and may be used to monitor the activity of the general public in the hope of deterring or identifying those responsible for urban crime and disorder. Initially, the police service was lukewarm towards the use of CCTV surveillance, regarding the need to provide operators to monitor the cameras and other staff to examine the tapes as labour intensive (Goold, 2004: 71). Subsequently, however, the service has accepted that the availability of CCTV images 'greatly assists in the investigation of crime and disorder' (House of Lords Select Committee on the Constitution, 2009: para 74). Such images have played an important role in the early identification and subsequent prosecutions of suspects in high-profile cases that have included the IRA terrorist campaign in the 1990s, the 1999 Brixton nail bomber and the July 2005 terrorist attacks in London (Gerrard et al., 2007: 7).

Around £500 million of public money has been invested in CCTV in the decade up to 2006 and it is estimated that there are around 4 million CCTV cameras in the UK (House of Lords Select Committee on the Constitution, 2009: para 70). One estimate suggested that an individual in Great Britain going about their everyday life might be photographed by up to 300 cameras on 30 different systems (Norris and Armstrong, 1999: 42).

The main legislation that regulates the use of CCTV in public spaces (most of which is owned by local authorities) is the 1998 Data Protection Act. Additionally, operators monitoring public spaces are required to possess a licence from the security industry.

The spread of the use of CCTV has its critics. It has been alleged that it 'poses a significant threat to personal privacy and individual freedom' and undermines the 'value of privacy as a public good' (cited in House of Lords Select Committee on the Constitution, 2009: paras 100 and 102). Nor has there been adequate research conducted into the impact of CCTV on the investigation of crime (House of Lords Select Committee on the Constitution, 2009: para 80).

Automated Number Plate Recognition (ANPR)

ANPR was invented in 1976 by the Police Scientific Development Branch. It operates through a camera (which may be an existing CCTV or road-rule enforcement camera) and optical recognition software in order to read vehicle number plates. Its rationale was to deny criminals the use of the road. It enables the police to gather data and track the movement of targets that include organised criminal gangs and terrorist suspects. It can also cross-check the car number plates that it has read against stolen or suspected vehicles logged on the PNC's databases.

Officers who use technical equipment such as number plate recognition are able to make a significantly higher number of arrests than those who do not use it. The problems with this technology include the quality of images and also the civil liberties issues arising from the police monitoring of innocent members of the public.

Communication applications

Technology may aid the process of communication both between the forces that comprise the police service and between the service and other criminal justice agencies.

A key recent technological development is called Airwave. This is a digital police radio communications service that provides improved mobile data provision that enables the speedier deployment of officers to incidents and the quicker relay of information regarding events. It is used by all police forces in the UK, thus enabling them to communicate by radio, telephone or text messages. It became fully operational throughout England and Wales in 2006, replacing the existing analogue radio systems. The Airwave radio network is an example of a technology that was centrally procured and implemented across all forces, allowing for consistent standards, economies of scale and operational efficiency (Home Affairs Committee, 2008: para 201).

QUESTION

To what extent have police methods to tackle crime since c.1960 posed a fundamental threat to the citizens' personal rights and freedoms?

In order to answer this question you would draw upon the material referred to above and consult some of the key material contained in the references. The main issues to be considered are:

- The changing nature of crime since 1960 as the context for introducing changes to police methods;
- Key changes that have been introduced by the police in this period to tackle crime (these issues have been discussed above);
- How these changes might pose a threat to the citizens' personal rights and freedom;
- The defences that exist to defend the personal rights and freedoms of the citizen (these include the 1998 Human Rights Act and the 2001 Regulation of Investigatory Powers Act, and it would be helpful to give some examples as to how these protections operate);
- A conclusion as to whether changes introduced into policing in this period have eroded citizens' personal rights and freedoms.

REFERENCES

ACPO (2003) *Manual of Guidance on the Police Use of Firearms.* London: ACPO.

Alderson, J. (1996) 'A Fair Cop', *Red Pepper*, 24. [Online] Red Pepper Archive www.web. archive.org/web/19970712055954/www.redpepper.org.uk/xfaircop.html [accessed on 24 April 2009].

Audit Commission (1993) *Helping with Enquiries.* Abingdon: Audit Commission.

Barnett, A. (2000) 'Fury at Police DNA Database', *The Observer*, 11 June.

Bassett, D., Haldenby, A., Thraves, L. and Truss, E. (2009) *A New Force.* London: Reform.

Bichard, Sir M. (2004) *The Bichard Inquiry Report.* House of Commons Paper 653. London: TSO.

Carrabine, E., Iganski, P., Lee, M., Plummer, K. and South, N. (2004) *Criminology: A Sociological Introduction.* London: Routledge.

Coaker, V. (2009) Speech in the House of Commons, 2 March, HC Debs, Vol 488, Col 41–42WS.

Cowan, R. and Hyder, K. (2005) 'Met Targets Gangs' Grip on Minorities', *The Guardian*, 25 March.

Crown Prosecution Service (2008) *Allegations of Criminal Offences against the Police.* [Online] www.cps.gov.uk/legal/a_to_c/allegations_of_criminal_offences_against_the_ police/#a01 [accessed on 15 April 2009].

Fisher, Sir H. (1977) *Report of an Inquiry into the Circumstances Leading to the Trial of Three Persons Arising out of the Death of Maxwell Confait and the Fire at 27 Doggett Road, London, SE6.* House of Commons Paper 80. London: House of Commons.

Flint, C. (2004) 'Parliamentary Under-Secretary of State's Foreword', in Home Office, *Police Science and Technology Strategy 2004–2009.* Science Policy. London: Home Office.

Gerrard, G., Parkins, G., Cunningham, I., Jones, W., Hill, S. and Douglas, S. (2007) *Home Office National CCTV Strategy.* London: Joint Home Office/ACPO Team.

Gifford, T. (1984) *Supergrasses: The Use of Accomplice Evidence in Northern Ireland.* London: The Cobden Trust.

Goold, B. (2004) *CCTV and Policing: Public Area Surveillance and Police Practices in Britain.* Oxford: Oxford University Press.

Her Majesty's Inspectorate of Constabulary (HMIC) (2005) *Closing the Gap – A Review of 'Fitness for Purpose' of the Current Structure of Policing in England and Wales.* London: Home Office.

Her Majesty's Inspectorate of Constabulary (HMIC) (2009) *Get Smart: Planning to Protect – The Protective Service Review 2008.* London: HMIC.

Hillier, M. (2007) Speech in the House of Commons, 10 December, HC Debs, Vol 469, Col 84W.

Hillier, M. (2008a) Speech in the House of Commons, 7 January, HC Debs, Vol 470, Col 287W.

Hillier, M. (2008b) Speech in the House of Commons, 29 February, HC Debs, Vol 472, Col 1433.

Home Affairs Committee (2005) *Police Reform.* Session 2004–05, Fourth Report, House of Commons Paper 307. London: TSO.

Home Affairs Committee (2008) *Policing in the Twenty-first Century.* Session 2007–08, Seventh Report, House of Commons Paper 364. London: TSO.

Home Office (1999) *The Stephen Lawrence Inquiry: Report of an Inquiry by Sir William Macpherson of Cluny.* Cm 4262. London: TSO.

Home Office (2003) *Building Safer Communities Together.* London: Home Office, Police Reform – Performance Delivery Unit.

Home Office (2004a) *One Step Ahead: A 21st Century Strategy to Defeat Organised Crime*. Cm 6167. London: TSO.

Home Office (2004b) *Police Science and Technology Strategy 2004–2009*. London: Home Office, Science Policy Unit.

House of Lords European Union Committee (2004) *Judicial Cooperation in the EU: The Role of Eurojust*. Session 2003–04, 23rd Report. House of Lords Paper 138. London: TSO.

House of Lords Select Committee on the Constitution (2009) *Surveillance: Citizens and the State*. Second Report, Session 2008–09. House of Lords Paper 18. London: TSO.

Justice (2004) *Response to White Paper 'One Step Ahead – A 21st Century Strategy to Defeat Organised Crime*. London: Justice.

Loveday, B. (2006) *Size Isn't Everything: Restructuring Policing in England and Wales*. London: The Policy Exchange.

McIntosh, M. (1971) 'Changes in the Organisation of Thieving', in S. Cohen (ed.), *Images of Deviance*. Harmondsworth: Penguin.

McNulty, T. (2007) Speech in the House of Commons, 26 November, HC Debs, Vol 468, Col 197W.

Morton, J. (2002) *Supergrasses & Informers and Bent Coppers* (Omnibus edition). London: Time Warner.

Morton, J. (2003) *Gangland* (Omnibus edition). London: Time Warner.

NABIS (2009) 'Welcome to NABIS'. National Ballistics Intelligence Service. [Online] www.nabis.police.uk/home.asp [accessed on 7 June 2009].

Norris, C. and Armstrong, G. (1999) *The Maximum Surveillance Society: The Rise of CCTV*. Oxford: Berg.

Owen, T., Bailin, A., Knowles, J., MacDonald, A., Ryder, M., Sayers, D. and Tomlinson, H. (2005) *Blackstone's Guide to the Serious Organised Crime and Police Act 2005*. Oxford: Oxford University Press.

Rimington, S. (1994) 'Security and Democracy – Is There a Conflict?' The Richard Dimbleby Lecture, BBC Television, 12 June.

Sprague, O. (2009) *Tasers: Oral and Written Evidence, 5 May 2009, Mr Oliver Sprague and ACC Simon Chesterton*, Home Affairs Committee, session 2008–2009. London: TSO, House of Commons Paper 494.

Tilley, N. (2003) 'Community Policing, Problem-oriented Policing and Intelligence-led Policing', in T. Newburn (ed.), *Handbook of Policing*. Cullompton, Devon: Willan Publishing.

Walker, N. (2000) *Policing in a Changing Constitutional Order*. London: Sweet and Maxwell.

3
Police powers

CHAPTER AIMS

The aims of this chapter are:

- To analyse the concept of discretion in connection with the use of police powers;
- To examine the allocation of powers to the police in the formative years of new policing and analyse the way in which police powers developed in the twentieth century;
- To evaluate the importance of the 1984 Police and Criminal Evidence Act in relation to the powers of the police;
- To consider the balance that has been struck in connection with police powers and the liberty of the subject;
- To discuss the development of the police complaints machinery and evaluate the effectiveness of the complaints procedure;
- To evaluate the nature of and responses to corruption in the police service.

Discretion

Although police work is governed by formal rules and procedures, these are tempered by the exercise of discretion by police officers at all levels of the service.

The term 'discretion' conjures up a variety of images. These include 'rule-bending', the application of 'tact', 'sympathy', 'understanding' and 'common sense' or the exercise of independent judgement by professionals to a situation with which they are faced. It has been argued that discretion 'refers to the freedom, power, authority, decision or leeway of an official, organisation or individual to decide, discern or determine to make a judgement, choice or decision, about alternative courses of action or inaction' (Gelsthorpe and Padfield, 2003: 1).

There are several factors that influence the exercise of discretion. These include 'process' (practitioners have been provided with the ability to screen out or divert cases from the criminal justice system based on legal or practical considerations), 'environment' (actions undertaken by practitioners will be influenced by community views concerning appropriate courses of action) and 'context' (practitioner's decisions are influenced by 'internal' organisational and occupational factors). What are termed 'illicit considerations' (factors such as class, race and gender underpin a professional's actions) may also influence the manner in which discretion is utilised (Gelsthorpe and Padfield, 2003: 6–9).

Discretion can be used in both negative and positive ways. It has been concluded that discretion 'is a force for ill when it leads to unjustifiable decisions (negative discrimination) and inconsistency (disparity), but it can be a good thing in that it provides a mechanism to show mercy which, even if defying precise definition, many would recognise as being necessary to the conception and delivery of justice' (Gelsthorpe and Padfield, 2003: 6).

The police service and discretion

Police officers at all levels of the service possess a considerable degree of discretion (or what has been termed 'mandated flexibility') (Gelsthorpe and Padfield, 2003: 1), but they do not possess complete freedom as to how they exercise it. 'Judgements or choices are in practice much constrained, not only by formal (and sometimes legal) rules but also by the many social, economic and political constraints that act upon the exercise of choice' (Gelsthorpe and Padfield, 2003: 3).

Chief constables

The principle of constabulary independence that developed during the course of the nineteenth century with regard to enforcing the law was affirmed in the case of *Fisher v. Oldham Corporation* [1930]. This meant that no outside body could dictate to a chief constable how the law should be enforced. The 1964 Police Act placed police forces under the 'direction and control' of their chief officers, giving them the ability to determine the law enforcement priorities for their forces (a task in which Watch Committees in towns had historically been involved). One reason for the need to exercise discretion was that it was impossible to enforce every law and thus a choice had to be made as to what was the most important for a particular force. A key problem with this situation was that decisions could be based on the personal views or prejudices of the most senior officers.

The exercise of discretion by chief officers was subject to constraints, one of which was the intervention of the judiciary (and, ultimately, the European Court of Human Rights), especially when it appeared that a chief officer was choosing not to enforce the law. This issue arose in 1968 and 1973 when Raymond Blackburn brought cases against the Metropolitan Police Commissioner in connection with legislation concerned with illegal gambling and the distribution of obscene material, but interventions of this nature have been sporadic. Further, judges have usually declined to interfere with what they regard as police operational decisions even when, as was the case in *R v. Chief Constable of Devon and Cornwall ex parte Central Electricity Generating Board* [1981], they perceived that chief constable's decision was founded on incorrect assumptions.

The ability of chief officers to determine priorities for their force was considerably constrained by the 1994 Police and Magistrates' Courts Act, which enabled the Home Secretary to set key priorities for the entire police service in England and Wales. This issue is discussed in Chapter 6.

Junior officers

Junior officers are required to exercise their discretion in a number of key aspects of their work. It underpins their conduct 'on the streets' where they may be required to exercise their judgement as to whether the law is being broken and, if so, what action to take. Often discretion at this level of police work is a decision which has to be taken on the spur of the moment. If an officer uses his or her discretion to arrest a person, other discretionary actions follow (for example, what crime to charge the suspect with, whether to release on bail or remand in custody).

The origins of this form of discretion are legal, based upon the fact that a constable's authority 'is original and not delegated, and is exercised at his own discretion by virtue of his office, and on no responsibility but his own' (*Enever v. The King* [1906]). A further, practical, justification for the existence of discretion at this level stems from the impossibility of police managers to effectively supervise every action taken by an officer. It also reflects the impossibility of police enforcement of all laws.

Although a junior officer's conduct has never been totally free of constraints, concern was expressed that officers had too free a rein in enforcing the law, which could become influenced by their personal or collective biases. As a result, legislation such as the 1984 Police and Criminal Evidence Act and the 2000 Race Relations (Amendment) Act sought to impose controls on how some of the more contentious displays of discretion (in particular the use of stop and search powers) were exercised.

Police powers

The role of the police, as stated in 1829 by Metropolitan Police Commissioner Sir Richard Mayne in his instructions to the newly-formed Metropolitan Police, was:

- To prevent crime;
- To protect life and property;
- To preserve public tranquillity.

To these functions others may be added:

- Bringing offenders to justice (which, until the creation of the Crown Prosecution Service, included the prosecution of offenders);
- 'Befriending the public'. The latter responsibility entails performing a wide range of activities which have little to do with law enforcement but which involve answering requests by the public for assistance, whatever the nature of the problem. This is known as the 'service function' of policing.

The police possess a range of methods through which they carry out their roles. They may rely on the authority of their office to achieve a desired outcome, but they can also to translate their individual authority into power through their ability to summon aid to deal with a confrontational situation.

Additionally, police officers are provided with a range of formal powers that augment their informal methods to achieve the outcomes they feel to be appropriate in their dealings with members of the public. When the new system of policing was set up in the early years of the nineteenth century, the police were provided with common law powers, and as late as 1929 it was argued that a constable was 'a citizen in uniform' (Royal Commission on Police Powers and Procedure, 1929). Some of these historic powers remain, for example, the common law power to arrest for a breach of the peace.

However, as the nineteenth century progressed, the police were given powers additional to those possessed by ordinary members of the general public. These powers were granted by legislation, often of local jurisdiction and applied to officers who worked in a particular part of the country. This meant that police powers lacked a national framework.

Changes affecting the nature of crime and the role and responsibilities of the police after 1945 necessitated a re-examination of police powers. This was provided for in the 1984 Police and Criminal Evidence Act (PACE), which has been described as 'the single most significant landmark in the modern development of police powers' (Reiner, 2000: 176).

The 1984 Police and Criminal Evidence Act

The legislation gave the police a number of key powers, including the ability to:

- Stop and search a person or a vehicle in a public place;
- Enter private property, search the premises and seize material found there (with or without a warrant);
- Arrest;
- Take fingerprints and other non-intimate samples;
- Detain a person in custody.

The Act also rationalised these powers across England and Wales, providing a national raft of police powers.

However, the 1984 Act was/is not the only source of police powers. As has been noted above, powers derived from common law also remained, although they were reduced in number following the enactment of the 1984 legislation. Powers have also been allocated to the police by other legislation. This situation has in part arisen from a recent tendency to respond to law and order problems by creating new offences, which often require the police to be given additional powers in order to enforce them. The key police powers are discussed in the following sections.

Stop and search

PACE provided the police with powers to stop and search a person or a vehicle in a public place to enable officers to allay or confirm their suspicions about individuals without first exercising their power of arrest. Safeguards relating to the exercise of these powers were provided by Codes of Practice, which are discussed below. Although most stop and searches (around 92% of those carried out in 2006/07) are carried out under PACE (Rollock, 2009: 57), other legislation has also provided police officers with similar powers. These additional measures included section 60 of the 1994 Criminal Justice and Public Order Act, which accounted for 44,659 stops in 2006/07, and section 44 of the 2000 Terrorism Act, which formed the basis of 37,000 searches in 2006/07 (Rollock, 2009: 58).

Other legislation containing stop and search provisions includes the 1968 Firearms Act, the 1971 Misuse of Drugs Act, the 1979 Customs and Excise Management Act, the 1982 Aviation Security Act, the 1985 Sporting Events (Control of Alcohol etc.) Act and the 1997 Knives Act.

Entry, search and seizure

PACE authorised a magistrate to issue a warrant to the police if they were unable to obtain consent to conduct a search. A warrant could only be issued in connection with what the Act categorised as a serious arrestable offence in order to obtain evidence which was likely to be significant to the investigation. In order to obtain a warrant, the police must specify to the magistrate the crime that is being investigated and the nature of the evidence they anticipate to be produced in the search.

Under the 1984 legislation, some items were not covered under the provisions of a general warrant (although separate authorisation may be obtained to gain access to them). These included legally privileged material (such as letters between a solicitor and his or her client) and what the Act defined as 'excluded material' or 'special procedure material' (such as medical records).

Sections 17, 18 and 32 of PACE permitted the police to enter premises without a search warrant. The legislation contained conditions which applied to the exercise of these powers. For example, under section 32, the police could enter and search premises occupied by a person who had already been arrested, provided that there were reasonable grounds to suspect that evidence relating to the offence for which the arrest was made will be uncovered.

Other powers of this nature were contained in the 1971 Misuse of Drugs Act and the 1988 Road Traffic Act.

Photographs, fingerprints and samples

PACE provided the police with powers to take photographs, fingerprints and samples from persons arrested on suspicion of having committed a crime. These powers were subsequently developed in Codes of Practice issued under the authority of the 1984 legislation.

In 1995, new Codes of Practice took into account a number of developments that had taken place since the implementation of PACE (in 1986), including the provisions of the 1994 Criminal Justice and Public Order Act relating to the taking of intimate and non-intimate body samples for forensic analysis and identification procedures (Bucke and Brown, 1997: 1). One consequence of the 1995 Codes was to redefine saliva and mouth swabs as non-intimate samples, which could thus be taken if a suspect refused to voluntarily supply a sample. Additionally, non-intimate samples could be taken for recordable offences rather than serious arrestable offences, as had been the case previously, thus vastly expanding the range of offences for which samples could be taken (Bucke and Brown, 1997: 42).

The 2005 Serious Organised Crime and Police Act amended a number of sections of PACE to enable photographs of suspects to be taken at places other than police stations and for fingerprints to be taken without a suspect's consent under specified circumstances. The definition given to intimate samples in PACE was extended by this legislation to include 'a swab taken from any part of a person's genitals (including the pubic hair)' and the definition of what constituted a non-intimate sample was extended.

Arrest

Arrests may be made on the basis of a warrant issued by a magistrate or a judge (for example, if a person fails to attend court after a summons has been issued). PACE permitted an arrest to be made without a warrant for serious offences (termed 'serious arrestable offences'), such as murder, which could be exercised by the criterion of a reasonable belief that an offence was being committed.

Section 28 of PACE stipulated the requirements that need to be adhered to for an arrest to be legal. These included the requirements that a person must be informed as soon as is practicable that he or she is under arrest and the reasons for the arrest. The person arrested must subsequently be cautioned before being questioned.

Some offences were not arrestable and were alternatively dealt with by a police officer reporting the wrongdoer, who might subsequently be summoned to appear in court. Section 25 of PACE, however, provided for general powers of arrest which applied when a person who had committed a minor offence to which the powers of arrest would not usually apply was deemed by a police officer not to have given a true name or address.

However, it was argued that these arrest provisions were complicated and confusing to police officers. Accordingly, the 2005 Serious Organised Crime and Police Act amended the power of arrest provisions of the 1984 Police and Criminal Evidence Act. The 2005 legislation extended the power to arrest without a warrant to cover a much broader range of offences, provided that certain criteria (in particular the necessity criteria) were met, as were stipulated in the Act. Additionally, powers available to the police in connection with 'serious arrestable offences' (such as powers to obtain search warrants or to detain arrested persons without charge for up to 96 hours) became applicable to all indictable offences (Owen et al., 2005: 72–77).

However, the new power to arrest without a warrant also meant that a number of summary offences, which had previously been arrestable under PACE, no longer attracted the 'trigger powers' of entry and search under the new arrangements. This embraced 17 offences previously listed under section 24 of PACE (Home Office, 2007).

Detention

Prior to PACE, a person who had been detained in custody was required to be charged with an offence and brought before the courts as soon as was practicable. The defence of the citizen against arbitrary detention by the authorities was guaranteed by *habeas corpus*, a writ that compelled the authorities who were holding a person in custody to present him or her to the courts in order to ascertain the validity of the detention. *Habeas corpus* dates from the Anglo-Saxon period and was placed on a statutory basis in the 1679 Habeas Corpus Act (or in Scotland the 1701 Wrongous Imprisonment Act).

However, this procedure failed to provide totally effective protection to a citizen's civil liberties, a key weakness being that a person who was being detained by the police was usually unlikely to be able to communicate his or her whereabouts to others who could initiate the *habeas corpus* procedure. This could result in lengthy periods of detention.

Accordingly, PACE imposed restrictions on the period of detention. Under the legislation, detention in custody would normally last for a period of 24 hours, although an officer of the rank of superintendent could add a further 12 hours. If a further extension was required, it had to be granted by a magistrate, and could extend to a total period of 96 hours. At that stage a person should either be charged with an offence or released. The 2006 Terrorism Act provided for an elongated period of detention (termed 'pre-charge detention') for a period of 28 days for those suspected of having committed terrorist offences.

Treatment in custody

The way in which a person held in custody was treated by the police was governed by Judges' Rules (introduced in 1912). These were non-statutory guidelines and the perception that they were not always rigidly adhered to by police officers investigating a crime was made public knowledge in connection with the treatment of three boys who had been charged with the murder of Maxwell Confait in 1972 (Fisher, 1977). Interviews did not require the presence of a solicitor and the frequent absence of detailed notes sometimes gave rise to the fabrication of confessions (a procedure known as 'verballing'). This report resulted in the appointment of a Royal Commission on Criminal Procedure in 1978 (Royal Commission on Criminal Procedure, 1981), and this and the report by Lord Scarman (Home Office, 1981) formed the background to the 1984 Police and Criminal Evidence Act.

To correct abuses that sometimes arose in police stations, PACE introduced the tape recording (and more recently the video recording) of interviews conducted by police officers and laid down guidelines as to how these interviews should be conducted. The legislation also provided for those held in custody to obtain legal representation, and in 1991 a revision of the PACE Codes emphasised a suspect's right to legal advice. It has been noted that since the introduction of PACE there has been a rise in the number of suspects requesting legal advice (Bucke and Brown, 1997: 70).

PACE also provided for the supervision of a suspect by the new post of 'custody officer'. The custody officer's role entails ensuring that the rights of an arrested person held in custody are adhered to and keeping a custody record. The custody officer has legal responsibility for persons held in custody and is required to determine if there is sufficient evidence to charge a person who had been arrested. If this is not the case, the custody officer may release the suspect with no further action being taken against him or her, or bail the suspect to return to the police station at a future date to enable further enquiries to be made before determining whether the suspect should be charged.

Right to silence

Historically, a person who had been arrested was not required to answer any subsequent questions put to him or her by a police officer. This was known as the 'right of silence'. However, perceptions that this right was abused led to restrictions being placed upon it.

The 1994 Criminal Justice and Public Order Act enabled the courts to draw inferences from a suspect's refusal to answer questions under four circumstances: (1) when a defendant uses a defence in court that he or she had failed to mention earlier when questioned or charged by the police; (2) when a defendant aged 14 years or over refuses to give evidence at a trial; (3) when a suspect, having been issued with a 'special warning' under the Act, fails to account for incriminating objects, marks or substances, or; (4) fails to account for his or her presence at a particular place (Bucke and Brown, 1997: 34 and 37).

Changes to the right of silence brought about by the 1994 legislation were reflected in the caution that an arrested person receives before being questioned. This was amended to state:

> You do not have to say anything but it may harm your defence if you do not mention now anything you later rely on in court. Anything you do say will be given in evidence.

The impact of this reform was to reduce the overall use of the right of silence by suspects, although factors that included the seriousness of the offence and racial and gender differences exerted an influence on suspects' use of silence. African-Caribbeans were found to be more likely to exercise this right than other racial groups, and men were more likely to exercise it than women (Bucke and Brown, 1997: 35–36).

Civil liberties and police powers

A key issue affecting police powers concerns the liberty of the subject – the need to ensure that the citizens' rights are properly safeguarded in their dealings with the police. In order to protect the liberties of the subject, a number of constraints have been developed. These include the 1998 Human Rights Act that requires police officers to ensure that their actions accord with the European Declaration of Human Rights (including interpretations handed down by the European Court of Human Rights).

More recently, the 2007 Corporate Homicide Act created a new statutory offence whereby an organisation was guilty of corporate manslaughter (in Scotland, corporate culpable homicide) if the way in which its activities were managed or organised caused a death and amounted to a gross breach of a relevant duty of care (which imposes an obligation on an organisation to take reasonable steps to protect a person's safety) to the dead person (Ministry of Justice, 2007: 3 and 8). There have been 2,000 deaths in custody between 1995 and 2005, but only 10 verdicts of unlawful killing have been secured (Grieve, 2007). Pressure from the House of Lords forced the government into agreeing that deaths in custody (either in police stations or in prisons) would be incorporated into to the measure through delegated legislation.

Additionally, the police service is required to comply with the requirements of the 1974 Health and Safety at Work Act in connection with its dealings with members of the general public. In 2007, the Crown Prosecution Service undertook proceedings against the Metropolitan Police Service alleging that the force had failed to provide for the health, safety and welfare of John Charles de Menezes on 22 July 2005. This case resulted in a fine of £175,000 plus costs of £385,000 being imposed.

The 1984 Police and Criminal Evidence Act (PACE) Codes of Practice

The usage and conditions under which police powers granted by the Police and Criminal Evidence Act can be exercised and what the police can and cannot do when implementing them is regulated by provisions contained in the Act itself and in detailed Codes of Practice. There are currently eight Codes of Practice, introduced in February 2008, that provide safeguards regarding the use of police powers and the protection of civil liberties.

PACE Codes of Practice are separate from the parent 1984 legislation. They constitute a form of delegated legislation that was issued by ministers following a statutory process of consultation and that required the approval of both Houses of Parliament. The current procedure governing this was amended in the 2003 Criminal Justice Act, making for a more limited consultation process outside Parliament (Gibson and Watkins, 2004: 26). Although the Codes impose obligations on the police service, breach of them does not automatically lead to criminal or disciplinary proceedings, although it may form the basis of a disciplinary hearing. This gave rise to the possibility that safeguards governing activities such as stop and search were 'presentational rules' ('ones that exist to give an acceptable appearance to the way that police work is carried out') which might be disregarded by officers on the streets (Smith and Gray, 1983: 171).

Furthermore, the Codes are accompanied by 'Notes for Guidance'. These amplify the content of the Codes but their legal status is less clear (Harlow and Rawlings, 1997: 157–158) and there have been occasions when they have not been strictly complied with.

Complaints against the police

Police officers do not enjoy total discretion in the exercise of their duties and their actions are subject to a number of informal and formal constraints. Examples of the former include the impact made by police culture on the actions of officers, and the latter comprises the requirements to operate in accordance with the law and the police service's code of behaviour.

The current code of behaviour is contained in the Standards of Professional Behaviour for Police Officers. These were introduced in the 2008 Police (Conduct) Regulations following the 2005 Taylor Review and the considerations of its recommendations by a working party of the Police Advisory Board for England and Wales, the Independent Police Complaints Commission (IPCC) and the Home Office. They incorporate considerations of ethics and conduct that set out the professional standards of behaviour required of a police officer.

The Standards impose a number of obligations on officers that include the requirement to act with honesty and integrity, to treat members of the public with respect and courtesy, to act with fairness and impartiality, to ensure that when on duty they are fit to carry out their responsibilities and to act in a professional manner when on duty (Home Office 2006, 2008). If these requirements are not met, the officer becomes the subject of a disciplinary hearing (which has been considerably streamlined for low-level misconduct matters) and, for serious offences (those that constitute 'gross misconduct'), may be dismissed from the service.

The new procedures removed the former sanctions of requirement to resign, reduction in rank, reduction in pay, fine, reprimand and caution, and replaced them with management action, written warning and final warning (Crown Prosecution Service, 2008: 8). The standards of proof in disciplinary hearings are based upon the civil law test of the balance of probabilities. The vast majority of misconduct cases (around 96% in the Metropolitan Police Service) arise as the result of internal allegations or investigations rather than from complaints by members of the general public (Taylor, 2005: 8), and the focus of the new system is to develop and improve as opposed to blame and punish (Crown Prosecution Service, 2008: 8).

The police complaints machinery

Formal machinery has been developed to investigate claims that officers have committed offences either against the law or against the Standards of Professional Behaviour for Police Officers. This section discusses the development of this mechanism, which is referred to as 'the police complaints machinery'. Its use should be set in the context that 'the number of public complaints and internal disciplinary matters are very small when measured against the myriad of public contacts and extensive range of police service activity' (Taylor, 2005: 3).

For many years, complaints by the public against police officers were handled internally, a procedure that commenced when the first two police commissioners in London (Charles Rowan and Richard Mayne) invited aggrieved members of the public to refer complaints directly to them (Lewis: 1999: 2). Perceptions that this was an ineffective way to combat police misbehaviour resulted in the development of formal machinery to handle complaints made against individual police officers. There have been three main developments to achieve this: (1) the establishment of the Police Complaints Board in the 1976 Police Act; (2) its replacement by the Police Complaints Authority in the 1984 Police and Criminal Evidence Act; and (3) the formation of the Independent Police Complaints Authority in the 2002 Police Reform Act.

The Police Complaints Board

The 1964 Police Act placed police forces under the control of chief constables, thereby making these officers vicariously liable for torts committed by officers under their command. It also introduced a common system for handling complaints by members of the general public against police officers. The 1976 Police Act considerably developed this procedure by establishing a Police Complaints Board (PCB), the role of which was to consider complaints alleging that an officer had breached Police Disciplinary Regulations.

Under the provisions of the 1976 Act, all complaints against police officers made by members of the public were to be monitored by the force's deputy chief constable. The complaint was then investigated either by officers from that force's Complaints and Discipline Department or by those drawn from another force. If this led the deputy chief constable to believe that a criminal offence may have been committed, a file was sent to the Director of Public Prosecutions (DPP), who would then decide whether or not to prosecute that officer. Following the establishment of the Crown Prosecution Service, this body decided whether to prosecute officers, although it is still performed in the name of the DPP.

However, if the deputy chief constable felt that the investigation had revealed no evidence of a criminal offence, or if the Director of Public Prosecutions decided not to initiate a prosecution, the deputy chief constable was empowered to prefer a disciplinary charge against the officer who had been complained against. It was at this stage that the Police Complaints Board became involved. It was sent a copy of the investigating officer's report, accompanied by a memorandum from the deputy chief constable indicating if it was intended to institute disciplinary proceedings or, if not, why this was not deemed to be an appropriate course of action. In the latter circumstance, the PCB was able to recommend that disciplinary charges should be brought and ultimately could insist on it. Alternatively, it could call for further investigations into the matter.

The introduction of the PCB as a lay element in the system of investigating complaints against police officers was criticised both within and outside the police service. It resulted in the resignation of the Metropolitan Police Commissioner, who objected to the dilution of the authority of chief officers, whom he deemed more likely to arrive at the truth and take effective action in connection with such issues (Mark, 1978: 207–209). A number of other criticisms were made against the operations of the 1976 Act (which are discussed in Hewitt, 1982: 12–25).

These included allegations that the Director of Public Prosecutions was insufficiently zealous in prosecuting officers who had acted improperly and that the Police Complaints Board adopted a perverse interpretation of the 'double jeopardy' rule, whereby sending a file to the DPP was deemed to constitute a trial. The PCB would not thus recommend disciplinary proceedings that relied on the same evidence should the DPP determine not to initiate a prosecution. This situation was, however, revised following criticism from the courts in the case of *R v.*

Police Complaints Board, ex parte Madden in 1982, and the view that a Crown Prosecution Service decision not to prefer a criminal charge did not automatically mean that an officer was excluded, for disciplinary proceedings based on the same facts was upheld in a later decision (*R v. Chief Constable of Thames Valley Police ex parte PCA, sub norm R v. Metropolitan Police Disciplinary Board ex parte Director of Metropolitan Police Complaints Bureau* [1996] COD 324 DC (cited in Crown Prosecution Service, 2008: 15).

Additionally, the public had a negative perception of a procedure where complaints against the police were investigated by the police themselves. Although this practice is normal in professions, it failed to 'command the confidence of the public' (Home Office, 1981: 115). Aggrieved citizens were loath to make an official complaint, one consequence of which was the increased tendency for those alleging police wrongdoing to resort to the civil courts for a remedy. The burden of proof in civil cases is less than that required in criminal proceedings (the 'balance of probabilities' rather than 'beyond a reasonable doubt') and a complaint was thus easier to prove.

The Police Complaints Authority

The 1984 Police and Criminal Evidence Act sought to respond to some of the criticisms of the police complaints machinery. The main reforms that were instituted were:

- *The abolition of the Police Complaints Board*: the PCB was replaced by a Police Complaints Authority (PCA). This consisted of a chair, deputy chair and 11 members of the public drawn from a wide variety of backgrounds. The budget of the PCA was around £3 million in 2000 (Home Office, 2000);
- *An enhanced role for the PCA*: the remit of the PCA was extended to cover criminal as well as disciplinary complaints involving police officers. All serious complaints made against or involving police officers (including death, serious injury, actual bodily harm, corruption and serious arrestable offences) were automatically notified to this body, which was empowered to *supervise* their investigation. It could also supervise the investigation of complaints submitted to it by chief constables or police authorities of the force concerned. Supervision included approving the appointment of an investigating officer and imposing requirements on the conduct of an investigation. When investigations were supervised by the PCA, the report from the investigating officer was presented directly to this body, which then transmitted it to the chief constable or police authority;
- *Overruling powers*: the PCA had the power to overrule a chief constable and instruct this officer to send a copy of a report to the DPP for action in the courts, or to recommend (and, ultimately, insist) that disciplinary charges should be brought;
- *The introduction of conciliation*: this process applied to minor complaints when the complainant wanted an explanation or an apology for a police officer's actions. Conciliation (which did not involve the PCA) was conducted in a less adversarial climate to that which had previously governed the handling of complaints against the police.

The amendments introduced in 1984 provided a half-way house between the independent and internal investigation of complaints and were intended to render unnecessary any fundamental changes to the structure of police accountability. It was anticipated that these reforms would result in improved standards of police behaviour and would secure better relationships between the police and public, especially in urban areas. However, in spite of the reforms that were enacted in 1984, it was alleged that officers who were accused of committing serious offences were still dealt with inadequately. This perception arose from issues discussed below.

No link with civil actions   Instances where those alleging police misconduct towards them resorted in a civil case rather than using the disciplinary system were often not understood by the general public. The police often settled these claims out of court (often for large sums of money, although the Court of Appeal issued guidelines in 1997 which stated that a ceiling of £50,000 was appropriate for complaints alleging assaults) yet usually refused to accept any liability. Their motives in adopting this course of action were generally to save money that would need to be expended to defend cases of this nature. Details of these awards and the circumstances that prompted payment were not always made public and officers involved in such actions frequently escaped any sanction since no official complaint had been made against them.

Most complaints were thrown out   The reasons for complaints being thrown out included the absence of adequate evidence to support them, the ability of officers against whom complaints have been made to exercise the right to silence, and the very high standard of proof ('beyond a reasonable doubt') required to substantiate them. Thus during the year ending 31 March 1998, the PCA dealt with 9,608 complaint cases which involved 18,354 individual complaints. However, only 1,130 disciplinary outcomes resulted (Police Complaints Authority, 1998: 11–13).

Officers guilty of disciplinary offences may escape sanction   There were a number of ways in which officers were able to avoid disciplinary action being taken against them. They could retire (thereby keeping full pension rights), take extended sick leave, resign or agree to an 'admonishment' (that is, a reprimand). Around 80% of complaints made between 1987 and 1999 were dealt with by the latter course of action (Smith, 1999).

Lack of transparency   A key problem affecting public faith in the work performed by the PCA was that investigations into complaints which were submitted as a report to the PCA were subject to Public Interest Immunity Certificates, and thus the public had no access to them. Further, the reasons why the DPP decided not to prosecute an officer were not made public.

Role of the Crown Prosecution Service   Decisions by the Crown Prosecution Service (CPS) not to prosecute officers were sometimes contentious, and led to accusations that it was too protective of abuses of power by the police. The role of the CPS was especially delicate in connection with cases involving deaths in custody or arising from the use of lethal force by firearms officers. In 1997 an inquiry was initiated under the chairmanship of Judge Gerald Butler. It reported in 1999. This report suggested that in two of the cases reviewed by the judge, the CPS had taken too pessimistic a view of the prospects of securing a conviction. The judge advised that the CPS should prosecute officers when there was a case to answer, and be more willing to seek counsel's advice than it had in the past (Butler, 1999).

In 2005, an article in *The Independent* newspaper stated that since 1993, 30 members of the public had been shot dead by police marksmen, not one of whom had been convicted of any crime (Verkaik and Bennetto, 2005). One explanation for this was that the level of evidence required by the CPS to mount a prosecution had been set too high. It was alleged that a claim by the police of self-defence was likely to block a prosecution (Verkaik, 2005).

Lack of independence   Perhaps the main weakness with the operations of the police complaints machinery following the enactment of the 1984 Police and Criminal Evidence Act was that the police service remained responsible for conducting investigations. Outside involvement in these matters was limited, the PCA's supervisory role extending to only around one-third of cases. This situation provoked a perception, whether founded or not, that police officers investigating their colleagues did not always pursue a complaint with the vigour which they would deploy in other criminal matters. Additionally, members of the PCA were appointed and dismissed by the Home Secretary, who could in some cases give guidance to them. This raised the possibility that PCA members could be subjected to outside pressure in the performance of their duties.

Reforms introduced by post-1997 Labour governments

Following the 1999 Macpherson Report (Home Office, 1999), Labour's Home Secretary at the time, Jack Straw, introduced reforms which entailed replacing the police disciplinary code with a code of conduct (which, since 2008, has been the *Standards of Professional Behaviour for Police Officers*). Breach of the code of conduct made an officer liable for disciplinary proceedings and new regulations which covered police conduct and efficiency. These reforms included lowering the burden of proof that was required to substantiate complaints (reducing this test to the civil one of 'the balance of probabilities'), removing their 'right of silence', and introducing a six-week, 'fast track' system to deal with serious allegations.

The Home Office also commissioned a study to examine whether an independent system was needed and could be afforded. This had been introduced for the Royal Ulster Constabulary by the 1998 Police (Northern Ireland) Act, where an independent ombudsman was given responsibility for investigating complaints against officers.

The Independent Police Complaints Commission

The 2002 Police Reform Act introduced a new method of handling complaints made against police officers (and also civilian support staff) in England and Wales. This replaced the Police Complaints Authority that had formerly dealt with these matters. The work of the Independent Police Complaints Commission (IPCC) entailed overseeing the whole of the police complaints system. Its particular objective was to raise public confidence in the police complaints system (Crown Prosecution Service, 2008: 3). Under the new system, which commenced on 1 April 2004, complaints against the police can be investigated in one of four ways:

- Independently, using investigators employed by the IPCC. Initially, 72 investigators were employed. Their role was to investigate the most serious cases, such as police shootings. These investigators can be former police officers or from other backgrounds (Hardwick, 2009).
- Managed by the IPCC, but using police officers to carry out the task of investigation.

In these first two cases, it is the responsibility of the IPCC to refer a report of an investigation to the DPP.

- Supervised by the IPCC, with the investigation conducted by police officers. This procedure is similar to the way in which the PCA formerly carried out supervised investigations, and in this case those who conduct the investigation will inform the IPCC whether it is their intention to refer the matter to the DPP. However, the IPCC possesses the power to insist on this course of action if the investigators were not minded to pursue it.
- Local resolution, when a complaint is investigated by the local police force's Professional Standards Department with no IPCC involvement. The complainant is required to agree to this course of action. It has now been extended to deal with complaints against senior officers. It was envisaged that most complaints would be dealt with in this manner, which was similar to the previous practice of informal resolution.

The new system provided additional rights for complainants that included the ability to appeal to the IPCC against the non-recording by the police of a complaint (although these do not have to be made at a police station), the manner in which a complaint is investigated, the outcome of an investigation, or a decision by the police to stop an investigation against the wishes of the complainant. Complaints could also be taken from persons not directly involved in a dispute, such as witnesses to an event of others who were 'adversely affected' by it. Unlike the former PCA, the IPCC may also scrutinise actions (using the 'call-in' procedure) that have not been made the subject of an official complaint.

The Act also removed the anomaly whereby civil actions against the police were not tied in with the complaints procedure. The Act required chief officers and police authorities to examine civil proceedings brought by the public against the police to ascertain if the claim contained a 'conduct matter' (which is defined in the Act as an action undertaken by a person serving in the police service which may constitute either a criminal offence or warrant disciplinary proceedings). If it was decided that a civil case involved a conduct matter, it is recorded as such by the force. Some categories of conduct matter must be referred to the IPCC to determine how the issue will be investigated. Those not referable to the IPCC may be dealt with by the force. The IPCC is empowered to compel police forces to hold disciplinary hearings and may, under certain circumstances, present evidence at these hearings.

The role of the IPCC in disciplinary matters is wider than that possessed by the PCA and includes the ability to call for a disciplinary hearing to be held in public in certain circumstances where this course of action is in the public interest. The IPCC can also present a disciplinary case where it gave direction to the force about taking disciplinary action (Taylor, 2005: 8).

The new system is superintended by a team of commissioners (initially numbering 18). Their role is to set, monitor and enforce standards relating to the investigation of complaints across England and Wales. They are provided with powers to inspect any part of the complaints procedure, carry out force inspections and seize documentation relevant to a complaint. Police authorities are provided with specific responsibilities. Under the new system they are required to communicate with complainants and other interested parties on the progress of an investigation, its provisional findings, any disciplinary actions which were proposed in the investigating officer's report, and the outcome of these actions (Wadham, 2004: 21). Providing copies of an investigating officer's report to the complainant was an innovation introduced by the new system.

The IPCC handles, on average, approximately 30,000 complaints each year. Of these, around half are concerned with incivility or rudeness, 400 alleged serious assault and there were abut 100 deaths. Of these 30,000 complaints in 2008, the IPCC investigated 110 and managed 120 (Hardwick, 2009).

The IPCC in operation

Although it is likely that the new system will be more effective than its predecessors, there are issues that will need to be addressed in order for the system to command the confidence of the general public. It is important that the IPCC is adequately funded to ensure that investigating officers are not overburdened with excessive caseloads. Starving oversight bodies of funds is an extremely effective way for governments to neuter their impact (Lewis, 1999: 94). The large volume of complaints arising from the policing of the G20 protests in 2009 led the chair of the IPCC to suggest the need for additional Home Office resources in order to cope with these investigations (Hardwick, 2009).

There is also the danger of a lack of cooperation by the police service. Police culture may hinder investigations. There exists an 'exceptionally strong unwritten code that police must stick together at all times' and this may help to cover up police wrongdoing (Lewis, 1999: 23). Although investigators from within the service may be well placed to overcome restrictions of this nature, a particular problem affects examination by those not from the police service. They may face what has been referred to as the 'blue wall of silence' or 'code of secrecy', which rests on the assumption that police officers will look out for each other (Kappeler et al., 1998: 309) and thus hinder attempts to investigate complaints of police misconduct.

In addition, senior officers may seek to hinder an independent investigation of a complaint. This problem emerged following the shooting by officers of the Metropolitan Police of an innocent young Brazilian who had been mistaken for a suicide bomber. Following this incident, the Metropolitan Police Commissioner contacted the Home Office arguing that this error should be internally investigated as an external investigation might have an adverse impact on national security and intelligence and would also undermine the morale of his force's firearms section. The Home Office overruled the Commissioner, but it was alleged that IPCC investigators were kept away from the scene of the shooting for several days (Cowan et al., 2005) on the direct orders of the Commissioner, Sir Ian Blair (Dodd, 2005; Hardwick, 2009).

There is also the problem of perceived CPS bias towards police officers. The decision as to whether criminal prosecutions are brought is determined by the Code for Crown Prosecutors (Crown Prosecution Service, 2008: 4). In 2008, around 100 lawyers who specialised in handling police complaints resigned from the IPCC's advisory body. Their concerns included allegations of inadequate oversight of investigations conducted by police officers, extreme delays in resolving complaints and favouritism being displayed towards the police.

Police corruption

Wrongdoings by police officers may go beyond abuse of power and constitute corruption. What is termed 'police corruption' is a difficult term to define and embraces a wide range of activities, including:

- *Collaboration with criminals*: this involves officers participating in a range of activities and is especially likely to arise from involvement with informants. Leaking information to criminals ('information-based corruption'), which may enable them to keep one step ahead of the police, is an important aspect of this form of corruption (Miller, 2003: 10 and 15).
- *Abuse of the office*: this is done to obtain perks and privileges for personal gain and involves behaviour such as accepting a bribe or other form of inducement in return for turning a blind eye to criminal activity.
- *Theft*: this arises in connection with money (or property such as drugs) which comes into the hands of the police as the result of apprehending a criminal. The officer(s) involved may then commit further illegal acts such as drug trafficking.
- *Intimidation*: this involves officers putting mental or physical pressure on a suspect to confess to having committed a crime or on vulnerable witnesses to give false evidence.
- *Suppression of evidence*: this entails failing to disclose to the defence material gathered during the course of an investigation which might undermine the prosecution's case or aid that of the defence.
- *Fabrication of evidence*: this entails the police manufacturing (or 'planting') evidence in order to secure a conviction.

Police corruption may be carried out by individual officers or by a team of officers, typically members of a squad (Miller, 2003: iii). The latter is less common than the former. The explanations that have been put forward to explain this behaviour consist of a number of work-based factors that include demoralisation with the job, the existence of opportunities that can be exploited for corrupt purposes (such as access to information or inadequate supervision), and the organisation's culture and values, which may act as an incentive to obtain results regardless of the methods used to obtain them. Non-work-related reasons (such as relationship problems, alcohol abuse and contacts with criminals arising from leisure pursuits) may also account for corrupt behaviour (Miller, 2003: 18–24).

Other explanations draw a distinction between constant factors that may influence corrupt behaviour, such as discretion, inadequate supervision of an officer's actions and peer group secrecy, and variable factors such as the ability of police officers to exploit law violation for personal gain when the law in question is widely flouted by members of the general public (Newburn, 1999: 14–27).

A distinction is often drawn within the police service between those forms of improper conduct motivated by the desire to benefit the officer(s) undertaking the activity (for example, receiving a bribe from a criminal who wishes to avoid arrest) and behaviour that is 'bent for the job', in the sense of seeking to aid the police to further organisational objectives (such as securing the arrest and conviction of a dangerous criminal). Both forms of behaviour may be deemed to be corrupt (Punch, 1985) but there is a tendency (at least historically) to view the latter form of behaviour as different in character from the former.

The scale of corruption

Since 'corruption' is a difficult term to define, the extent to which it occurs is hard to measure. However, it has been argued that 'between about one half and one per cent of police staff (both officers and civilians) were potentially (though not necessarily) corrupt' (Miller, 2003: ii).

Corruption in the police is not a new phenomenon and arose, for example, in connection with the activities of Sergeant George Goddard in the 1920s. He was alleged to have amassed a 'fortune' derived from protection money (Morton, 1993: xvi). Since 1945 there have been a number of high-profile allegations of police corruption.

The first was initiated by Sir Robert Mark when he was Commissioner of the Metropolitan police. This led to the departure of 478 police officers, although only 80 were dealt with through the courts or disciplinary proceedings (Campbell, 1999) and 13 were jailed. The second was Operation Countryman, mounted in 1978 to investigate the City of London and Metropolitan Police forces. Here, allegations of corrupt association between the police and criminals were the central concern, but the investigation resulted in only four officers being prosecuted.

In 1989 the West Midlands Serious Crimes Squad was disbanded and an investigation was initiated into its activities. A particular cause of concern was the methods used by officers to obtain confessions. Although this enquiry led to a number of convicted criminals being freed by the Court of Appeal, no officer was convicted of an offence. In the early 1990s an investigation, known as 'Operation Jackpot', was mounted into allegations of corruption at Stoke Newington police station in Hackney, London. Alleged police malpractice at this station resulted in the Metropolitan Police paying £1 million in damages and costs, and one officer was jailed for drug dealing.

The fifth case of alleged police corruption became public knowledge when Sir Paul Condon informed the House of Commons Home Affairs Committee in 1997 that there were between 100 and 250 corrupt officers in his force (which amounted to 0.5–1.0% of the strength of the force). Although he stated that this figure was 'numerically lower than in the 1970s', he conceded that 'however tiny that is in percentage terms, the damage they can do to the reputation and morale of the overwhelming majority of officers is enormous' (Home Affairs Committee, 1998). It was subsequently reported in *The Guardian* on 3 March 2000 that between 110 and 120 officers were allegedly guilty of serious misconduct. By that date, 75 persons had been charged with corruption, including 26 serving police officers and 11 former officers. Six serving Metropolitan police officers were suspended because of continuing corruption-related investigations.

The final case involved the South Wales Police, where accusations of wrongful imprisonment based on fake police interview notes, false or missing evidence, bribes or intimidation were made over two decades. This prompted the Welsh Assembly in October 2000 to ask the Home Secretary to launch a public inquiry.

The investigation of corrupt behaviour

Corruption investigations are handled by police forces, which may deploy specialist Professional Standards Units to investigate such matters. The techniques used to root out corruption have become increasingly sophisticated, involving the use of supergrasses and surveillance techniques (Campbell, 1999). The issue of corruption was addressed in an HMIC report into the broader area of integrity. This made a number of recommendations that included the need for proper guidelines covering gifts and gratuities and for the introduction of more effective supervision of officers handling informants (Her Majesty's Inspectorate of Constabulary, 1999).

However, convictions relating to corrupt behaviour are difficult to obtain for a number of reasons, including officers who are the subject of investigation being aware of standard police investigative methods, and thus being adept at covering their tracks (Miller, 2003: 26). For this reason, alternative solutions to dealing with the problem are often pursued, such as the use of police disciplinary procedures (Miller, 2003: 28) and placing emphasis of methods to prevent the problem from occurring. Guidance in this area has been provided by the Association of Chief Police Officers (ACPO), whose innovations included the formation of a Presidential Task Force on Corruption in 1999. Their work was subsequently taken over by the ACPO Professional Standards Committee. The methods that can be deployed to prevent corrupt behaviour include promoting an ethical culture within the organisation through the use of methods that rely heavily on good leadership and the setting of appropriate standards in the workplace (Miller, 2003: 35). Enhanced information security has been put forward as a 'cornerstone' in corruption prevention strategies (Miller, 2003: 37).

QUESTION

Evaluate the importance of the 1984 Police and Criminal Evidence Act in connection with the development of police powers.

The material required to answer this question is contained in the above discussion. You should also consult some of the material that is cited in the references. To answer this question you would:

- Consider the basis on which police powers rested before the enactment of PACE and the problems posed by this situation;
- Analyse the key developments introduced by PACE in connection with police powers;
- Evaluate the adequacy of PACE and the Codes of Practice subsequently issued under this legislation in safeguarding the rights of the public in their dealings with the police;
- Present a conclusion based on the arguments you have presented above as to whether PACE constituted a key landmark in the development of police powers.

================================ REFERENCES ================================

Bucke, T. and Brown, D. (1997) *In Police Custody: Police Powers and Suspects' Rights under the Revised PACE Codes of Practice.* Research and Statistics Directorate, Home Office Research Study 174. London: Home Office.

Butler, G. (1999) *Inquiry into Crown Prosecution Service Decision-making in Relation to Deaths in Custody and Related Matters.* London: TSO.

Campbell, D. (1999) 'Police in New Scandal', *The Guardian*, 27 February.

Cowen, R., Dodd, V. and Norton-Taylor, R. (2005) 'Met Chief Tried to Stop Shooting Enquiry', *The Guardian*, 18 August.

Crown Prosecution Service (2008) *Guidance on the Handling of Allegations of Criminal Offences against Persons Serving with the Police.* London: Crown Prosecution Service.

Dodd, V. (2005) 'Met Chief Tried to Block Shooting Inquiry', *The Guardian*, 1 October.

Fisher, Sir H. (1977) *Report of an Inquiry into the Circumstances Leading to the Trial of Three Persons Arising out of the Death of Maxwell Confait and the Fire at 27 Doggett Road, London, SE6.* House of Commons Paper 80. London: House of Commons.

Gelsthorpe, L. and Padfield, N. (2003) 'Introduction', in L. Gelsthorpe and N. Padfield (eds), *Exercising Discretion: Decision-making in the Criminal Justice System and Beyond.* Cullompton, Devon: Willan Publishing.

Gibson, B. and Watkins, M. (2004) *Criminal Justice Act 2003: A Guide to the New Procedures and Sentencing.* Winchester: Waterside Press.

Grieve, D. (2007) Speech in the House of Commons, 11 July, HC Debs, Vol 462, Col 1566.

Hardwick, N. (2009) Oral Evidence to the Home Affairs Inquiry into *Policing of G20 Protests*, 21 April.

Harlow, C. and Rawlings, R. (1997) *Law and Administration.* Cambridge: Cambridge University Press.

Her Majesty's Inspectorate of Constabulary (1999) *Police Integrity: Securing and Maintaining Public Confidence.* London: HMIC.

Hewitt, P. (1982) *A Fair Cop: Reforming the Police Complaints Procedure.* London: National Council for Civil Liberties.

Home Affairs Committee (1998) *Police Disciplinary and Complaints Procedure*, First Report, Session 1997/8, House of Commons Paper 258–1. London: TSO.

Home Office (1981) *The Brixton Disorders, 10–12 April 1981: Report of an Inquiry by the Rt. Hon. The Lord Scarman, OBE.* Cmnd 8427. London: HMSO.

Home Office (1999) *The Stephen Lawrence Inquiry: Report of an Inquiry by Sir William Macpherson of Cluny.* Cm 4262. London: TSO.

Home Office (2000) *Complaints against the Police*: A Consultative Paper. London: Home Office Operational Policy Unit.

Home Office (2006) *New Code of Professional Standards for Police Officers.* London: Home Office.

Home Office (2007) *Review of the Police and Criminal Evidence Act (PACE) 1984: Summary of Responses to the Public Consultation Exercise (16 March–31 May 2007).* London: Home Office, Policing Powers and Protection Unit.

Home Office (2008) *Police and Criminal Evidence Act 1984 CODE A.* London: Home Office. [Online] www.police.homeoffice.gov.uk/publications/operational-policing/pace-code-a-amended-jan-2009?view=Binary [accessed 22 March 2009].

Kappeler, V., Sluder, R. and Alpert, G. (1998) *Forces of Deviance: Understanding the Dark Side of Policing* (2nd edition). Prospect Heights, IL: Waveland Press.

Lewis, C. (1999) *Complaints against the Police: The Politics of Reform*. Annandale, NSW: Hawkins Press.

Mark, Sir R. (1978) *In the Office of Constable*. London: Fontana.

Ministry of Justice (2007) *A Guide to the Corporate Manslaughter and Corporate Homicide Act, 2007*. London: Ministry of Justice.

Miller, J. (2003) *Police Corruption in England and Wales: An Assessment of Current Evidence*. London: Home Office, Online report 11/03.

Morton, G. (1993) *Bent Coppers*. London: Little Brown.

Newburn, T. (1999) *Understanding and Preventing Police Corruption: Lessons from the Literature*. Police Research Series Paper 110. London: Home Office Research, Development and Statistics Directorate.

Owen, T., Bailin, A., Knowles, J., MacDonald, A., Ryder, M., Sayers, D. and Tomlinson, H. (2005) *Blackstone's Guide to the Serious Organised Crime and Police Act 2005*. Oxford: Oxford University Press.

Police Complaints Authority (1998) *The 1997/8 Annual Report of the Police Complaints Authority*. House of Commons Paper 805. London: TSO.

Punch, M. (1985) *Conduct Unbecoming*. London: Tavistock.

Reiner, R. (2000) *The Politics of the Police* (3rd edition). Oxford: Oxford University Press.

Rollock, N. (2009) *The Stephen Lawrence Inquiry 10 Years On: An Analysis of the Literature*. London: The Runnymede Trust.

Royal Commission on Criminal Procedure (1981) *The Royal Commission on Criminal Procedure Report*. Cmnd 8092. London: HMSO.

Royal Commission on Police Powers and Procedure (1929) *Report of the Royal Commission on Police Powers and Procedure*. Cmd 3297. London: HMSO.

Smith, G. (1999) quoted in H. Mills 'Rogue Police a Law unto Themselves', *The Guardian*, 14 September (online). Available at: www.guardian.co.uk/uk/1999/feb/14/lawrence.ukcrime1 [accessed 14 June 2009].

Smith, D. and Gray, J. (1983) *Police and People in London* (Vol. IV). London: Policy Studies Institute.

Taylor, B. (2005) *Review of Police Disciplinary Arrangements, Report*. London: Home Office.

Verkaik, R. (2005) 'Level of Evidence Has Been Set Too High, Say Lawyers', *The Independent*, 21 October.

Verkaik, R. and Bennetto, J. (2005) 'Shot Dead by Police 30: Officers Convicted 0', *The Independent*, 21 October.

Wadham, J. (2004) 'A New Course for Complaints', *Policing Today*, 10(1): 21.

4

The methods of policing

CHAPTER AIMS

The aims of this chapter are:

- To identify the methods used to police local communities from 1829 onwards and evaluate the strengths and weaknesses of these methods;
- To evaluate contemporary methods of policing;
- To discuss the reassurance agenda and consider the methods of policing that were developed to deliver it;
- To evaluate developments since 1945 that have led to police functions being carried out by private sector organisations.

The policing of local communities

This section analyses the various methods through which policing has been delivered to local communities since the early part of the nineteenth century.

Preventive policing

As is argued in Chapter 1, the emphasis of nineteenth-century police work was upon the prevention of crime. This was implemented by 'home beat' policing, whereby a police officer was allocated a small geographic area that he would patrol on foot and thus become acquainted with its inhabitants. It was believed that the physical presence of an officer in uniform was sufficient to reduce the level of crime within an area, so that the crime prevention role of the police was an essentially passive task.

By the early decades of the twentieth century the bulk of police work was performed by officers who were assigned to a small geographic area and whose activities were underpinned by random patrol work. However, although this style of policing, which was exemplified by the post-war BBC television programme, *Dixon of Dock Green*, was popular with the public (Skogan, 1990), it was widely viewed as having a negligible impact on crime levels (an opinion subsequently upheld by Jordan, 1998: 67) and the benefits with which it was associated (especially securing good relationships between police and public) were not easily quantifiable. A number of additional issues were posed by home beat policing:

- *It was costly in terms of personnel*: as late as the 1960s, urban patrol work followed what was termed 'the fixed point system', whereby officers patrolled between a series of contact points (such as police boxes) at preset times (Chatterton, 1979). This was an expensive use of personnel, especially in a period when many urban police forces found it difficult to recruit to their establishment figure.
- *It was laborious work*: the work was often undemanding and monotonous and lacked the glamour associated with other aspects of police work, particularly that performed by the CID.
- *It was out of date*: home beat policing did not facilitate the use of technology (including motor vehicles) which was needed to combat the increased sophistication and mobility of criminal activity. It was also detrimental to the specialisation of functions within police forces, a development that was increasingly required to respond to changing patterns of crime and disorder.
- *It was hard to gauge efficiency*: the extent to which crimes were actually prevented by this method of policing was incapable of any objective assessment. It was therefore difficult to ascertain whether this was an effective use of personnel.
- *Its objectives were unclear*: the objectives of random patrol work are not clearly defined for those undertaking the task, and officers who carry it out primarily conduct self-initiated activities (amounting to around 47% of total shift time according to a later American study) (Famega et al., 2005: 549–550).

Reactive policing

During the 1960s the preventive orientation of patrol work began to be replaced by a reactive focus. This change was actively promoted by the Home Office (Home Office, 1967), which led to forces reducing the number of officers who patrolled on foot or on bicycles in favour of the use of motorised vehicles. This was dubbed 'fire brigade policing' by Sir Robert Mark, who later became Commissioner of Police in London. It involved redirecting patrol work to respond to events after they had occurred rather than seeking to forestall them, and was thus developed at the expense of preventive patrol by uniformed officers.

Reactive policing was implemented by the 'unit beat' method, which was intimately associated with the use of cars (initially panda cars) and two-way radios. It was supplemented by technological developments such as the Police National Computer and the computer-aided despatch of officers to incidents. The rise of the 'technological cops' (Alderson, 1979: 41–42) meant that random foot patrol increasingly assumed a low status and low priority within police forces, with patrol work being performed mainly by officers driving from one incident to another.

By the 1970s, methods of reactive policing had been widely adopted by forces throughout England and Wales. The main benefit of this was that it provided tangible measurements, so that efficiency could be judged (such as response times and arrest figures), and it enabled the police service to increase its output without the need to raise the number of officers who were employed. The approach was underpinned by an implicit assumption that speedy response times to incidents would facilitate the apprehension of criminals. It was also initially assumed that the increased efficiency that derived from reactive policing would improve the level of satisfaction held by the public towards the police, which is a key determinant of public confidence in the service. However, any benefits were obtained at the expense of the police's relationship with the general public, especially in urban areas.

A number of specific criticisms were levelled against reactive policing and the methods used to perform it. These included:

- *The lack of intimate knowledge of local communities*: officers who performed most of their work patrolling in cars saw no need (and, indeed, would have found it difficult) to establish relationships with the 'ordinary' people they policed. This objection had been raised when suggestions had been previously made to introduced motorised policing (Bottoms and Stevenson, 1992: 29). The police service's inability to communicate with people other than those they met in 'conflict and crisis' situations (Alderson, 1979: 41–42) resulted in accusations of insensitive policing (Weatheritt, 1982: 133).
- *Stereotyping*: with no intimate knowledge of different neighbourhoods, the police had a tendency to stereotype them and the people who lived in them. This sometimes resulted in the use of police powers in a random fashion. There was considerable criticism of the way in which stop and search powers were used against black youths, implying a perception by the police that all members of black communities posed a problem for society. Accusations of this nature tended to alienate the public, reduce their level of cooperation with the police and erode the legitimacy of the police function within the affected communities.
- *It down-valued the role of the general public in police work*: policing by reactive methods was almost entirely delivered by the police themselves, who saw no need to involve the public in their operations. This meant that consulting with the public and seeking to construct good relationships with them were not viewed as important activities, one consequence of which was that the flow of information from the public to the police concerning crime was reduced, enhancing police reliance on stereotyping and using powers in a random fashion.
- *It emphasised law enforcement as the prime police function*: this was at the expense of other activities, especially the service role of policing that was a key aspect of policing by consent. Additionally, the prominence given to law enforcement had an impact on the types of people seeking careers in the police service.
- *The visible police presence was removed from communities*: officers patrolling in cars were no substitute for bobbies on the beat whose physical presence provided communities

with a sense of reassurance and security. In this sense, policing became depersonalised. It was transformed into a function performed by officers who were outsiders to the communities in which they operated.

- *Efficiency*: there was little evidence to support the perception that faster response rates increased the chances of catching a criminal at or near the scene of the crime. An American study suggested that immediate response to all reports of serious crimes led to on-scene arrests in only 29 of every 1,000 cases. It was argued that citizen reporting time, not police response time, most influenced the possibility of on-scene arrest. Marginal improvement in police response times was predicted to have no real impact on the apprehension or arrest of offenders (Spelman and Brown, 1984: xi).
- *It did not solve the root problems of crime*: the emphasis placed by the police on response meant that there was no attempt to address the underlying issues that caused crime to occur.
- *Initially, responses were not adequately prioritised*: this might mean that crimes were responded to in the order in which they were reported rather than according to their level of seriousness. Subsequently, forces introduced graded response to counter such difficulties.

Some of these problems resulted from the tactics used to implement reactive policing, rather than the method itself. It had not been envisaged that foot patrol would be entirely abandoned. It was also assumed that the 'collator system' (which involved an officer, usually of the rank of sergeant, recording snippets of intelligence gathered by officers while performing their duties in particular areas) would provide the police with an acceptable level of knowledge of local communities.

Other difficulties that exerted an adverse impact on reactive policing arose not because of the weaknesses of policing methods but because of factors such as a large increase in the demand made by the general public for police assistance. These increased demands were a significant factor in undermining reactive policing because officers were effectively swamped by the volume of work to which they were required to respond (Baldwin and Kinsey, 1982: 35).

Community policing

The 1981 disorders were a catalyst to change since methods of policing play an important part in influencing police–public relationships. The police service responded to criticisms of reactive policing by diverting some of its resources into proactive methods. These were implemented through a range of techniques that were individually or collectively referred to as 'community policing'. A particular objective of these varied initiatives was to shift the ethos of policing away from law enforcement (and the control function which underpinned this) towards the service function of policing that was founded on the general duty to befriend the community.

Proactive policing emphasised the need for the police to prevent crime rather than merely react to it, and like preventive policing it was directed at limiting the opportunities for crime to occur rather than focusing on those who committed it.

But unlike old-style preventive policing, the proactive style required the police to assume an active role and undertake a range of measures designed to prevent the occurrence of crime.

This proactive philosophy was particularly associated with John Alderson, Chief Constable of Devon and Cornwall from 1973 until 1982. Alderson presented his community policing proposals as a coordinated package of measures (which are discussed in detail in Moore and Brown, 1981). The key features of this approach embraced a belief that the police could not wage an effective war against crime single-handedly, but required the involvement of local people and a multi-agency approach, involving agencies in the public and voluntary sectors. Additionally, attempts were made to construct a sense of community.

Alderson perceived the police to be at their most effective when they reinforced community values or standards of behaviour. There was thus a need to mobilise the perceived common interests shared by members of communities and direct these to combat crime. This would enable the police to 'plug into' community values when called upon to intervene in connection with crime. However, the fragmentation of communities or the absence of community values was often a feature of post-war urban living. An attempt to remedy this problem was thus a key feature of Alderson's community policing initiatives in Exeter. The police took a lead in establishing local bodies, such as tenants' and residents' associations, which were designed to bond citizens together and help develop a community spirit that could be directed towards the maintenance of social harmony.

During the 1980s, in the wake of the Scarman report (Home Office, 1981), most chief constables adopted methods under the general heading of 'community policing' that typically operated alongside reactive strategies, by which officers on foot patrol were backed up by mobile response units. Community policing initiatives included an increased commitment to foot patrol (those who performed this work being given new titles such as 'neighbourhood' or 'area' constable or 'community beat officers') and the development of community liaison or contact departments which sought to formalise police relationships with specific groups of local inhabitants. Neighbourhood Watch schemes were also encouraged on a national basis to develop a sense of community.

Critique of community policing

One rationale of community policing was to reconstruct consent and the underlying requirement of legitimacy, thereby reducing the intensity of the demand for increased accountability of the police to the public that had been made in places such as Merseyside and Greater Manchester during the early 1980s. In this sense, consent was described as a surrogate form of accountability (Brogden, 1982: 197). For this reason, those on the left of the political spectrum who sought enhanced police accountability were often sceptical of community policing initiatives introduced by the police. Such criticisms included the perception that the police exercised too dominant a position in local affairs and that multi-agency ventures and police involvement in community development were designed to enable decisions related to resource allocation to be taken by the police instead of local government (Short, 1982: 80). Initiatives related to constructing a sense of community were viewed as 'an exercise in social engineering by the police (Weatheritt, 1987: 18), whose aim was to produce a 'village community' (Fletcher, 2005: 63).

In addition, reactive policing remained an important aspect of police work. Towards the end of the twentieth century it was estimated that reactive policing accounted for 75% of arrests compared to 24% arising from proactive methods of policing (Phillips and Brown, 1998: xiii).

Contemporary styles of policing local communities

Towards the end of the twentieth century new methods, based upon earlier reactive and proactive initiatives, were put forward to police local communities.

Problem-oriented policing

Problem-oriented policing (POP) is preventive in nature. It was developed in America by Herman Goldstein (Goldstein, 1979, 1990) as a rejection of the professional model of policing which entailed 'tight central control, standard operating procedures and increasing use of cars, computers and modern communications technologies' (Bullock and Tilley, 2003: 2). The development of POP was based on the perception that demands placed upon the police service meant that key issues to the community were often neglected (Tilley, 2003: 318) and that 'the active involvement of the community and external agencies is often vital to the identification of problems and the development of strategies to solve them' (Leigh et al., 1998: 5). The involvement of other agencies in delivering a response to crime tends to reorient the work of police officers operating in neighbourhoods who then become responsible for coordinating activities to combat crime.

The basic premise of POP 'is that the core of policing should be to deal effectively with underlying police-recurrent problems rather than simply to react to incidents calling for attention one by one as they occur' (Bullock and Tilley, 2003: 1). This approach places the application of scientific methods at the heart of policing (Ekblom, 2002; Bullock and Tilley, 2003: 5–6; John and Maguire, 2003: 38) and involves a range of processes:

- Identifying and analysing recurrent problems;
- Interrogating their underlying sources;
- Finding some points of intervention that will block causes and risk factors. This intervention need not be concerned with the law enforcement aspects of policing. For example, repeat victims of crime could be given financial aid to improve levels of security;

- Implementing the initiatives that have been devised;
- Evaluating the success of initiatives put forward to respond to identified problems.

There are various models of problem-solving which guide activities of this nature, including SARA (Scanning, Analysis, Response, Assessment). This was used in early POP initiatives in Leicestershire and Cleveland (Leigh et al., 1998: vi). Other established POP tools include the Problem Analysis Triangle (PAT), which provides a framework within which recurrent problems of crime and disorder can be analysed in order to identify where crime prevention initiatives can be most usefully directed.

The introduction of POP was designed to bring a number of advantages to the delivery of contemporary policing. In particular, POP attempts to move the focus of police decision-making away from managers and towards front-line officers, who are in a better position to understand the causes and possible solutions for problems (John and Maguire, 2003: 65). It has been argued that 'officers must know the underlying issues locally, be in contact with the community, have information to help understand the nature of the underlying problems that generate clusters of incidents, be supported by senior officers in attempting to solve problems imaginatively and tailor problem-solving to emerging local issues' (Jordan, 1998: 73). This enables police resources to become more directly related to community needs.

POP serves to enhance the role of police officers working in neighbourhoods, especially when the response to crime entails activities being performed by other agencies since they become responsible for coordinating activities to combat crime. In this sense, police officers are transformed from 'thief-takers' into 'crime managers'.

The implementation of POP

POP was introduced into police forces in England and Wales during the 1980s and was applied with slightly more vigour towards the end of the 1990s (Leigh et al., 1996, 1998). As an incentive to induce police forces to adopt this approach, following the 1997 comprehensive spending review, around £30 million over three years was ear-marked for the Targeted Policing Initiative. It funded schemes to help the service develop and implement a problem-oriented approach to its work.

However, progress in applying a problem-oriented approach to policing remained patchy (HMIC, 1998) and many forces were identified as being a long way off from implementing it fully (HMIC, 2000). There are several reasons which might explain the relatively slow progress of this approach to police work. These are considered below.

Reluctance to change

Beat officers may be reluctant or unwilling to make changes to their work practices. In Leicestershire (where the introduction of POP in the East Area was analysed by Leigh et al., 1996) it was discovered that 'many beat officers ... were cynical, hostile to form filling, reluctant or unable to analyse incident data and apt to fall back on traditional policing methods' (Leigh et al., 1998: v). Subsequently, reference was made to the presence in that area of 'a core of cynical officers who took a jaundiced view of POP, regarding it as faddish nonsense or a bureaucratic imposition' (Leigh et al., 1998: 7).

Complexity

Considerable social science skills are required in connection with problem identification, the analysis of their causes and the evaluation of strategies to respond to these issues. However, these skills are not necessarily to be readily found within the police service (although personnel such as policy analysts can be recruited as support staff) or may require expenditure in the form of software (such as the INSIGHT incident software package that was developed in Leicestershire during the 1990s) (Leigh et al., 1998: v). Further, these activities are time-consuming and to be performed may require sacrifices to be made to other aspects of police service provision (Goldstein, 2003; Matassa and Newburn, 2003: 213).

Efficiency

It has been argued that 'POP is interpreted and implemented in too many ways to permit any firm conclusion' to be made to this question (Stockdale and Whitehead, 2003: 244). It has further been asserted that the assessment of outcomes in monetary terms is insufficiently developed to be able to assess whether POP is cost effective (Stockdale and Whitehead, 2003: 249).

Zero tolerance

POP is a preventive style of policing that seeks to address the causes of problems in order to avoid their future repetition. Zero tolerance is a reactive response to crime based on enforcement procedures.

Zero tolerance policing was launched on the back of the 'broken windows' thesis that was put forward in the 1980s (Wilson and Kelling, 1982). It entailed strenuously addressing petty offending (such as broken windows, graffiti or abandoned cars) which gave the impression that nobody cared about an area. This uncaring attitude encouraged an area to slide into crime since it 'creates fear on the part of citizens in a neighbourhood' who respond by withdrawing physically from public places, 'and when they do so, they withdraw those kinds of normal social controls that tend to operate. Once that social control has gone ... what you have then is an invitation to perpetrators of serious crime' (Kelling and Coles, 1998: 8).

However, those associated with the development of the concept of 'broken windows' were sceptical of the concept of zero tolerance policing' (Kelling and

Coles, 1998: 9). Although both zero tolerance and broken windows emphasised the need to control minor transgressions of the law, zero tolerance placed considerable emphasis on the law enforcement aspects of policing, delivered in what was termed a 'hard-edged' or 'confident' manner (Dennis and Mallon, 1997). It thus had no place for interventions that sought to tackle the root causes of crime.

Zero tolerance policing has an aim akin to that of a moral crusade – regaining control of the streets on behalf of law-abiding people and seeking to overcome the 'culture of fear' that existed within them (Furedi, 1997). This approach concentrated on 'ordinary' crime that troubled large sections of the public rather than serious crime, and it targeted local concerns. It was adopted in American cities such as New York, where it seemed to have a major impact on the level of crime.

However, there were shortcomings identified with zero tolerance policing. Its imperative to demonstrate success in the war against crime might lead to the use of improper practices in the belief that the end justified the means. Its effectiveness was uncertain: zero tolerance policing might reduce crime in selected areas by displacing it elsewhere. The approach relied on the 'short sharp shock' working over a brief period of time and this might not be sustainable as a longer-term police method. It has also been argued that the success of this method of policing in New York might have been due to the large increase in numbers of police officers rather than the tactic itself.

However, zero tolerance policing may have a legitimate role to play in conjunction with POP, which may embrace zero tolerance aspects as a partial solution to an indentified problem (especially one of a short-term nature), conducted alongside other, longer-term approaches that are designed to remedy its more deeply rooted causes. These two approaches have also been amalgamated to produce a new method of policing. This was termed 'order maintenance' and was put forward by the then prime minister, Tony Blair, at the 1998 Labour Party conference. It was to be applied to 25 crime 'hot spot' areas throughout Britain that were identified through the use of methods such as crime pattern analysis. This proposed a more targeted use of police patrols and blended the reactive aspects of zero tolerance with crime prevention based upon the use of problem-oriented and 'intelligence-led' policing.

Intelligence-led policing

Intelligence-led policing seeks to move away from reactive responses to crime in favour of pre-emptive operations that are based upon the analysis of intelligence that is already available in order to establish features such as crime trends and patterns. The information derived from this approach then informs police operations that may target individuals, activities or locations. This approach is derived from a perception that the police service was failing to address 'the systemic sources of crime and crime patterns' (Tilley, 2003: 313). It thus seeks to improve the standard of police performance and was especially directed at improving the detection rates of crime.

Intelligence-led policing requires the collection of vast stores of information, employing devices which include the use of informants, varied forms of surveillance and technological, and academic applications such as offender profiling. It enables specific groups of offenders (especially prolific offenders) or particular patterns of behaviour to be targeted and then eliminated. These developments indicate a move towards establishing the management of risk as a police role (Neyroud, 1999).

Although POP makes considerable use of intelligence as the basis of intervention, it is not the same as intelligence-led policing. In particular, intelligence-led policing focuses on law enforcement as a response to crime and does not necessarily require the involvement of outside agencies (Bullock and Tilley, 2003: 8), although it may serve to act as the enforcement role of community safety (Tilley, 2003: 321).

The National Intelligence Model

The National Intelligence Model (NIM) was developed within the National Criminal Intelligence Service. It was adopted by the Association of Chief Police Officers (ACPO), who viewed it as a mechanism that would blend existing methods of policing (including community policing, intelligence-led policing and POP) ultimately to provide a vehicle 'through which all major police business is channelled and delivered' (John and Maguire, 2003: 38). It aimed to provide a common approach (or a 'standard template', Home Office 2004: 29) to the gathering, analysis and dissemination of information, thus providing a decision-making framework and giving senior officers a clear strategy within which to deploy resources. In particular, it was the major vehicle through which intelligence-led policing would be delivered (Tilley, 2003: 321).

NIM identified three levels of crime: Level 1 concerned local criminality that could be handled within a BCU; Level 2 related to crime and major incidents affecting more than one BCU; and Level 3 concerned crime operating at a national or international level. NIM set a framework for tackling crimes at all these levels on the basis of a clear threat assessment. It was essentially a business model – 'a means of organising knowledge and information in such a way that the best possible decisions can be made about how to deploy resources, that actions can be co-ordinated within and between different levels of policing, and that lessons are continually learnt and fed back into the system' (John and Maguire, 2003: 38–39).

The 2003 National Policing Plan required all forces to adopt NIM, which was to be implemented by all forces to commonly accepted minimum standards by April 2004. In 2005 an ACPO Code of Practice was issued by the Home Secretary under the provisions of the 2002 Police Reform Act to provide a statutory basis for the introduction of NIM minimum standards and basic principles.

The reassurance agenda and neighbourhood policing

One difficulty posed by the styles of policing that have been discussed above is that they did not satisfactorily address a key concern of the public, that of the fear of crime. Although statistics suggested that the level of crime began to fall during the 1990s, the public's fear of crime remained high. This had an adverse impact on public confidence towards the police service. The Labour government's remedy to this situation derived from the reassurance agenda, which aimed to address this 'confidence deficit'.

The reassurance agenda

The reassurance agenda was promoted following an assessment conducted by Her Majesty's Inspectorate of Constabulary (2001), which was followed by a number of initiatives that included the safer neighbourhoods programme. The national reassurance policing programme was initiated between 2003 and 2005 and entailed the adoption the neighbourhood policing in a small number of trial sites in eight police forces. This also emphasised the importance of involvement with the public in selecting problems and designing remedies to them. Particular attention was to be devoted to tackling what were termed 'signal crimes and disorders'. These were activities (including anti-social behaviour) that had an adverse impact on people's sense of security and caused them to alter their beliefs or behaviour. Success in tackling these would thus have a disproportionate impact on neighbourhoods, especially in alleviating their fear of crime, and serve to strengthen community cohesion.

Neighbourhood policing

Neighbourhood policing was the method chosen by the Labour government to deliver the reassurance agenda. Suggestions to advance the concept of neighbourhood policing were made in a White Paper which advocated 'the spread of neighbourhood policing … to every community', and 'the greater involvement of communities and citizens in determining how their communities are policed' (Home Office, 2004: 6–7). This approach effectively remorphed community policing and was universally applied throughout England and Wales during 2008. 'Neighbourhood' often equates with local government ward boundaries but this is not always the case. Its underlying ethos is preventive and the operations of neighbourhood policing teams are guided by the Ten Principles of Neighbourhood Policing (ACPO, 2006: 10).

It has been noted that a central aspect of Labour's Third Way agenda was to develop a sense of responsibility and citizenship by treating citizens as key stakeholders in the services they use (Giddens, 1998). Neighbourhood policing was compatible with this approach. It sought to provide people who lived and worked in an area with:

- Access;
- Influence;
- Interventions;
- Answers;

concerning the policing of their community and the manner in which problems are addressed (National Policing Improvement Agency, 2008, quoted in Casey, 2008: 23). It entailed creating structures and processes to promote engagement with the public (Singer, 2004: 7), thus promoting a collaborative approach to problem-solving. This is achieved in ways that include meetings held with the general public (the term Police and Communities Together – PACT – often being used) and the provision of information to local communities by the police regarding local crime (Casey, 2008: 24).

The virtues of neighbourhood policing extend beyond tackling local issues to embrace matters that include gathering intelligence that might relate to more serious forms of criminality, including terrorism. The justification for this approach is that it is rare within a community for one single individual to be in possession of a full range of information relating to criminal activity. Instead several individuals may possess snippets of knowledge and information that a dedicated neighbourhood police officer can pull together and translate into a coherent picture (Innes, 2006). It was in this sense that it has been argued that neighbourhood policing 'should be a golden thread that runs through every aspect of policing. It is not something to be separated, that in some way is totally detached from our counter-terrorist thrust, for example' (Home Affairs Committee, 2008a: para 259).

Neighbourhood policing teams

Neighbourhood policing is delivered by teams who take 'an intelligence-led, proactive, problem-solving approach to enable them to focus on and tackle specific local issues' (Home Office, 2004: 7). These teams are composed of uniformed police officers, Police Community Support Officers (PCSOs) and Special Constables.

Uniformed police officers   Although uniformed police officers play an integral part in neighbourhood policing teams, they are unable to fulfil all of the tasks required to undertake this activity, especially in connection with providing a constant uniformed presence within a neighbourhood to reassure the public that it is a safe and secure environment.

A study in 1996 estimated that although around 55% of a police force's strength was theoretically classed as operational patrol, the nature of policing meant that an average sized force of around 2,500 officers serving a population of 1 million citizens had only 125 officers (or 5% of its strength) to conduct patrol work and that most of this was carried out in cars rather than on foot (Audit Commission, 1996: 10–11). This implied that there would need to be an enormous, and costly, recruitment of additional police officers to make any significant improvement in this area of activity, a view that was held by a later enquiry that estimated: 'to get one more officer permanently out on patrol would require employing an additional five officers', a solution that the investigation argued was 'not cost effective' (Singer, 2004: vi–vii). It is thus necessary to supplement the work performed by uniformed officers by other personnel.

The Special Constabulary   An alternative solution to the use of uniformed police officers is to place increased emphasis on the Special Constabulary to carry out routine patrol functions.

The Special Constabulary was formed in 1831 under the provisions of the Special Constables Act, and consists of members of the general public who volunteer their services to perform a limited number of hours of police work in their spare time. Special Constables are unpaid, although they receive out-of-pocket expenses. They are given a limited amount of training, delivered (since a recommendation made by a Police Advisory Board for England and Wales report in 1981) at weekend residential training courses. They exercise full police powers for the areas in which they are appointed.

During the 1990s the Special Constabulary was reinvigorated to undertake routine patrol tasks. In 1993 the Home Secretary announced the establishment of the Parish Constable scheme in rural areas. This involved deploying Special Constables to provide a foot patrol presence and address nuisance and minor crime, and parish wardens (who were not members of police forces) to channel information and advice between the police and community. This scheme was subsequently extended throughout the country as part of the Neighbourhood Constable initiative. In 2000 a £700,000 recruiting scheme was launched to boost recruitment to the Special Constabulary.

Police Community Support Officers   The 2002 Police Reform Act enabled chief constables to designate suitably skilled and trained civilians to exercise powers and undertake specific functions which could be in one of four categories – investigating officer, detention officer, escort officer and Police Community Support Officer (PCSO). The provision of a visible police presence within neighbourhoods has been associated with the latter of these categories, resulting in the creation of PCSOs. The bulk of their work is performed on patrol and their prime purpose is to act as the eyes and ears for neighbourhood policing teams. PCSOs receive less training and are paid less than members of regular police forces and neither are they equipped in the same manner.

PCSOs are funded by a combination of central government and local authority grants and are employed by both police forces and local councils. Home Office funding has been ring-fenced until 2011. In September 2008, 15,470 PCSOs were employed by the 43 police forces in England and Wales (Bullock and Mulchandani, 2009: table 3).

PCSOs have fewer powers than police officers. Their key power is to detain for 30 minutes to await the arrival of a constable and they may use reasonable force in order to achieve this end. Initially, they had various powers designated to them at the discretion of individual chief constables. This created a wide variation in what PCSOs could and could not do, leading to uncertainty among the public and adding to the media's negative stereotype. In order to address this, in December 2007 all PCSOs across England and Wales were provided with a common set of 20 standard (or core) powers. These were drawn up by the Home Secretary but allowed chief constables flexibility on other powers.

In total, 53 powers can be designated to PCSOs, to which some local authority bylaws can also be added (NPIA, 2008: 11). These additional powers range from the confiscation of alcohol and tobacco from minors to the ability to detain a person for a specific period of time. Some chief constables have given all of these powers to PCSOs, whereas others have only given some. The power of detention has only been provided to PCSOs in 50% of forces (Home Office, 2007).

Reviews of PCSOs have suggested that if forces try to use them in a back-office role to provide administrative support in order to free up officers, it is likely that their visibility and impact on reassurance would decline (HMIC, 2004: 144). A recent evaluation of the deployment, use and effectiveness of PCSOs highlighted concerns of role drift and variation, with some PCSOs being engaged in tasks that are seen as outside their core remit of high-profile patrol in neighbourhoods, such as roads policing and offender management (NPIA, 2008: 34–35).

Plural policing Initiatives

Plural policing entails an enhanced role for organisations other than the police service to perform patrol work. These effectively constitute a second tier of police service providers. The organisations supplying work of this nature may be located in either the public or private sectors, or embrace aspects of both in areas such as funding and the status of those performing the work. This has given rise to what has been referred to as 'hybrid' policing bodies (Johnston, 1993).

These developments have resulted in what has been described as 'a pluralized, fragmented and differentiated framework of policing' (Crawford, 2003: 136), a key concern of which is to tackle the fear of crime and fill the gap caused by the removal of a number of 'secondary social control occupations' (Jones and Newburn, 2002), such as park keepers and guards on public transport. Plural policing provides an important example of the implementation of a strategy of 'responsibilisation' (Garland, 2001), whereby the responsibility for crime prevention has been 'hived off' from the central state to be performed by local bodies such as local authorities and commercial organisations. This approach has become intimately associated with the objective of community safety.

A number of local authorities have funded law enforcement initiatives and routine patrols in areas such as housing estates. Those who perform these activities are local authority employees and the main advantage of local government performing work of this nature is that they are locally accountable.

In March 2000, proposals for paid neighbourhood wardens to patrol housing estates and inner-city streets were announced. This led to the development of a system of neighbourhood wardens (or neighbourhood safety patrols, as they are sometimes called) throughout England and Wales. Their purpose is to offer a semi-official presence in communities which suffer from disorderly and anti-social behaviour committed by young people, thereby providing assurance in these areas and reducing the fear of crime. Further developments based on wardens have subsequently evolved. The Street Wardens programme, which was initiated in 2001, extended the concept of neighbourhood wardens beyond residential areas. In 2002, Street Crime Wardens were introduced as an aspect of the government's Street Crime Initiative in the ten police forces with the highest levels of street crime.

Typically, neighbourhood warden schemes are operated by private companies that obtain funding from a range of central sources (including, initially, money provided from the Office of the Deputy Prime Minister). The employer provides wardens with basic training, for example, in the area of drug awareness. Wardens do not possess police powers. Their main role is to relieve the police service from low-level tasks (especially patrol work), but they may perform additional functions, such as acting as professional witnesses (for interventions such as anti-social behaviour orders) and providing the police with intelligence. Their working arrangements with the police are governed by guidelines prepared by ACPO in 2000 and protocols entered into by local police forces and the wardens' organisers. Problems with this initiative include the relatively low wages paid to wardens, the uncertain long-term status of the funding, and the possibility that the presence of wardens in one area will merely transfer anti-social activities and crime to neighbouring areas where there are no wardens.

The development of plural policing has prompted suggestions that mechanisms need to be established to supervise closely all agencies and bodies engaged in the delivery of policing policy (Loader, 2000). This objective was advanced by the 2002 Police Reform Act, which enabled chief constables to set up Community Safety Accreditation Schemes. These allowed police forces to work in closer cooperation with local authorities, housing associations and private security companies. Chief constables could designate wardens, security guards and others as Accredited Community Safety Officers who would have powers to deal with anti-social behaviour (although such powers would be more limited in scope than those possessed by PCSOs).

The private policing sector

Plural policing is also associated with initiatives undertaken within the public or private sectors to establish policing arrangements. Typically, these were performed by persons whose jurisdiction was confined to specific geographical areas or places.

The performance of such police-related functions is not a new development. As has been observed in Chapter 1, private security organisations figured prominently in the late eighteenth century, when deficiencies in the old policing system resulted in widespread criminal activity, such as theft and highway robbery. This led to ventures that were initially privately financed, including the Bow Street Runners and the Marine Police Establishment. In the 1840s and 1850s railway companies funded their own police organisations to protect towns from workers who were engaged in railway construction.

More recently, some state agencies established their own police forces, including the Atomic Energy Authority and the Ministry of Defence. The boundary between these private policing bodies and the regular police is difficult to draw precisely, and in some cases (most notably concerning the British Transport Police) has effectively been eliminated.

Some functions performed through private policing arrangements are carried out by bodies that operate as private sector companies. These are often referred to as 'commercial policing' organisations and they exist to make a profit from the work they carry out, which is typically conducted within the framework of a contract between the company and its clients. The following section discusses their work in greater detail.

Nature of the work performed by commercial policing bodies

The role performed by commercial policing organisations can be broadly divided into two areas – security work and detective work. Security work includes activities such as guarding premises, the manufacture, installation and provision of security devices, retail security and guard duty. Detective work is typically carried out by private investigators and includes activities such as monitoring personal relationships, tracing those who owe money, working on behalf of solicitors on civil and criminal matters (such as insurance fraud and tracing missing persons), and examining allegations of white-collar crime, such as theft by employees. Some aspects of detective work, such as industrial espionage and functions concerned with defending the state against subversion, are controversial.

The growth of commercial policing

The precise size of the commercial policing sector is unknown, but it considerably dwarfs the numbers employed as regular police officers. A study published in

1998 suggested that this sector employed around a third of a million workers (Newburn and Jones, 1998). The total market size of the private sector in security work rose from £807 million in 1987 to £2.1 billion by 1992 (Smith, 1994) and was estimated by *The Guardian* on 26 April 2000 to be worth around £3 billion. The sizeable growth of commercial policing is a post-war phenomenon and has occurred in two 'waves'.

The first 'wave' of commercial policing

The first period of growth of commercial policing bodies occurred in the 1950s and the 1960s. A boom in consumerism resulted in the growth of private property ownership, requiring owners to seek ways to protect their goods, premises and money. In addition, British workers' longstanding dislike of bank accounts also meant that large sums of money for employees' wages had constantly to be collected from banks and taken to firms and factories, leading to the employment of security guards to protect the payroll. The expansion of commercial policing arrangements in this period made it possible, by the 1970s, to describe this sector as 'a second-string police force in this country' (Draper, 1978: 168).

The second 'wave' of commercial policing

A further growth phase occurred during the 1980s as a result of a more affluent society as well as other developments. The increased emphasis on crime prevention after 1980 required individuals and organisations to take responsibility for the protection of their property. This encouraged the growth of commercial policing organisations offering security services that included various forms of patrol or guard work and the installation of security devices, alarm systems, and so on. The involvement of the private sector in such crime prevention activities led to the assertion that security had become commodified, that is 'distributed by market forces rather than according to need' (Garland, 1996: 463).

'Mass private property', meaning property in private ownership but which is open to the public (Shearing and Stenning, 1981), such as shopping malls and night clubs, also grew dramatically in the 1980s. Although the police would respond to crime committed at such venues, they were not authorised to provide a routine presence there. Instead, such services had to be provided by commercial bodies. The expansion of the night-time economy, fuelled by alcohol-based leisure industries, has provided a further boost to the employment of security personnel such as club doormen (Crawford, 2003: 154).

The privatisation policies of Conservative governments in 1979–1997 emerged as the product of 'globalisation', one feature of which was 'hollowing out', involving the state shedding its peripheral activities that became discharged by other agencies (Leishman et al., 1996: 10–11). The police service was not exempt from this process. As with other public service sectors, it was subject to the discipline of the market in order to promote efficiency through competition. This was achieved by 'load shedding', whereby services traditionally undertaken by the police were ceded to commercial or voluntary providers (Johnston, 1992: 12).

The extent to which privatisation eroded traditional policing functions to the benefit of the commercial sector has, however, been disputed. Although some functions, such as prisoner escort duties, were relinquished, it has been argued that the 'privatisation of policing has been relatively limited and ... not extensive enough to explain the large growth in private security over the longer period' (Newburn and Jones, 1998: 31).

In addition, much of the work performed by private policing agencies (especially in connection with detective work) is concerned with issues or disputes affecting private parties, underpinned totally or significantly by civil law. This suggests that the growth of the commercial policing sector has not necessarily occurred at the expense of the functions of the regular police, since many of the issues handled by commercial organisations are not, and never have been, performed by the police service.

Problems associated with commercial policing

There are a number of problems associated with the role performed by commercial policing organisations.

Coordination

The increase in the number of police functions carried out by the private sector has resulted in 'a world of fragmented, plural policing' (Loader, 2000). This justifies attempts to coordinate the activities of bodies which perform police tasks at the local level, perhaps by establishing local police commissions, as were advocated by the Patten Commission on Northern Ireland which reported in 1999.

Standards

The backgrounds of those who work in the private policing sector has not traditionally been subject to the same rigorous checking as the procedures employed by regular police forces. In 1999, it was suggested that 10,000 of the 80,000 people who applied for work in private sector security companies each year possessed some sort of criminal record, and in 24,000 instances the crimes involved ranked above minor offences (Home Office, 1999: 25). This problem is partly explained by the poor rates of pay in some sectors of the industry.

The training and methods used by commercial companies have also been subjected to criticism. Regular police officers undergo a two-year period of probationer training. They operate in accordance with procedures laid down by the 1984 Police and Criminal Evidence Act and its related Codes of Practice, and their conduct is further is regulated by the Standards of Professional Behaviour for Police Officers and the Police Complaints Procedure.

The personnel employed by commercial bodies are not regulated in the same rigorous manner, and the use in some areas of activity (such as debt collection) of a system of 'payment by results' may induce employees to resort to methods that would not be tolerated by regular police forces. Training has not traditionally received a high priority in the industry, although the establishment in 1990 of the Security Industry Training Organisation (SITO) sought to remedy this deficiency.

Accountability

A particular problem affecting accountability is that commercial agencies that receive a contract to perform policing activities may contract this out to another organisation which may in turn subcontract the work to another body or individual. If something goes wrong, it is very difficult to pin-point blame and hold wrongdoers accountable for their actions.

There are a number of trade associations that organisations in the commercial sector may join. These include the National Approval Council for Security Systems, the British Security Industry Association, the Association of British Investigators, the Association of Professional Investigators, and the International Professional Security Association. These trade associations seek to set standards for the industry on matters such as recruitment, qualifications, training and fees charged. Some of these regulatory bodies have the theoretical ability to expel members who contravene acceptable standards of behaviour. However, since membership is purely voluntary, their ability to control the commercial sector meaningfully is significantly limited.

In recent years inspectorates (such as the Inspectorate of the Security Industry, established in 1992) have been set up to supplement existing machinery to supervise the operation of the industry. Some local authorities have also introduced registration schemes for specific activities (especially in connection with door staff in clubs) that typically entailed vetting procedures and training courses.

Privatisation may not benefit the public

Although privatisation has been argued to benefit the consumer (in that competition keeps charges low), it may also affect them adversely. They may be required to pay for services at the point of delivery that were previously financed from taxation, resulting in the danger that the ability to pay will determine the standard or level of services consumers receive.

It has been observed that 'one of the central paradoxes of crime prevention and security provision is that there is often an inverse relationship between activity and need' (Crawford, 2003: 161). If the level of security reflects a person's (or community's) ability to pay, the notion of common good that underpins regular policing is eroded (Newburn and Jones, 1998: 32). This may result in crime being displaced to neighbourhoods that are unable or unwilling to pay for their own security, and may thus contribute to other people's feelings of insecurity.

The relationship between the private and public policing sectors

The relationship between private sector policing organisations and the regular police service has become closer in the post-war period. The private sector may perform services for the legal system, including delivering court orders and serving summonses. However, there is no precise definition as to which activities should remain in the public domain and which should be located elsewhere.

An independent committee of inquiry set up under the joint auspices of the Police Foundation and Policy Studies Institute sought to establish the relationship between the regular police and private bodies. Its report concluded that only sworn police constables should be able to arrest, detain and search citizens, and search and seize property under statutory powers; that only they should be able to bear arms and exercise force for the purpose of policing; and that only they should have the exclusive right of access to criminal records and criminal intelligence for the purposes of operational policing. It was proposed that other groups and agencies not having these powers could engage in a number of policing activities 'to complement and supplement what sworn constables do' (Cassels, 1994: 19).

Reforms to commercial policing

The most important reform to commercial policing has been stricter regulation by the state. The control that it has exerted since 1945 was initially fashioned on a piecemeal basis, directed at the practices utilised by some commercial concerns (such as the 1970 Administration of Justice Act, the 1973 Guard Dogs Act and the 1974 Consumer Credit Act). Compulsory registration and licensing, which can be used to exert control over standards, has long been a requirement in most American states and in many European countries, but successive UK governments shied away from instituting this. This reform was suggested by the 1972 Younger Committee on Privacy in connection with private detective work, but was not subsequently acted upon. However, the 1987 Emergency Provisions Act (which applied only to Northern Ireland) introduced a licensing system for security firms in that country.

In 1999 the Labour government announced its intention to establish a self-financing private Security Industry Authority (SIA). This would vet the background of individuals wishing to form companies or seek employment in a wide range of activities concerned with private security (including club 'bouncers') and would grant licences only to those judged to be 'fit persons' (Home Office, 1999).

Reform was implemented in 2001 when the Private Security Industry Act established the Security Industry Authority (SIA), which became operational in 2003. Its role is to issue licences to people working in specifically designated sectors of the security industry. In order to obtain a licence from this body, the applicant is required to undergo an age, identity and criminal records check and be able to demonstrate that he or she has the appropriate skills and training required for the type of work to be carried out. Applicants can be required to undertake a course of SIA-approved training in order to obtain a licence.

The aim of these innovations is to raise levels of professional skills in the industry. SIA inspectors are empowered to enter certain types of premises to ensure that security staff hold valid licences and persons operating in the industry without a licence are liable, on conviction at a magistrates' court, to a penalty of six months' imprisonment, a £5,000 fine, or both. The SIA has also created a public register of approved security firms. The main aim of this reform is to prevent undesirable persons (including those with criminal records) from working as doormen. One weakness of this reform, however, is that it is restricted to personnel employed by security organisations. 'In-house' security staff, employed directly by the organisation in which they operate, are exempt from regulation (Crawford, 2003: 151).

There have, however, been difficulties with the effectiveness of the licensing system, which were brought to light in November 2007. It was found that licences to work in the security industry had been granted to a possible 10,000 non-EU nationals who were illegal immigrants. The problem arose because there was no unified system for carrying out right-to-work checks on those seeking a licence from the SIA. Those applying for licences from the SIA were not asked to confirm their right to work in the UK on their application form, and the SIA had no legal responsibility to vet applicants in this regard.

The Home Affairs Committee concluded that 'the licence application form would be an expedient means of ensuring consideration of the immigration status of security industry workers' (Home Affairs Committee, 2008b: 6). Changes were subsequently introduced to SIA procedures whereby right-to-work checks conducted by the Border and Immigration Agency on all non-EU applicants were integrated into the SIA licence process.

QUESTION

Evaluate the strengths and weaknesses of the current system of neighbourhood policing.

The basis of the answer to this question is found in material in this chapter and in Chapter 10. You should also consult literature cited in the references related to neighbourhood policing. To answer this question you should:

- Consider the context in which the current system of neighbourhood policing was advanced (the reassurance agenda);
- Discuss the key features of neighbourhood policing (in particular the importance of community engagement) and the manner in which it is delivered;
- Analyse the benefits that neighbourhood policing brings both to the policing of local communities but also to policing in general;
- Evaluate any problems you perceive with this approach;
- Present a conclusion based on your previous arguments which might indicate how any current shortcomings can be overcome and the future direction of this method of policing.

REFERENCES

ACPO (2006) *Practical Advice on Professionalising the Business of Neighbourhood Policing*. London: CENTREX.

Alderson, J. (1979) *Policing Freedom*. Plymouth: Macdonald and Evans.

Audit Commission (1996) *Streetwise: Effective Police Patrol*. London: HMSO.

Baldwin, R. and Kinsey, R. (1982) *Police Powers and Politics*. London: Quartet Books.

Bottoms, S. and Stevenson, K. (1992) *Crime Prevention*. Oxford: Oxford University Press.

Brogden, M. (1982) *The Police: Autonomy and Consent*. London: Academic Press.

Bullock, K. and Tilley, N. (2003) 'Introduction', in K. Bullock and N. Tilley (eds), *Crime Reduction and Problem-oriented Policing*. Cullompton, Devon: Willan Publishing.

Bullock, S. and Mulchandani, R. (2009) *Police Service Strength England and Wales, 30 September 2008*. London: Home Office Statistics Bulletin, Research, Development and Statistics.

Casey, L. (2008) *Engaging Communities in Fighting Crime – A Review by Louise Casey*. London: The Cabinet Office.

Cassels, Sir J. (1994) *Independent Committee of Inquiry into the Role and Responsibilities of the Police*. London: The Police Foundation and Policy Studies Institute.

Chatterton, M. (1979) 'The Supervision of Patrol Work under the Fixed Points System', in S. Holdaway (ed.), *The British Police*. London: Edward Arnold.

Crawford, A. (2003) 'The Pattern of Policing in the UK: Policing Beyond the Police', in T. Newburn (ed.), *Handbook of Policing*. Cullompton, Devon: Willan Publishing.

Dennis, N. and Mallon, R. (1997) 'Confident Policing in Hartlepool', in N. Dennis (ed.), *Zero Tolerance Policing in a Free Society*. London: Institute of Economic Affairs.

Draper, H. (1978) *Private Police*. Harmondsworth: Penguin.

Ekblom, P. (2002) 'Towards a European Knowledge Base', paper presented at EU Crime Prevention Network Conference, Aalborg, October 2002, quoted in K. Bullock and N. Tilley, 'Introduction', in K. Bullock and N. Tilley (eds), *Crime Reduction and Problem-orientated Policing*. Cullompton, Devon: Willan Publishing.

Famega, C., Frank, J. and Mazerolle, L. (2005) 'Managing Police Patrol Time: The Role of Supervisor Directives', *Justice Quarterly*, 22 (4): 540–559.

Fletcher, R. (2005) 'The Police Service: From Enforcement to Management', in J. Winstone and F. Pakes (eds), *Community Justice: Issues for Probation and Criminal Justice*. Cullompton, Devon: Willan Publishing.

Furedi, F. (1997) *Culture of Fear.* London: Cassell.

Garland, D. (1996) 'The Limits of the Sovereign State: Strategies of Crime Control in Contemporary Societies', *British Journal of Criminology*, 35(4): 445–471.

Garland, D. (2001) *The Culture of Control.* Oxford: Oxford University Press.

Giddens, A. (1998) *The Third Way.* Oxford: Polity Press.

Goldstein, H. (1979) 'Improving Policing: A Problem-orientated Approach', *Crime and Delinquency*, 25 (2): 234–258.

Goldstein, H. (1990) *Problem-orientated Policing.* New York: McGraw-Hill.

Goldstein, H. (2003) 'On Further Developing Problem-orientated Policing: The Most Critical Need, the Major Impediments and a Proposal', in J. Knutsson (ed.), *Problem-Orientated Policing: From Innovation to Mainstream.* Cullompton, Devon: Willan Publishing.

Her Majesty's Inspectorate of Constabulary (HMIC) (1998) *Beating Crime: HMIC Thematic Inspection Report.* London: Home Office.

Her Majesty's Inspectorate of Constabulary (HMIC) (2000) *Calling Time on Crime: A Thematic Inspection on Crime and Disorder.* London: Home Office.

Her Majesty's Inspectorate of Constabulary (HMIC) (2001) *Going Local – The BCU Inspection Handbook.* London: HMIC.

Her Majesty's Inspectorate of Constabulary (HMIC) (2004) *Modernising the Police Service: A Thematic Inspection of Workplace Modernisation.* London: HMIC.

Home Office (2008a) *Policing in the Twenty-First Century.* Session 2007–8, Seventh Report, House of Commons Paper 364. London: TSO.

Home Affairs Committee (2008b) *Security Industry Authority: Licensing of Applicants.* Third Report Session 2007–08. House of Commons Paper 144. London, TSO.

Home Office (1967) *Police Manpower, Equipment and Efficiency.* London: Home Office.

Home Office (1981) *The Brixton Disorders, 10–12 April 1981: Report of an Inquiry by the Rt. Hon. The Lord Scarman*, OBE. Cmnd 8427. London: HMSO.

Home Office (1999) *The Government's Proposals for Regulation of the Private Security Industry in England and Wales.* Cm 4254. London: TSO.

Home Office (2004) *Building Communities, Beating Crime: A Better Police Service for the 21st Century.* Cm 6360. London: TSO.

Home Office (2007) PCSO Powers. [Online] www.police.homeoffice.gov.uk/publications/community-policing/PCSOs_Audit_Table_May_2007_1.pdf?view=Binary [accessed on 23 March 2009].

Innes, M. (2006) 'Policing Uncertainty: Countering Terror through Community Intelligence and Democratic Policing' *The Annals of the American Academy of Political and Social Science*, 605: 222–241.

John, T. and Maguire, M. (2003) 'Rolling Out the National Intelligence Model: Key Challenges', in K. Bullock and N. Tilley (eds), *Crime Reduction and Problem-oriented Policing.* Cullompton, Devon: Willan Publishing.

Johnston, L. (1992) *The Rebirth of Private Policing.* London: Routledge.

Johnston, L. (1993) 'Privatisation and Protection: Spatial and Sectoral Ideologies in British Policing and Crime Prevention', *Modern Law Review*, 56 (6): 771–792.

Jones, T. and Newburn, T. (2002) 'The Transformation of Policing', *British Journal of Criminology*, 42: 129–146.

Jordan, P. (1998) 'Effective Policing Strategies for Reducing Crime', in P. Goldblatt and C. Lewis (eds), *Reducing Offending: An Assessment of Evidence on Ways of Dealing with Offending Behaviour*. Research Study 187. London: Home Office.

Kelling, G. and Coles, C. (1998) 'Policing Disorder', *Criminal Justice Matters*, 33, Autumn: 8–9.

Leigh, A., Read, T. and Tilley, N. (1996) *Problem-Oriented Policing: Brit Pop 1*. Crime Prevention and Detection Series Paper 75. London: Home Office.

Leigh, A., Read, T. and Tilley, N. (1998) *Problem-Oriented Policing: Brit Pop 2*. Police Research Series Paper 93. London: Home Office, Policing and Reducing Crime Unit.

Leishman, F., Cope, S. and Starie, P. (1996) 'Reinventing and Restructuring: Towards a "New" Policing Order', in F. Leishman, B. Loveday and S. Savage (eds), *Core Issues in Policing*. Harlow: Longman.

Loader, I. (2000) 'Plural Policing and Democratic Governance', *Social and Legal Studies*, 9 (3): 323–345.

Malassa, M. and Newburn, T. (2003) 'Problem-orientated Evaluation? Evaluating Problem-orientated Policing Initiatives', in K. Bullock and N. Tilley (eds), *Crime Reduction and Problem-orientated Policing*. Cullompton, Devon: Willan Publishing.

Moore, C. and Brown, J. (1981) *Community Versus Crime*. London: Bedford Square Press.

National Policing Improvement Agency (NPIA) (2008) *Neighbourhood Policing Programme: PCSO Review*. London: NPIA.

Newburn, T. and Jones, T. (1998) 'Security Measures', *Policing Today*, 4 (1): 30–32.

Neyroud, P. (1999) 'Danger Signals', *Policing Today*, 5 (2): 10–15.

Phillips, C. and Brown, D. (1998) *Entry into the Criminal Justice System: A Survey of Police Arrests and Their Outcomes*. Home Office Research Study 185. London: Home Office, Research and Statistics Directorate.

Shearing, C. and Stenning, P. (1981) 'Modern Private Security: Its Growth and Implications', in M. Tonry and N. Norris (eds), *Crime and Justice: An Annual Review of Research* (Vol. 3). Chicago: University of Chicago Press.

Short, C. (1982) 'Community Policing – Beyond Slogans', in T. Bennett (ed.), *The Future of Policing: Papers Delivered to the Fifteenth Cropwood Round-Table Conference, December 1982*. Cropwood Conference Series 15. Cambridge: Cambridge Institute of Criminology.

Singer, L. (2004) *Reassurance Policing: An Evaluation of the Local Management of Community Safety*. Home Office Research Study 288. London: Home Office.

Skogan, W. (1990) *The Police and Public in England and Wales: A British Crime Survey Report*. Home Office Research Study Number 117. London: Home Office Research and Planning Unit.

Smith, Sir J. (1994) Speech to a Fabian Society Conference, Ruskin College, Oxford, 9 January, quoted in *The Guardian*, 10 January.

Spelman, W. and Brown, D. (1984) *Calling the Police: Citizen Reporting of Serious Crime*. Washington, DC: US Government Printing Office.

Stockdale, J. and Whitehead, C. (2003) 'Assessing Cost-effectiveness', in K. Bullock and N. Tilley (eds), *Crime Reduction and Problem-oriented Policing*. Cullompton, Devon: Willan Publishing.

Tilley, N. (2003) 'Community Policing, Problem-oriented Policing and Intelligence-led Policing', in T. Newburn (ed.), *Handbook of Policing.* Cullompton, Devon: Willan Publishing.

Weatheritt, M. (1982) 'Community Policing: Does it Work and How Do We Know?', in T. Bennett (ed.), *The Future Policing.* Cambridge: Cambridge Institute of Criminology.

Weatheritt, M. (1987) 'Community Policing Now', in P. Willmott (ed.), *Policing and the Community.* Discussion Paper 16. London: Policy Studies Institute.

Wilson, J. and Kelling, G. (1982) 'Broken Windows', *Atlantic Monthly*, March: 29–38.

5

The police service and the criminal justice system

CHAPTER AIMS

The aims of this chapter are:

- To evaluate the role performed by the police service in bringing offenders to justice;
- To discuss the emergence of the multi-agency approach to policing;
- To analyse the involvement of the police service in partnership work in connection with the prevention of crime and community safety;
- To consider the role played by the police service in the management of offenders;
- To evaluate developments affecting policing that are associated with securing a 'joined-up' approach to criminal justice policy.

Introduction

The criminal justice system performs a wide range of functions. These include:

- The prevention of crime;
- The investigation of crime;
- Delivering an appropriate response to those who have committed minor crime which does not require prosecution (which includes restorative justice);
- The prosecution of offenders;
- The infliction of an appropriate penalty on those who have committed crime;
- The administration of the penalty that has been served on an offender whether in the community or in custody;
- The provision of practical aid and advice to the victims of crime.

In recent years, the role performed by the police service within the criminal justice system has been subject to a number of developments which have provided contemporary policing with an orientation that is different from that devised in the service's formative years in the nineteenth century. This chapter seeks to illustrate the changing way through which the police service performs its functions within the criminal justice system by focusing on three areas of work: bringing offenders to justice; the prevention of crime; and managing offenders.

Bringing offenders to justice

The police service has always played a key role in bringing offenders to justice by investigating crime and (until the creation of the Crown Prosecution Service) prosecuting offenders. This section briefly discusses the role performed by the police in connection with those who have committed a criminal offence.

Crimes may be brought to the attention of the police in a variety of ways that include an officer's personal encounter with a criminal action or through the reporting of an alleged crime to the police by a member of the public (Burrows et al., 2000: v). The person reporting the crime may be a victim or a third party, such as a bystander or witness to a criminal action. In these latter circumstances, the role of the police is to record the crime, which may entail a direct entry by an officer on to the force's crime recording systems or may involve officers submitting a hand-written report that is then inputted on to such a system. This activity generates a crime record which commences the process of investigation involving interviews conducted on a face-to-face basis or (in the case of minor crimes) over the telephone.

Police responses to offending behaviour

Police officers have a number of choices they can make dealing with an alleged law-breaker. These are discussed below.

'No-criming'

The action may be judged not to constitute a criminal offence which thus terminates police involvement. One survey suggested that only 47% of crime allegations were eventually recorded as crimes, a shortfall that especially affected allegations relating to personal and property offences (Burrows et al., 2000: vii and ix).

Historically, 'no-criming' decisions were undertaken by a range of police personnel, including Crime Management Units or station officers, and were largely explained by the practice of the police to insist that an allegation should be substantiated before being a crime record was produced (Burrows et al., 2000: viii–ix). Subsequently, guidance relating to the recording of an offence was provided by the National Crime Recording Standard and Home Office Counting Rules. However, the system of crime recording is reliant upon human interpretation of details of an incident and errors may be made, even in connection with 'no-criming' violent crime (HMIC, 2009: 5).

Informal warnings

A transgression may be dealt with by an officer giving an informal warning. This has no legal status and is equivalent to a telling off. It may be accompanied by a 'recommendation' that should the offender repeat his or her behaviour, a more severe response will be delivered. Early intervention warnings, which may be given by any agency in connection with anti-social behaviour, are of a similar status to informal warnings since they have no legal consequences.

Reprimands and formal warnings

A criminal action may result in a reprimand or formal warning. These procedures were introduced by the 1998 Crime and Disorder Act and apply only to juveniles (aged 10–17). They are designed to avoid repeat cautioning, with a presumption that a juvenile who has been reprimanded and goes on to commit a further offence within two years of that reprimand will be officially warned (and automatically referred to the Youth Offending Team (YOT) for assessment).

Formal cautions

A formal caution is delivered to a person who admits to having committed a minor offence and is delivered by, or under the authority of, a senior police officer. This does not constitute a conviction (since the person has not been taken to court), but is recorded on the Police National Computer and may be taken into account if the person who has been cautioned commits a further offence. The 2003 Criminal Justice Act introduced the *conditional caution*, which enables measures such as community work and reparation to the victim to be added to the caution. This approach facilitates the involvement of agencies other than the police service in formulating responses to offending behaviour.

One difficulty with this approach is that the courts are not involved in sentencing offenders and the police and/or the Crown Prosecution Service (CPS) may use the sanction of a caution inappropriately in relation to offences that warrant a more severe penalty. In 2008/09 39,952 recorded cases of actual bodily harm (ABH) were dealt with by police forces in England and Wales in this manner, without referring the cases to the CPS. ABH can, on conviction by a court, carry a penalty of five years' imprisonment. In the same period, 734 cases of the more serious grievous bodily harm (GBH) were dealt with in the same way (BBC, 2009).

A different procedure exists in Scotland, where a system of fiscal fines has applied since the passage of the 1987 Criminal Justice (Scotland) Act. This enables the procurator fiscal to offer a person charged with a minor offence the opportunity to pay a fine or a sum of money as compensation to a person harmed by the offence without a court appearance and without getting a criminal conviction.

Summary justice

'On-the-spot' justice, sometimes referred to as 'summary justice', is a further response to minor criminal actions. The 1988 Road Traffic Act introduced fixed penalty notices for a range of minor traffic offences and this approach was built upon in the 2001 Criminal Justice and Police Act, which introduced a penalty notice for disorder (PND). These apply to England and Wales and entail on-the-spot fines of £50 or £80 being handed out (usually by police officers) to those who have committed various forms of anti-social behaviour or minor criminal actions such as theft to the value of £200 or criminal damage to the level of £500. A key reason for their use is to save police time that would otherwise be spent on processing paperwork. A PND can be challenged, in which case the offender may be taken to court or the PND may be dropped, but if the offender fails to pay the fine, it is raised and becomes enforced by the courts (Morgan, 2008: 13).

This approach is also used in Scotland. The Scottish Executive's 2004 Antisocial Behaviour etc. (Scotland) Act provided new powers for the police to issue fixed penalty notices for a broad range of offences of an anti-social behaviour nature.

Charging

The ultimate power of the police is to formally charge a person with having committed a criminal offence. If this course of action is preferred, the police may free the person on police bail or detain him or her in police custody pending an appearance in the magistrates' court. The system of police bail was initially provided for in the 1976 Bail Act and was designed to enable the police to conclude their enquiries before deciding whether to charge a person and, if so, with what offence. The procedure also enabled the police (if they wished) to place restrictions on a person's movements (termed 'conditional bail'). Decisions relating to police bail were traditionally made at a police station, but the 2003 Criminal Justice Act introduced a system of 'street bail', whereby a police officer could grant bail to a person who had been arrested without having to convey him or her to a police station. The main rationale for this reform was to enable police officers to spend more time out on the streets.

The prosecution of offenders

The introduction of new policing arrangements in England and Wales in the early years of the nineteenth century was not accompanied by the establishment of a prosecution authority. Accordingly, all prosecutions were conducted either by private persons or by the police. The creation of the office of the Director of

Public Prosecutions in 1879 introduced a new element into prosecution policy, but its powers were limited and the police (advised by lawyers but whose advice was neither independent nor binding) carried the great majority of prosecutions. For this reason, magistrates' courts were commonly known as 'police courts', although by the 1960s most large police forces had solicitor's departments that conducted this kind of work.

One difficulty with the dual role played by the police in conducting investigations and mounting subsequent prosecutions was that this might give them a vested interest in securing a positive outcome. This situation could result in pressure being applied to a suspect to admit guilt with the consequent possibility that a miscarriage of justice might arise. Accordingly, the two tasks were separated by the 1985 Prosecution of Offences Act, which established the Crown Prosecution Service. The CPS is an independent authority that conducts criminal prosecutions on behalf of the state. It is headed by the Director of Public Prosecutions (DPP) and the Attorney General is responsible to Parliament for its conduct.

Initially, the police would investigate an alleged offence and would then charge the person if it was decided to arrest him or her for this offence. The role of the Crown Prosecution Service was (and still is) to review case files prepared by the police and to decide whether to proceed or to discontinue them. In arriving at these decisions, CPS lawyers are guided by the Code for Crown Prosecutors, which is prepared by the DPP and lays down guiding principles relating to decisions regarding prosecution. These emphasise the need for:

- There to be a realistic prospect of securing a conviction (the evidential test): historically, police officers believed that this resulted in excessive preparation for minor cases even where the defendant was likely to plead guilty;
- The public interest to be served by pursuing a prosecution.

If the CPS decides to pursue a prosecution, it then determines what precise charge is brought, following guidelines contained in the Code for Crown Prosecutors. Legal Guidance is prepared by the CPS to aid these decisions.

Problems affecting police–CPS relations

Initially, a number of problems affected police–CPS relations. These included:

- Scepticism by the police service as to whether the creation of the CPS was required and of the motives that brought it about.
- The police were especially concerned about the high level of dropped cases as a result of CPS performance targets requiring successful convictions. The CPS would only proceed with watertight cases that were certain to secure convictions and this meant that some offences were not charged at all and others were downgraded in order to make them easier to prove in court.

- Inadequate liaison and working relationships between both agencies. This problem was compounded by both agencies using different organisational boundaries. Initially, the CPS was organised into 31 areas, but in 1993 this was reduced to 13. The police service used 43 in England and Wales.

Problems of this nature resulted in reforms that were designed to secure a more harmonious working relationship between the police service and the CPS.

Organisational reform

In 1999 (derived from proposals contained in Glidewell, 1998), the CPS was reorganised so that CPS areas coincided with those used by police forces in England and Wales (save that one area embraces all of London, incorporating two police forces – the Metropolitan Police Service and the City of London Police). Each of the 42 CPS areas is headed by a chief crown prosecutor.

Reforms affecting charging decisions

The belief that the CPS was too isolated from the police forces that sent cases to it (Glidewell, 1998) resulted in the initiation of pilot schemes which included CPS lawyers assuming responsibility for charging defendants. These experiments were advanced by the 2003 Criminal Justice Act, which provided for the involvement of the CPS in decisions relating to conditional cautioning and also regarding the charge to be bought against a person whom the police decided should be prosecuted for an offence. Charging for the most serious offences was transferred (on a phased-in basis) from the police to the CPS in 2004. One consequence of this is the presence of CPS lawyers in police stations. Traditionally, advice from the CPS was obtained through visits that had to be undertaken by police officers and were frequently time consuming (Sergeant, 2008: 30).

Evaluation of reforms to police–CPS relationships

A report into the operations of the Crown Prosecution Service (Justice Committee, 2009) discussed statutory charging arrangements that were introduced by the 2003 Criminal Justice Act. It referred to the beneficial impact this had exerted on discontinuance rates, which in magistrates' courts had declined to 13.2% by March 2008 compared to a figure of 36% before statutory charging was introduced. Nonetheless, there were issues with the system that were deemed capable of improvement, in particular in connection with delays at the stage when the police were ready to charge but awaiting the decision of a CPS prosecutor. Difficulties of this nature had resulted in suggestions (for example, in the Flanagan (2008) report) that the charging powers of the police should be restored in cases to be heard at the magistrates' court. However, the Justice Committee heard evidence on other solutions, including enhancing the role of CPS Direct, which allowed charging decisions to be given by telephone out of hours.

The report also referred to other developments affecting police–CPS relations, including the development of the 'prosecution team' involving close liaison between the two services, especially in the early stages of an investigation. One danger with this, however, was the perception that such a close relationship undermined the independence of the CPS. The Justice Committee therefore argued that inspection and scrutiny processes should maintain an oversight of the relationship between the two agencies.

Multi-agency policing

Initially, the police performed discrete functions within the criminal justice system. However, the need to work more closely with other agencies (and more recently with third sector, community-based organisations) has increasingly played an important part of modern police work. This section briefly describes the history of multi-agency policing.

The multi-agency approach was based on a belief that crime could be most effectively prevented by various bodies working together rather than leaving the entire burden of crime fighting in the hands of the police (Moore and Brown, 1981: 52). Street crime, for example, might be deterred by more adequate street lighting, the improved layout of housing estates or alterations to public transport time tables. However, such approaches were not universally pursued. It could not be taken for granted that individual agencies appreciated the need for cooperation, and even if they did, tunnel-vision parochialism often served as an impediment to locally-oriented inter-agency operation.

A number of community-oriented, multi-agency initiatives involving the police service and other bodies were pursued in the 1980s. This entailed joint action by public, private or voluntary sector organisations, which was designed to prevent crime within specific localities. If the gelling of working practices took place within the confines of a partnership organisational structure, the term 'inter-agency' rather than 'multi-agency' was often applied (Crawford, 1998).

Multi-agency work poses a number of challenges. The professionals involved in multi-agency work may view a specific issue from the perspective of their own organisation and find views expressed by other professionals, who adopt a different perspective, difficult to accept. Securing effective leadership of an organisation drawn from personnel from several agencies may be difficult to achieve and information-sharing between partner agencies is also a crucial ingredient to successful multi-agency operations. However, cooperation, even within departments of one agency such as the police service, was not always readily forthcoming, as was revealed by the report into child abuse in Cleveland in 1987 (Butler-Sloss,

1988). In addition, relatively limited progress has been made in pursuing technological developments to enable agencies such as the police service and the CPS to share information. Multi-agency work requires the development of a number of common standards to govern the type and quality of service that each participating agency can expect from another. These are usually embodied in Service Level Agreements (SLAs). Many of these issues are discussed in more detail in the following sections.

The prevention of crime (1): Multi-agency initiatives before 1997

Several proposals were put forward from the late 1970s regarding the desirability of using multi-agency initiatives to combat crime. This objective was particularly directed at crime prevention, which became a major concern for central government with the establishment of the Home Office Crime Prevention Unit in 1983.

The multi-agency approach had previously been recommended in connection with juvenile offending (Home Office, 1978). A subsequent Government Circular 8/84 (issued by the Home Office and four other Departments) recognised that the police alone could not tackle crime and disorder and thus also encouraged multi-agency work (Home Office, 1984). The approach also featured in the Five Towns initiative in 1986 and the Safer Cities Programme, phase I of which commenced in 1988 (phase II being taken over by the Department of the Environment and launched in 1992). The latter comprised initiatives that utilised both situational and social crime prevention measures that were managed by organisations such as the National Association for the Care and Resettlement of Offenders (NACRO) and Crime Concern rather than local government.

In 1990, a Home Office publication stated that well-planned and well-executed inter-agency schemes were to be found throughout the country (Home Office, 1990a: 1). Subsequently, central government encouraged the adoption of multi-agency solutions to crime prevention in 1990 (Home Office, 1990b) and 1994 (Department of the Environment, 1994). The 1990 circular was endorsed by ten government departments and the 1994 circular served to popularise the role of police architectural liaison officers, who had been appointed in some police forces in the late 1980s.

The Morgan report

A major catalyst to increase the involvement of the police service in multi-agency crime prevention initiatives that were spearheaded by local government came with the publication of a report prepared by the Home Office Standing Conference on Crime Prevention, which was chaired by James Morgan, in 1991.

This was set up to monitor 'the progress made in the local delivery of crime prevention through the multi-agency approach in the light of the guidance contained in the booklet accompanying 44/90' (Home Office Standing Conference on Crime Prevention, 1991: 10). Its proposals advocated that local government should be given a dominant role in advancing such developments. The report stated that 'the local authority is a natural focus for coordinating, in collaboration with the police, the broad range of activities directed at improving community safety' (Home Office Standing Conference on Crime Prevention, 1991: 19). It argued that 'the lack of a clear statutory responsibility for local government to play its part fully in crime prevention has clearly inhibited progress' (Home Office Standing Conference on Crime Prevention, 1991: 20).

The Morgan report also introduced the concept of 'community safety', as opposed to crime prevention, arguing that the latter term suggested that crime prevention was solely the responsibility of the police. Partnership was thus seen as the appropriate direction in which to develop future policy. The new designation asserted the important role that communities should play in crime prevention strategies and sought to stimulate greater participation from all members of the general public in the fight against crime. It would also enable fuller weight to be given to activities that went beyond the traditional police concentration on 'opportunity reduction' methods of crime prevention, and would encourage greater attention to be paid to social issues (Home Office, 1991: 13 and 20–21).

Problems impeding the development of multi-agency crime prevention work

There were, however, a number of problems associated with multi-agency crime prevention work in the period before 1997, in particular in connection with an enhanced role for local government in this area of activity. The relationship between the police service and local government was an impediment to progress in this direction, and this problem became more acute following Labour's defeat at the 1979 general election, which resulted in the rise of the 'urban left' in several local councils. These authorities tended to view the police with suspicion and sought to democratise the operations of policing whereby police priorities were determined by local people rather than the chief constables. Although some chief officers (most notably John Alderson in Devon and Cornwall) appreciated the need for inter-agency cooperation to fight crime, Labour-controlled local authorities often viewed these suggestions with scepticism, perceiving inter-agency work as a pretext for the police takeover of local government services.

The negative views held by a number of Labour-controlled local authorities towards cooperation with the police in multi-agency crime prevention initiatives were mirrored by the attitude displayed by post-1979 Conservative governments towards local government. This made it unlikely that central government would support local government playing a lead role in coordinating multi-agency crime prevention partnerships, as had been argued in the Morgan report. Therefore, no central funding was made available to implement any of the proposals contained in the Morgan report (a situation confirmed in Home Office, 1993).

Progress in involving local government in multi-agency work related to crime prevention was also impeded by the attempt to distinguish between the core and ancillary tasks of policing during the early 1990s and give priority to the former. Multi-agency crime prevention work was generally viewed as an ancillary task of policing, which resulted in a number of forces disbanding their headquarters community affairs departments, which frequently had a history of close cooperation with other agencies, including local government.

The prevention of crime (2): Partnership work after 1997

The 1998 Crime and Disorder Act placed a statutory duty on police forces and local authorities (termed 'responsible authorities') to act in cooperation with police authorities, health authorities and probation committees in multi-agency bodies which became known as crime and disorder reduction partnerships (CDRPs), although this designation did not appear in the legislation. In Wales, CDRPs are termed community safety partnerships (CSUs). The role of these partnerships was to develop and implement a strategy for reducing crime and disorder in each district and unitary local authority in England and Wales. They act as the engine of community safety initiatives and provided an important new mechanism to secure the involvement of communities in preventing crime and disorder.

The subsequent development of CDRPs

The 2002 Police Reform Act amended the 1998 legislation. Police and fire authorities became responsible authorities as defined by the 1998 legislation in April 2003, and in the following year were joined by Primary Care Trusts in England (and health authorities in Wales). Crime and disorder reduction partnerships were required to work closely with drug action teams in areas with a two-tier structure of local government and to integrate their work with drug action teams in areas which had a unitary structure of local government by April 2004. This latter requirement did not specify a merger of the two bodies, but required them to undertake appropriate arrangements to secure integration.

The 2002 Act also enabled CDRPs to merge where this course of action seemed appropriate in order to tackle issues traversing a number of related local authority areas. An example of this would be crime committed in one CDRP where the perpetrators lived in a neighbouring CDRP area. Preventive measures could thus be coordinated across local authority boundaries.

The powers of CDRPs in connection with drug misuse and anti-social behaviour were amended by the 2002 Police Reform Act, the 2003 Anti-social Behaviour Act and the 2006 Police and Justice Act. The latter legislation expanded the role of CDRPs to include alcohol and other substances in addition to drugs. In 2010, derived from the 2009 Policing and Crime Act, the role of CDRPs was expanded to include reducing re-offending and the probation service has been included as a statutory member.

The operations of CDRPs

The starting point of the process to reduce crime and disorder in each locality was the preparation of a local crime audit (conducted by the local authority) that would form the basis of the local crime reduction strategy. This emphasised the role of CDRPs as mechanisms to bring together agencies and also to engage with communities. It required all local service providers to record crime and in this way local 'hot spots' could be identified. To do this, local authorities developed tools such as geographic information systems (GIS) (Loveday, 2005: 74), in which data relating to crime can be stored and subsequently analysed in order to present findings in the form of maps or charts.

The audit also had to take into account the views of the public who lived and worked in the local authority area concerning crime and disorder. This required a detailed process of popular consultation, in particular with groups deemed 'hard to reach'. One intention of this was to give ordinary members of the general public the opportunity to influence the policy-making agenda. The CDRP would then formulate priorities, and a three-year strategy to tackle crime and disorder would be published.

CDRPs are required to produce a three-year rolling partnership plan (the first of which was for 2008–11) in place of a three-year strategy based on an audit of crime. This is based on a strategic assessment of crime and disorder, using a range of partner data. The partnership plan contains the objectives required to be implemented, how these will be delivered (in particular specifying the contribution of partners to support the delivery of the priorities), the manner in which performance against priorities will be assessed and the way in which the partnership will engage with its communities. Progress in attaining these objectives is monitored (through the mechanism of a strategic assessment produced every year) so that adjustments can be made as required.

CDRPs also provide a mechanism for the pooling of information collected by the participants in the process, and in conducting community safety projects. The funding for these is scarce, with most initiatives being fixed-term projects conducted at the neighbourhood level. Funding sources include the Home Office crime reduction programme or regeneration programmes.

Most local authorities have established community safety units (CSUs), whose main roles are to ensure the compliance of all local authority activities with section 17 of the 1998 legislation (which requires local authorities and police authorities to do all that they can reasonably do to prevent crime and disorder when exercising their functions) and also to link the local authority and the CDRP. CSUs also act as the first port of call for local people who have concerns regarding crime and disorder (and who prefer to report the matter in this way rather than having to contact the police), and may deliver initiatives designed to prevent crime, including tackling anti-social behaviour. They also provide the police with a link to local government when seeking to pursue multi-agency responses to crime and anti-social behaviour.

The work of CDRPs is supervised by the nine government offices for the regions. These were established in 1994 to coordinate regional activities to meet the targets of their sponsoring departments. They are headed by a regional crime director and since 2007 by a regional office minister.

Each of the nine regional offices has a Home Office Crime Reduction Team that is responsible for liaising with CDRPs operating in the region. Its work includes providing guidance, support and training to these partnerships, monitoring the performance of projects that have been funded by the Home Office, and ensuring that an appreciation of crime reduction issues is reflected in the work performed by all government offices which operate in the region. It has been proposed to extend the feedback role of Home Office Regional Directors, whereby they would provide regular information to CDRPs on their performance relative to neighbouring CDRPs (National Audit Office, 2004: 7).

The Home Office also has a Crime Reduction Team, based within the machinery of the Welsh Assembly, whose work is to provide support to that country's community safety partnerships (in particular to ensure that they meet performance targets set by the Welsh Assembly and the Home Office). In addition, it ensures that community safety issues are adequately addressed in other aspects of the Assembly's work. The task to reduce crime and disorder in Wales is supervised by the Welsh Assembly, whose Minister for Social Justice and Regeneration has control over a crime fighting fund to provide for programmes of community safety.

Community safety is not a statutory function performed by local authorities in either Scotland or Northern Ireland. However, work of this nature is undertaken by Scottish Councils and voluntary and statutory bodies in Northern Ireland.

Problem-solving and evaluation

The need to identify local crime and disorder problems, devise solutions to them and monitor their effectiveness are key functions of CDRPs.

Problem-solving is a complex task that embraces the identification of problems, understanding their causes, devising solutions to address them and evaluating the success of the applied remedies with a view to making adjustments if these are not successful in remedying the problems. The latter is of considerable importance since 'without an understanding of the impact of any intervention, partnerships will be limited in their ability to repeat their successes or improve delivery of outcomes' (Home Office, 2007a: 85).

There is no statutory requirement imposed on CDRPs as to the procedures involved in problem-solving, but there are models available to guide their processes. These include SARA (Scanning, Analysis, Response, Assessment – a method relatively widely used within the police service) and PROCTOR (PROblem, Cause, Tactic/Treatment, Output, Result).

Evaluation goes beyond a consideration of the extent to which individual problems have been addressed to an analysis of the overall work of the CDRP. A key process through which the effectiveness or otherwise of partnership working can be assessed is performance management. This entails gathering data regarding the performance of the partnership and using this data to evaluate the success or otherwise of the work that it has carried out.

Initially, the performance of CDRPs was assessed through a number of mechanisms, including the Policing Performance Assessment Framework. This was replaced in 2008 by the Assessment of Policing and Community Safety (APACS). These enabled the performance of agencies operating in partnership to be more easily assessed because they allow indicators used by these separate bodies to be aligned, thereby providing a 'common language for the discussion of performance' (Home Office, 2007a: 17).

Issues posed by the operations of CDRPs

The effective operations of CDRPs require a number of issues to be addressed. These impact on the operations of all participants to the partnership process.

Leadership in a partnership setting

'Leadership of the partnership is crucial to the success in tackling the issues of the community', in particular by developing a strategic vision for the partnership, identifying priorities, outlining the means to attain them and evaluating performance (Home Office, 2007a: 22). A principal difficulty that needs to be overcome is that of dispersed leadership, which may undermine attempts by CDRP managers to achieve targets.

Leadership in a multi-agency setting is potentially difficult to achieve, perhaps resulting in one partner taking the lead. This may create resentment in other partners who effectively disengage themselves from the partnership process. Further difficulties may arise between the various agencies involved in the partnerships as a result as the different perspectives of these bodies, the differential power relationships between them and whether they succeed in gelling together behind common aims and objectives.

It has been argued that success in reducing crime dependes on generating a 'synergy' among those in partnership, and sharing a commitment to tackle crime that is most likely to arise when issues of genuine local concern are targeted. However, divisional police commanders and chairs of CDRPs typically rate their local probation service and local health service as less active than other key statutory partners due to resource constraints and competing priorities (National Audit Office, 2004: 3).

Following the enactment of the 2006 Police and Justice Act, significant changes were made to the governance structure of each partnership, requiring the creation of a 'strategy group' to exercise ultimate responsibility for the implementation of the partnership plan. The responsible authorities must be represented on this group by a senior official (such as the Basic Command Unit (BCU) commander), whose key role is to prepare and implement a strategic assessment and partnership plan. In two-tier areas, the role of the County Strategy Group is to coordinate the operations of the partnerships within the area, and this group is required to include the chairs of each of the District Strategy Groups.

Operational autonomy

Although the operations of CDRPs were initially scrutinised through the requirement that they produced three-year audits and strategies and the duty to report annually to the Secretary of State, they were initially given little central guidance as to how they should deliver their responsibilities. It was not until the enactment of the 2006 Police and Justice Act that national standards (in the form of 'hallmarks of effective partnerships') were introduced as minimum statutory requirements, reflecting what had been identified as good practice since their introduction in 1998 (Home Office, 2007a: 4). These were supplemented by subsequent regulations.

Inter-agency information-sharing

Inter-agency cooperation has not always been easy to achieve, one particular problem being the sharing of information. This is a crucial aspect of identifying priorities and delivering community safety initiatives, and is central to the strategic assessment process. However, although the 1998 Crime and Disorder Act permitted partners to share both personal and depersonalised information, it was subsequently noted that progress had often been 'sporadic' (Home Office, 2007a: 36). The 2006 Police and Justice Act introduced a duty on partnership agencies to disclose certain types of depersonalised information (but not personal data) to the other partners. It was argued that the first step in ensuring effective information-sharing involved establishing an information-sharing protocol and nominating designated liaison officers to facilitate the sharing of information (Home Office, 2007a: 36).

Localism versus centralism

The 'bottom up' system of objective-setting contained in the 1998 Act was threatened by the increased involvement of the Home Office in the operations and performance of CDRPs. This was evidenced in the setting of targets for CDRPs in connection with vehicle crime, domestic burglary and robbery, and the introduction of performance indicators for CDRPs that inevitably shifted the local crime prevention agenda on to outputs that were capable of measurement.

The emphasis exerted by the Home Office also tended to direct the work of CDRPs towards crime control activities to the detriment of longer-term measures concerned with addressing the causes of crime. The performance of CDRPs was monitored by the Home Office and, commencing in 2003/04, CDRPs were required to complete an annual report on the implementation of their crime and disorder reduction strategy. As has been noted above, additional control over CDRPs was also exerted after 2000 by the appointment of regional crime directors to each of the nine regional government offices in 2000, whose role was to improve the overall effectiveness of crime prevention.

These actions indicated a move towards centralisation in that 'CDRPs are increasingly subject to pressures to conform to national police agendas' (Loveday, 2005: 81). Some attempt to ameliorate this situation was put forward in the 2008–11 Crime Strategy. This promised to reduce the number of specific targets set for CDRPs within the safer communities Public Service Agreements (PSAs, see page 112), many of which would be replaced by a target to increase public confidence in agencies. This approach would ensure that the attainment of priorities felt to be important by local communities was placed at the forefront of agency action (Home Office, 2007b: 43).

Partnership work and specific crimes

In addition to partnership work that seeks to prevent a wide range of criminal and disorderly activities, machinery has also been created to provide for a partnership response to specific forms of criminal activity. This includes hate crime and the abuse of children, where a concern for the victims of crime underpins intervention.

Hate crime

The procedures for reporting and recording racist incidents were set out in a Code of Practice published by the Home Office in 2000 which applies to the police service and to any other statutory or voluntary groups that are responsible for recording these incidents. The involvement of agencies other than the police in recording these incidents has given rise to the development of multi-agency panels to develop strategies to tackle the problem, comprising local government agencies, the police and probation services, the Crown Prosecution Service and voluntary and community organisations such as the Citizens' Advice Bureau and

Victim Support. The structure and organisation of these panels is subject to variation across England and Wales and their operations are affected by problems that include police dominance, the absence of data-sharing and the lack of coordination between participating bodies (Docking and Tuffin, 2005: 29–31).

Child abuse

The police service is required to adopt a proactive multi-agency approach to preventing and reducing child abuse and neglect and safeguarding children (ACPO/NPIA, 2009: 9). There are a number of aspects to this approach.

Multi-Agency Risk Assessment Conferences (MARACs) constitute one multi-agency initiative through which the interests of children may be safeguarded. Although this machinery is focused on supporting those at repeat risk of domestic violence, it may also reveal allegations of child abuse.

Local multi-agency policy on child protection matters is the responsibility of Local Safeguarding Children Boards (LSCBs), which are accountable to and funded by each partner agency, including the police (ACPO/NPIA, 2009: 58–59). The role of these bodies is to bring the police, local authority and other local partners together in order to safeguard children and promote their welfare. Links are usually fashioned between LSCBs and other partnership mechanisms (such as MAPPAs and MARACs) (Home Office, 2009b: 94).

The key partner agency with whom the police work in responding to concerns regarding children and allegations of child abuse is children's social care. The Police and Children's Social Care agencies may jointly visit a child's home to establish his or her welfare. If there is reasonable cause to suspect that a child is suffering from (or is at serious risk of suffering) significant harm, a strategy meeting is convened at which the relevant agencies (including health professionals and school staff) provide information that forms the basis of decisions on future interventions. These may include a child protection conference and a child protection review conference (ACPO/NPIA, 2009: 96).

Partnership work – a conclusion

The development of partnership work has transformed the way in which contemporary policing is delivered. The 1998 Crime and Disorder Act placed partnership working on a statutory footing throughout England and Wales and this has subsequently matured so that 'inter-agency working has become second nature to many who work to improve the safety of our communities'. Partnership work has 'been a key factor in the significant and lasting progress that has been made in the fight against crime' (Coaker, 2007: 3) and was a key factor in the delivery of the government's 2007 Crime Strategy. It has been argued that police involvement in crimefighting partnerships 'will help us to build communities where local people have a say in tackling crime and anti-social behaviour, and can see and feel the difference made by front line agencies' (Home Office 2009b: 93).

Partnership work and the management of offenders

The police service has also been involved, alongside other criminal justice agencies, in the management of offenders. There are a number of dimensions to this role, examples of which are considered below.

Youth Offending Teams

Youth Offending Teams (YOTs) were established by the 1998 Crime and Disorder legislation as a multi-agency initiative to tackle youth offending that involves local authority education and social services departments, the probation and health services and the police. However, police involvement with other agencies in connection with youth offending pre-dated this legislation. It was relatively common for the police to liaise with outside bodies when juveniles committed criminal offences. Youths who came to the attention of the police (perhaps as a result of being called to a domestic dispute) and who were deemed by them to be at risk of becoming victims of crime in the home would often be subject to some form of multi-agency intervention coordinated by a police Child Protection Department.

YOTs perform a number of functions in relation to young offenders aged between 10 and 17. These include determining whether intervention (which may necessitate family group conferencing) is required in support of the new police final warning schemes, the aim of which is to prevent further re-offending. YOTs also coordinate a multi-agency response to develop and supervise intervention programmes. They prepare pre-sentence reports and other information required by the courts in criminal proceedings against juveniles, liaise with victims and supervise community sentences imposed by the courts. Additionally Aspects of operational policing that seek to combat youth offending (such as visits to schools) are also frequently conducted in collaboration with YOTs.

Despite this, the number of police officers seconded to work in YOTs is relatively small.

Information-sharing between the police service and YOTs is an important aspect of partnership work. A number of developments have taken place to enable the police service to undertake this form of cooperation. One of these is the Police Electronic Notification to YOTs (PENY) project. This was initiated in 2008 and seeks to provide YOTs with information regarding reprimands, final warnings, fixed penalty notices and charges in order to enable YOTs to make informed decisions about the youths who have been referred to them.

Further statutory requirements calling for Youth Offending Teams and the police and probation service to cooperate in connection with juveniles convicted of serious offences was provided by the 2000 Criminal Justice and Court Services Act, which was later augmented by the 2003 Criminal Justice Act.

In addition to their involvement with YOTs, the police may also be involved in other multi-agency initiatives designed to identify children at risk of offending before it happens. This may include sharing information with other agencies within the framework of interventions such as Youth Inclusion and Support Panels (YISPs). These are multi-agency groups which offer support on a voluntary basis to 8–13 year olds and their families who are deemed to present a high risk of carrying out criminal and anti-social behaviour.

Multi-Agency Public Protection Arrangements

In recent years, partnership work has been specially directed at prolific offenders who cause most harm within communities (Home Office, 2009b: 29). Action across agencies entails the identification of such offenders, monitoring them, offering opportunities for rehabilitation and securing fast-track punishment should they re-offend. Multi-Agency Public Protection Arrangements (MAPPAs) constitute an important aspect of this kind of work. MAPPAs allow agencies to cooperate to develop policies that seek to assess and manage the risk to the public posed by violent, dangerous or sex offenders when they are released from custody and placed back into the community.

The MAPPA process entails four stages: (1) identifying the offender, (2) sharing information between agencies, (3) assessing the risk (using assessment tools such as OASys), and (4) managing that risk.

Following the 1997 Sex Offenders Act, which required convicted sex offenders to register with the police, public protection panels were set up to facilitate information-sharing between relevant agencies in order to assess and manage the risk posed by these offenders. The 2000 Criminal Justice and Court Services Act also required the police and probation services (termed 'responsible authorities') to cooperate to make arrangements to assess and manage the risk posed by sex or violent offenders and others who presented a risk to the public when they were placed in the community. The 2003 Criminal Justice Act included the prison service as a responsible authority and placed a duty to cooperate on a range of other statutory and other social care agencies, including YOTs and local social services, education authorities and housing authorities.

There are three categories of offenders who are subject to MAPPA. Category 1 consists of registered sex offenders who have been convicted or cautioned since September 1997. The police have a responsibility to identify those in this category. Category 2 consists of violent or other sex offenders who have received a custodial sentence of 12 months or more since April 2001, a hospital or guardianship order or who have been disqualified from working with children. Those in this category are subject to supervision by the National Probation Service and are thus identified by this agency. Category 3 consists of other offenders deemed by the 'responsible authority' to pose a risk of serious harm to the general public. Those in this category are identified by the relevant responsible authority.

There are three levels of risk assessment: level 1 applies to offenders who present a low or medium risk and who can be managed by the agency that initially identified the offender; level 2 applies to offenders who are deemed to pose a higher level of risk that requires the involvement of more than one agency in devising risk management plans but who are not deemed to pose a risk appropriate to the next level; level 3 applies to offenders who pose a high risk or whose management in the community requires resources from more than one of the partnership agencies.

Risk management for high-risk offenders is implemented and overseen by a multi-agency public protection panel (MAPPP), which consists of senior managers from the participating agencies. The more routine cases are overseen by a lower-tier and more local committee known as a multi-agency risk assessment conference (MARAC) (Tilley, 2005: 542). Since 2003, the overall responsibility for MAPPA work was given to strategic management boards (SMBs) established by the responsible authorities to review and monitor the effectiveness of MAPPAs.

In 2003/04 there were 39,429 offenders being managed by MAPPAs: 62% were registered sex offenders (category 1), 32% were in category 2 and 6% in category 3 (Kemshall et al., 2005: 3). The initiatives that have been used to manage risk are wide-ranging and include tagging, supervised accommodation and accredited programmes.

Integrated Offender Management (IOM)

The approach embodied by MAPPA was adopted in a number of other programmes. These include the Prolific and other Priority Offenders (PPO) programme, which was established in 2004 to provide for a multi-agency response (led by CDRPs) whose aims are to deter, catch, convict, rehabilitate and resettle offenders who have committed disproportionate amounts of serious crime in their communities. Additionally, the Drug Intervention Programme (DIP) seeks to reduce the amount of drug-related crime through the use of partnership work with a number of agencies directed at drug users who have committed crime. These programmes were developed in the Integrated Offender Management (IOM) initiative that was initially piloted in five areas in 2008. This seeks to provide a coherent structure for the management of a wide range of repeat offenders aged 18 and over, whether subject to statutory supervision in the community or not.

This approach is based on multi-agency problem-solving and embraces identification, assessment, management and enforcement. Information and intelligence-sharing between agencies is the essential element underpinning this approach, which aims to ensure that agencies develop 'shared approaches to assessment and management of those who pose the highest risks and ensure co-ordinated access to the resources that will help offenders turn away from crime' (Ministry of Justice, 2008: 13).

Joined-up government

The involvement of the police service in the broader affairs of the criminal justice system has been advanced through developments that seek to provide a 'joined-up' approach to criminal justice policy. This refers to measures that have been pursued by the post-1997 Labour governments to ensure the greater coordination of public sector organisations whose work might contribute towards combating crime, whether these are mainstream criminal justice agencies (such as the police and probation service) or bodies such as education and social services that have not traditionally viewed crime-fighting as one of their functions.

Initially, reforms to achieve a joined-up approach in criminal justice policy were based on the multi-agency or partnership approach that was formalised in the area of youth justice and community safety through the development of Youth Offending Teams and crime and disorder reduction partnerships. The joined-up approach was also developed through other initiatives, including multi-agency performance targets. An early example of this was Public Service Agreements (PSAs), introduced in the 1998 Comprehensive Spending Review. These sought to coordinate the work of a number of government departments behind a common theme (the PSA), whose attainment was measured by a series of performance indicators. These themes embraced a wide range of government activity, including criminal justice affairs.

A further key reform that sought to promote a joined-up approach at a national level embracing the three criminal justice agencies was the creation of the Office for Criminal Justice Reform (OCJR). The OCJR consists of a cross-departmental team designed to aid criminal justice agencies to work together. It is responsible to the Home Secretary, Lord Chancellor/Secretary of State for Justice and the Attorney General. It is located within the Ministry of Justice's Criminal Justice Business Group. One mechanism through which the OCJR achieves joined-up government is the production of strategic plans that shape the future operations of criminal justice agencies, and into which the strategic plans of individual government departments are fitted.

An example is the strategic plan for the criminal justice system in England and Wales, *Working Together To Cut Crime and Deliver Justice* (Office for Criminal Justice Reform, 2007), which set out an approach whereby the key criminal justice agencies (police, prosecution, probation, prisons and youth justice system) cooperate in order to more effectively combat crime, bring more offenders to justice and help to tackle crime and reduce re-offending. The objectives contained in this strategy document were closely aligned with the Home Office Crime Reduction Strategy for 2008–11 (Home Office, 2007a), which set out the key areas that should be focused on (serious violence, anti-social behaviour, young people, designing out crime, reducing re-offending, partnership and building public confidence) (Home Office, 2007a: 3–5).

The broad objectives contained in strategic and national policy documents are translated into more specific objectives and targets by the National Criminal Justice Board (NCJB), whose role is to define 'the vision and targets and for the high level policy framework' within which the criminal justice system operates (Office for Criminal Justice Reform, 2007: 49). The NCJB works closely with the OCJR, the National Crime Reduction Board and the National Policing Board, and reports to the Criminal Justice System Cabinet Committee, which is also responsible for monitoring the delivery of criminal justice system PSA targets.

The objectives put forward by the NCJB are incorporated into local programmes by the Local Criminal Justice Boards, which are key delivery mechanisms to achieve NCJB strategic objectives. LCJBs were established in 2003. There are 42 of them and they are composed of the chief officers of each of the criminal justice agencies. They exist to secure close working relationships between the police, the CPS, the probation, prison and youth services at a local level and to ensure that these agencies work together effectively. LCJBs have been given an enhanced role to deliver services and the ability to tailor service improvement to local needs and priorities (Office for Criminal Justice Reform, 2007: 17 and 49).

LCJBs seek to coordinate the operations of criminal justice agencies at a local level. However, joined-up government seeks to incorporate agencies outside the criminal justice sector in the fight against crime, some of which work together in alternative partnership structures such as CDRPs. The work performed by a wide range of partnerships bodies is joined up through the mechanism of a community strategy. Future government policy intends to integrate the work of LCJBs and CDRPs in areas that include 'the alignment of plans, sharing analysis, joint communications or streamlining partnership meetings and governance resources' (Home Office, 2009b: 100).

The 2000 Local Government Act imposed a statutory duty on local authorities to prepare community strategies, and Local Strategic Partnerships (LSPs) were developed to drive these strategies forward. This approach was further developed in the 2007 Local Government and Public Involvement in Health Act, which provided for LSPs to become the main vehicle through which the government's sustainable community strategy would be advanced.

An LSP is a non-statutory, multi-agency, non-executive body whose boundaries are coterminous with those of a local authority (either a district or county council or a unitary authority). Their role is to bring together the public, private, voluntary and community sectors in order to tackle problems such as crime that require a response from a range of different bodies acting in an integrated manner. They are not a single organisation 'but a "family" of partnerships and/or themed sub-groups' (Home Office, 2007b: 130). Typically, the LSP develops themes to advance the local authority's community strategy. The delivery mechanisms of these themes are multi-agency bodies such as CDRPs.

The link between local strategic planning and national objectives is fashioned by Local Area Agreements (LAAs), whose content is informed by Public Service Agreements (PSAs) and the priorities contained in CDRP partnership plans. LSPs negotiate and deliver LAAs. LAAs establish the priorities for a local area, which are agreed between central government and the local authority, the LSP and other local-level partners. Their aim is to join up local public services (entailing the sharing of information and pooling of resources), thereby tailoring service delivery to local needs.

LAAs are structured around four policy areas: (1) children and young people, (2) safer and stronger communities, (3) healthier communities and older people, and (4) economic development and environment. They operate over a three-year planning cycle. In two-tier areas, LAAs are negotiated at county level but districts are also involved in formulating them.

The extent of joined-up government at a local level is now subject to an annual inspection regime known as the Comprehensive Area Assessment (CAA) (Audit Commission, 2009). It is being delivered jointly by six inspectorates (the Audit Commission, Ofsted, the Care Quality Commission, Her Majesty's Inspectorate of Constabulary, Her Majesty's Inspectorate of Probation and Her Majesty's Inspectorate of Prisons), and examines the workings of the LSP, the delivery of the community strategy and LAAs.

The CAA has two main elements: an area assessment that looks at how well local public services are delivering better results for local people in local priorities such as health, economic prospects and crime and safety, and how likely they are to improve in the future. There are also organisational assessments of individual public bodies including performance against targets and use of resources. The new CAA framework commenced in 2009 and provides an independent assessment of the work of partner agencies in improving outcomes and the quality of life for people living in local communities.

QUESTION

Analyse the role performed by partnership work to the operations of policing since 1997.

To answer this question you should:

- Discuss what you understand by the term partnership work;
- Evaluate the reasons for the development of partnership work since 1997;

- Indicate the mechanisms through which this objective is advanced, in particular referring to CDRPs;
- Analyse the manner in which partnership work impacts on the operations of contemporary policing, identifying its key strengths and weaknesses;
- Present a conclusion in which, drawing from arguments presented earlier, you assess how partnership work is likely to develop in the future.

REFERENCES

ACPO/NPIA (2009) *Guidance on Investigating Child Abuse and Safeguarding Children* (2nd edition). London: National Police Improvements Agency.

Audit Commission (2009) *What is CAA?* [Online] www.audit-commission.gov.uk/localgov/audit/caa/pages/whatiscaa.aspx [accessed 1 November 2009].

BBC (2009) *Panorama: Assault on Justice.* Screened on BBC One, 9 November.

Burrows, J., Tarling, R., Mackie, A., Lewis, R. and Taylor, G. (2000) *Review of Police Forces' Crime Recording Practices.* Research Study 204. London: Home Office Research and Statistics Directorate.

Butler-Sloss, E. (1988) *Report of the Inquiry into Child Abuse in Cleveland 1987.* Cm 412. London: HMSO.

Coaker, V. (2007) *Delivering Safer Communities: A Guide to Effective Partnership Working: Guidance for Crime and Disorder Reduction Partnerships and Community Safety Partnerships.* London: Home Office, Police and Crime Standards Directorate.

Crawford, A. (1998) 'Community Safety Partnerships', *Criminal Justice Matters,* 33 (Autumn): 4–5.

Department of the Environment (1994) *Planning Out Crime.* Circular 5/94. London: Department of the Environment.

Docking, N. and Tuffin, R. (2005) *Racist Incidents: Progress since the Lawrence Inquiry.* Home Office Online Report 42/05. London: Home Office.

Flanagan, Sir R (2008) *The Review of Policing Final Report.* London: Review of Policing.

Glidewell, Sir I. (1998) *Review of the Crown Prosecution Service: A Report.* Cm 3960. London: TSO.

Her Majesty's Inspectorate of Constabulary (2009) *Crime Counts: A Review of Data Quality for Offences of the Most Serious Violence.* London: HMIC.

Home Office (1978) *Juveniles: Cooperation between the Police and Other Agencies.* Circular 211/78. London: Home Office.

Home Office (1984) *Crime Prevention.* Circular 8/84. London: Home Office.

Home Office (1990a) *Partnership in Crime Prevention.* London: Home Office.

Home Office (1990b) *Crime Prevention: The Success of the Partnership Approach.* Circular 44/90. London: Home Office.

Home Office (1991) *Criminal Statistics.* Vol. IV: *Annual & Miscellaneous Returns.* London: Home Office.

Home Office (1993) *A Practical Guide to Crime Prevention for Local Partnerships.* London: HMSO.

Home Office (2007a) *Cutting Crime: A New Partnership 2008–2011.* London: Home Office.

Home Office (2007b) *Delivering Safer Communities: A Guide to Effective Partnership Working: Guidance for Crime and Disorder Reduction Partnerships and Community Safety Partnerships*. London: Home Office, Police and Crime Standards Directorate.

Home Office (2009a) *Cutting Crime Two Years On: An Update to the 2008–2011 Crime Strategy*. London: Home Office.

Home Office (2009b) *Protecting the Public: Supporting the Police to Succeed*. Cm 7749. London: TSO.

Home Office Standing Conference on Crime Prevention (1991) *Safer Communities: The Local Delivery of Crime Prevention through the Partnership Approach*. London: Home Office.

Justice Committee (2009) *The Crown Prosecution Service: Gatekeeper of the Criminal Justice System*. Ninth Report Session 2008/9 House of Commons Paper 186. London: TSO.

Kemshall, H., Mackenzie, G., Wood, J., Bailey, R. and Yates, J. (2005) *Strengthening Multi-Agency Public Protection Arrangements*. Home Office Development and Practice Report 45. London: Home Office.

Loveday, B. (2005) 'Police and Community Justice in Partnership', in J. Winstone and F. Pakes (eds), *Community Justice: Issues for Probation and Criminal Justice*. Cullompton, Devon: Willan Publishing.

Ministry of Justice (2008) *Punishment and Reform: Our Approach to Managing Offenders – A Summary*. London: Ministry of Justice.

Moore, C. and Brown, J. (1981) *Community Versus Crime*. London: Bedford Square Press.

Morgan, R. (2008) *Summary Justice Fast – but is it Fair?* London: Centre for Crime and Justice Studies.

National Audit Office (2004) *Reducing Crime: The Home Office Working with Crime and Disorder Reduction Partnerships*. Value for Money Reports. London: National Audit Office.

Office for Criminal Justice Reform (2007) *Working Together To Cut Crime and Deliver Justice: A Strategic Plan for 2008–2011*. C. 7247. London: TSO.

Sergeant, H. (2008) *The Public and the Police*. London: Civitas.

Tilley, N. (ed.) (2005) *Handbook of Crime Prevention and Community Safety*. Cullompton, Devon: Willan Publishing.

6

The control and accountability of the police service

CHAPTER AIMS

The aims of this chapter are:

- To consider the tripartite division of responsibilities for police work in England and Wales which was established by the 1964 Police Act;
- To examine initiatives pursued by Conservative governments towards the control and accountability of the police service between 1979 and 1997 and to analyse the impact of new public management on the police service in that period;
- To analyse policies pursued by post-1997 Labour governments in the control and accountability of the police service;
- To evaluate the extent to which reforms pursued by post-1979 governments have resulted in the centralisation of the police service;
- To evaluate the consequences of the empowerment agenda on the future direction of the police service.

The 1964 Police Act

By the middle of the twentieth century, responsibility for policing was shared by local government, central government and chief constables. However, the separation of responsibilities was unclear and disputes between chief officers and Watch Committees, which occurred in areas such as Nottingham in 1958 (Jefferson and Grimshaw, 1984: 40–41), justified the need to determine a more precise division between the three bodies, and in particular between chief constables and police authorities since this has a crucial bearing on the concept of constabulary independence. The 1964 Police Act sought to achieve this objective and its main provisions are outlined below.

Local government

The 1964 Police Act ended the direct control previously exercised by local government over policing outside London. Local responsibilities for policing would henceforth be discharged by a police committee (later termed a police authority). Although attached to the structure of local government (at county level), the police committee did not derive its powers by delegation from the local council (which had been the position previously), but directly from the Act itself. This provided the committee/authority with a considerable degree of independence from local government, whose main role (unless the police committee operated across more than one county) was confined to approving the police force budget, prepared by the police authority.

Two-thirds of the members of the police committee were councillors and the remaining third were magistrates who served in the area covered by the police force. The role of the police committee was to 'secure the maintenance of an adequate and efficient police force for their area' and this entailed the authority setting a budget for their force. The authority was also required to keep itself informed of how complaints by members of the public against police officers were dealt with by the chief constable.

Police authorities were given a number of powers to fulfil these responsibilities, including the appointment and dismissal of senior officers of the force and the provision and maintenance of premises, vehicles, clothing and other equipment. In addition, police committees acted as disciplinary authorities for the chief constable and deputy and assistant chief constables, and could require the chief constable to submit a report in writing relating to the policing of the area.

Chief constables

The 1964 Police Act placed each force under the operational 'direction and control' of its chief officer, whose prime responsibility was to enforce the law and maintain the Queen's peace. The legislation gave the chief constable a number of day-to-day functions in relation to the administration of the force, including the appointment and dismissal of officers up to the rank of chief superintendent, and the specific requirement to investigate all complaints made by the public against any junior officers.

Central government

The Home Secretary exercised a prerogative power to maintain law and order. The 1964 Police Act gave this Minister a range of strategic and tactical responsibilities that were designed to promote the overall efficiency of the police service.

These (adapted from Spencer, 1985: 37–38) included powers to:

- Pay or withhold the government grant to particular police authorities;
- Require police authorities to insist upon the retirement of their chief officer;
- Make regulations connected with the 'government, administration and conditions of service of police forces';
- Appoint inspectors of constabulary and instruct them to carry out duties designed to further police efficiency;
- Exercise control over the standard of equipment used by police forces;
- Supply and maintain a number of services available to the police service generally;
- Require a chief constable to submit a report on the policing of an area and to order a local enquiry on any police matter;
- Direct a chief constable to provide officers to another force under the mutual aid procedure;
- Exercise control over the amalgamation of forces;
- Act as the appeal body for officers found guilty of disciplinary offences.

An assessment of the 1964 Police Act

The 1964 Police Act gave rise to several subsequent problems.

Control of police responsibilities

The division of responsibilities provided for in the 1964 legislation was put forward in vague language. This created grey areas that could become a battleground as to who had the right to determine a particular activity. It was the backdrop of the notable disputes between chief constables and their police authorities in Greater Manchester and Merseyside, which centred on who should exercise responsibility for determining police priorities.

The tripartite system of control and accountability

For much of the nineteenth century the mechanism of police accountability had been straightforward. Outside London, policing was controlled by local government, to which the police were accountable for their actions. The subsequent involvement of central government and chief constables in police affairs complicated this historic form of accountability. It made for an unwieldy system of accountability in that the actions undertaken by the Home Office, chief constables or police committees could be vetoed by one or both of the other bodies. For example, a police authority was empowered to require a chief constable to produce a report on police activities. However, the chief constable could appeal to the Home Office to countermand this request. This system of checks and balances created an 'entanglement' of responsibilities, resulting in uncertain lines of accountability, and made it 'hard to find sufficient basis for calling any of the parties to account' (Home Office, 1993a: 7).

A further difficulty with the system of accountability that was established by the 1964 Police Act concerned the weakness of the sanctions that were available for the three parties to apply to one of the others. For example, the Home Office could withhold the government's grant if it deemed a police force to be operating inefficiently. But the practical impossibility of bankrupting a police force meant this penalty could never be applied, even in a situation where it might have been justified.

Conservative legislation affecting the governance of the police service 1979–97

Conservative governments between 1979 and 1997 enacted a series of measures that impacted on the governance of the police service. These are discussed below.

The 1984 Police and Criminal Evidence Act

The 1964 Police Act was followed by a series of police force amalgamations which reduced the number of forces from 126 in 1968 to 43 in 1974 (Loveday and Reid, 2003: 12). The creation of bigger forces operating over large geographic areas tended to create a sense of distance between the police and the public.

The immediate impetus to enacting the 1984 legislation derived from reports by Lord Scarman (Home Office, 1981) and the Royal Commission on Criminal Procedure (1981). The aim of the 1984 legislation was not to create new mechanisms of accountability, whereby police forces would become more answerable to the public for their actions, but instead to resurrect the consent of the public in areas where there was popular disaffection towards the police.

The only change that was made to the control and accountability of policing was the requirement in section 106 of the Act that the police had to consult with local communities on a regular basis. However, consultation did not alter the established power relationship between the police and public. It merely required the police to listen to what local people had to say regarding police affairs; it did not require them to act on the basis of what they had heard.

The 1985 Local Government Act

The 1985 Local Government Act abolished the Greater London Council (which exercised no responsibility for policing) and the six metropolitan county councils. The role previously performed by police committees in metropolitan counties were now discharged by joint boards, composed of magistrates and representatives from the constituent district councils. Section 85 of the 1985 Local

Government Act made joint boards subject to a much greater degree of central control in key areas of work for the first three years of their existence. However, the councillors who were appointed to serve on them lacked experience and were more willing to accept the chief constable's definition of their responsibilities (Loveday, 1987: 14–15).

The 1992 Local Government Act

This legislation created unitary local authorities. The main significance of this reform for the governance of the police was that it extended the number of localities where police authorities covered several local authority areas.

The 1994 Police and Magistrates' Courts Act

The police service and Conservative government enjoyed a cordial relationship during the early part of the 1980s. However, a perception arose within government that increased spending on the police service was not succeeding in reducing the levels of crime and disorder. This prompted a change of direction by the government and gave rise to a raft of reforms that were directed at its working practices (and in particular its performance culture). These were based upon the principles of new public management and sought 'to improve cost efficiency and performance effectiveness via the imposition of market disciplines on the police service' (Jones, 2003: 615) (see Box 6.1). This section will examine the concept of new public management and discuss the various initiatives that sought to promote this principle within the police service, the culmination of which was the 1994 Police and Magistrates' Courts Act.

BOX 6.1

THE KEY PRINCIPLES OF NEW PUBLIC MANAGEMENT

New public management has been described as 'a way of reorganising public sector bodies to bring their management and reporting closer to a particular conception of business methods' (Dunleavy and Hood, 1994: 9). Thus management techniques traditionally associated with the private sector (such as performance indicators, business plans, and the costing and market testing of all activities) were vigorously developed to redress perceived organisational inefficiencies and promote enhanced value for money. In particular, new public management:

(Continued)

(Continued)

- Emphasised the need for public services to be driven by concerns of efficiency, value for money and quality of service. This would be secured by methods that included the use of performance management techniques associated with the private sector, such as setting targets and performance indicators.
- Sought to provide public services with a consumer orientation whose power rested not on the political sanction of accountability, but rather on their ability to shop around and go elsewhere if a service was not being provided efficiently.
- Entailed organisational goals being set by central government while giving agency heads a considerable degree of freedom as to how these were attained. This approach is sometimes referred to described in terms of a 'steering/rowing' analogy.
- Led to public policy being implemented by a range of bodies rather than being the preserve of agencies that functioned as arms of the state. This goal was achieved by the processes that included 'hiving off' and compulsory competitive tendering.

The implementation of new public management

The introduction of the principles of new public management into the police service derived from a circular (Home Office, 1983) which sought to apply the 1982 Financial Management Initiative to the delivery of police services. The need to produce quantifiable evidence on which to base claims of organisational effectiveness was reinforced by subsequent circulars (such as Home Office, 1988a) and gave rise to associated developments that included expanding the role of the Her Majesty's Inspectorate of Constabulary (HMIC) to ensure that forces adopted 'the language of objectives and demonstrable achievement' (Weatheritt, 1986).

Initiatives based upon new public management that were developed after 1983 included policing by objectives and civilianisation. However, these had a relatively limited impact on the working practices of the police service during the 1980s, and resulted in more vigorous attempts to pursue new public management principles during the 1990s. The main developments are considered below.

Performance indicators   An important development that was designed to enhance police performance and productivity was the introduction of a range of centrally determined performance indicators, which related to those areas of police work for which quantifiable data could most easily be compiled. They particularly related to the goal of controlling crime (Martin, 2003: 161).

The performance indicators that were used were in the nature of output controls and were initially devised by a variety of bodies (including the Home Office, the Audit Commission, HMIC and ACPO) but, following the enactment of the

1992 Local Government Act, became the responsibility of the Audit Commission. The emphasis placed on quantifiable data meant that crime statistics generated by individual police forces became an important measure of police efficiency. A Home Office circular put forward a set of core statistics to be included in the chief constables' annual reports (Home Office, 1995b) and in 1995 the Audit Commission commenced the publication of 'league tables' containing comparative information on issues such as the level of crime, detection rates per police officer, and clear-up rates for all crimes in each of the 43 police forces in England and Wales.

In this way politicians and the public were able to assess police performance and ascertain whether good value for money was being achieved within the police service (Audit Commission, 1990a).

Core and ancillary functions   The responsibilities discharged by British police forces had not developed in a systematic manner but frequently arose from the fact that police stations were open 24 hours a day and thus attracted calls for assistance from members of the public and also other agencies, which resulted in the police providing 'a host of friendly supportive services to people in need' (Reiner, 1994: 13). Accordingly, the desire to improve police performance embraced an attempt to define the main tasks of policing with a view to abandoning activities that were of marginal important to the police service's core business.

In 1993 a Home Office review team was charged with distinguishing between core and peripheral (or ancillary) functions in order to determine what activities could be relinquished (or 'hived off') by the police. Its remit was to examine the services provided by the police, to make recommendations about the most cost-effective way of delivering core police services and to assess the scope for relinquishing ancillary tasks. Twenty-six areas were identified in which time and money could be saved if the police effort was streamlined or reduced, and it was recommended that these activities could either be off-loaded on to commercial or voluntary-sector providers or be made subject to the process of compulsory competitive tendering, which had been introduced in the 1988 Local Government Act (Home Office, 1995a).

However, it proved difficult to secure consensus within the police service as to what functions constituted core and ancillary activities. Ultimately, the government resolved this dilemma by enacting the 1994 Police and Magistrates' Court Act, which enabled the Home Secretary to define police priorities.

Consumerism   Attempts to reform the performance culture of the police service were associated with consumerism. This approach was especially based upon the Citizens' Charter, which was launched in 1991 and sought to improve the choice, quality, value for money and accountability of public services by ascertaining what the public expected of them and ensuring that services were delivered effectively. Consumerism aimed to enhance the rights and responsibilities of ordinary citizens through the avenue of market choice (Brake and Hale, 1992: 37) rather than through political structures of accountability, and was associated with developments that included reforms affecting the quality of service.

The objective of improving quality of service became the concern of a number of initiatives put forward by the police service that included quality awareness programmes, performance indicators, questionnaire surveys directed at the public and procedures such as activity analysis, which were designed to enable an officer's time on duty to be used to maximum effectiveness. These sought to ensure public satisfaction with the manner in which policing was delivered and were derived from methods employed by business, particularly from the Japanese adoption of Total Quality Management, which emphasised the importance of a commitment to quality from all levels of industry. In Britain, this is assessed by procedures associated with achieving BS5750 accreditation.

An important impetus to improving quality of service was a perception that public approval for police activities was declining (Home Office, 1988b). This prompted ACPO to initiate the Operational Policing Review, which was conducted under the supervision of the Joint Consultative Committee (consisting of officers from ACPO, the Superintendents' Association and the Police Federation). It was designed to assess the impact of reforms that had been initiated within the service on both police officers and the general public, and in particular to assess public expectations of policing and how these could be addressed.

The findings of this survey resulted in the publication of an ACPO strategic document that sought to create a corporate image for the police service, through the adoption of its statement of common purpose and values. This emphasised the need for the police to be 'compassionate, courteous and patient', to act without fear, favour or prejudice with regard to the rights of others and to be 'professional, calm and restrained' in the face of violence, applying only such force as was necessary to accomplish their duties. The police were charged with the responsibility for reducing the fears of the public and to reflect such priorities as far as they could in the actions that they took. The service was urged to respond to well-founded criticism with a willingness to change.

The ACPO document made a number of further recommendations relating to the behaviour of individual police officers. These included suggestions that each chief constable should draw up a policy statement on quality of service, in which responsibilities for its implementation were allocated throughout the police management hierarchy. This would emphasise the central responsibility of all officers to provide a fair, courteous and non-discriminatory service. It was proposed that customer satisfaction could be verified by the use of consultative and communicative procedures, including the use of questionnaires. The chief constable would have the responsibility to monitor the service provided by the police in conjunction with comments made by members of the public (ACPO, 1990).

Police forces responded to the ACPO document with their own measures. These included the production of policy statements based on the working party's report, and the establishment of departments charged with producing quality initiatives throughout the force. A major problem with quality of service initiatives was the extent to which the actions of individual police officers were positively affected. The initiatives needed to be effectively communicated within the organisation, explaining their rationale and how individual officers could contribute to their attainment. Without this, cultural resistance and bureaucratic or individual inertia would prevent the attainment of quality-enhancing objectives.

The Sheehy Inquiry   The aim of new public management to secure enhanced value for money and efficiency in the police service led to an examination of its internal management structure. This was initiated in 1992 when Home Secretary Kenneth Clarke appointed a team headed by Sir Patrick Sheehy to conduct an independent inquiry into the 'rank structure, remuneration and conditions of service of the police service' (Home Office, 1993b). However, police reaction was hostile to the majority of the recommendations that were put forward. As a result, the government (following a change of Home Secretary) failed to implement proposals relating to the reform of the rank structure or the introduction of performance-related pay. A further proposal, that of fixed-term contracts, was applied only to the most senior posts of ACPO rank.

The key provisions of the 1994 Police and Magistrates' Courts Act

Government initiatives to reform the performance culture of the police service ultimately resulted in changes affecting its governance, which were incorporated into the 1994 Police and Magistrates' Courts Act. This measure was depicted as the crystallisation of Conservative policy that rested on the pillars of value for money, setting priorities, self-help, consumerism and transparent stewardship (Morgan, 1989).

The 1994 Police and Magistrates' Courts Act introduced the following innovations to the governance of the police service:

- *National objectives*: the Home Secretary was empowered to set national objectives (later termed 'ministerial priorities' and now 'ministerial objectives') for the police service. The practical impact of this was that henceforth ministers and not chief constables would determine police priorities, thereby undermining the historic concept of constabulary independence.
- *Performance targets*: the legislation established performance targets to assess the attainment of national objectives laid down by the Home Secretary.
- *Cash limits*: it had been observed that, prior to the Act, the revenue grant paid by central government to police forces 'was not distributed ... according to a visibly objective assessment of need'. Nor, unlike most other areas of public expenditure, was the grant

cash-limited – 'the Home Office will meet 51% of forces' net expenditure, whatever it is' (Audit Commission, 1990b: 2). The Act introduced cash-limited budgets, thereby enhancing the government's control over expenditure.

- *Amalgamation of police forces*: simplified procedures were introduced for amalgamating forces. This was justified by the argument that the existence of 43 separate forces in England and Wales did not make the most effective use of resources available for policing (Home Office, 1993a: 41–42).
- *Reform of the status and role of police authorities*: the key role of police authorities was to draw up an annual, costed local policing plan containing a statement of national and local objectives, performance indicators and finances available. The new police authorities were free-standing bodies, divorced from the structure of local government, and to which the Home Office directly paid central government's financial allocation for local police work.
- *Reform of the composition of police authorities*: the composition of police authorities was also amended so that it would usually consist of 17 members: nine were councillors (chosen by local authorities in the police authority area and drawn from the political parties in proportion to their share of the vote), three were magistrates (selected by Magistrates' Courts Selection Panels) and the remaining five were independent members whose selection was determined by a local selection panel and the Home Secretary.

The governance of the police service

The 1994 legislation had implications for the role and responsibilities of all three parties to the tripartite division of responsibility for police affairs.

Police authorities   The existence of published objectives increased the ability of police authorities to hold chief constables to account for the way in which policing was delivered locally. Accountability was secured through the requirement that a chief constable had to prepare a general report at the end of each financial year that enabled objectives to be compared against performance. It has been observed that although at the outset many police authorities were content to play a minor role in determining objectives and targets and setting policing plans, they subsequently adopted 'a more active role in the policing plan process and [recognised] the critical importance of their role in monitoring performance and making sure that the chief constable delivers' (Henig, 1998: 8).

It has also been argued that the independent members of police authorities helped to make these bodies more assertive than their predecessors, thus promoting the importance of local issues within local policing plans (Savage, 1998: 4). Finally, the formation of the Association of Police Authorities (APA) in 1997 (representing police authorities in England, Wales and Scotland) was designed to strengthen the collective voice of these bodies in police affairs and also to guard against the isolation of individual authorities (see Box 6.2).

BOX 6.2

THE DEVELOPMENT OF POLICE AUTHORITIES

The role of police authorities has developed from the 1964 Police Act and now consists of the following:

- Setting the strategic direction for each force, which is contained in a three-year strategy plan (requiring the Home Secretary's approval). This includes requirements placed on forces by the Home Secretary's National Indicators and Public Service Agreements.
- Publishing an annual local policing plan and a best value performance plan, which establish policing priorities, performance targets and the allocation of resources.
- Holding the chief constable to account on behalf of the local community and reporting to the community on the performance of the police during the previous year by issuing an annual report.
- Setting the budget (a task that is performed through liaison with the force's Chief Officer Team) and deciding how much council tax should be raised for policing.
- Appointing the chief constable and senior officers (subject to the Home Secretary's approval) and requiring (with the Home Secretary's agreement) the chief constable to retire. The 2009 Policing and Crime Act established new arrangements for the appointment of senior officers. Henceforth appointments would be made by a police senior appointments panel consisting of members nominated by the Home Secretary, ACPO and the APA. It has been argued that this situation will strengthen ACPO's ability to exist as a 'self-perpetuating oligarchy' (Bassett et al., 2009: 11).
- Consulting with local people regarding the policing of the area and what they consider should be regarded a police priorities.
- Monitoring the performance of the force against the performance targets contained in the policing plan.
- Ensuring the force achieves best value by scrutinising police activity for possible improvements.

(Based on Docking, 2003; Home Affairs Committee, 2008: para 232.)

Chief constables The new controls introduced by the 1994 Police and Magistrates' Courts Act were strategic in nature and within their confines offered enhanced autonomy for chief constables by replacing existing Home Office controls over personnel and financial matters. One example of this was that chief constables, rather than the Home Office, would henceforth determine the number of police officers employed. In addition, the 1994 Act gave chief officers full management responsibility for all police personnel and operational control to direct local policing in accordance with a business plan drawn up within the context of the local policing plan and the cash-limited budget. Also, the chief constable played an important role in drawing up the draft version of the local policing plan for the police authority.

The Home Office One evaluation of the 1994 Police and Magistrates' Courts Act emphasised the extent to which enhanced central control was imposed over the entire service throughout England and Wales. This control was exerted by the Home Office and exercised through methods that included 'setting detailed targets, prescribing policing strategies, inspecting perform-ance and requiring the implementation of detailed action plans' (Loveday and Reid, 2003: 7).

This opinion asserted that chief officers were reduced in status and subjected to increased central control, whereby the service could be directed into areas stipulated in the Home Secretary's national objectives, assessed by the newly created Police Performance Unit at the Home Office, which monitored per-formance indicators, and relegated to providing services determined by police authorities in their local policing plan. It is further alleged that the police authorities were themselves subject to increased central direction exercised by the Home Office, effectively transforming them into an intermediary of central government and a direct agent of the Home Office (Loveday, 1994: 232). This opinion thus condemned the 1994 Act as an attempt to achieve a national police force without such an objective being openly declared (Alderson, 1994) and for its effect in transforming the police from a local service to a state police (Loveday, 1995: 156).

The introduction of centrally-imposed targets had considerable repercussions regarding the ability of central government to direct police resources into areas of work that were determined centrally to the detriment of local needs and concerns. However, this power has not been used to its full potential. Early analysis sug-gested that 'there is no clear evidence ... that national considerations dominate local ones' (Jones and Newburn, 1997: 47). Also, national objectives have often been uncontentious and framed following a process of consultation involving key bodies such as ACPO (Jones and Newburn, 1997: 36). Similarly, performance indicators, have been devised through a consultative process and have included suggestions made by the Inspectorate.

The 1996 Police Act

This measure consolidated a number of reforms that had been previously made to the governance of policing. Thus consultation, introduced under section 106 of the 1984 Police and Criminal Evidence Act, became governed by section 96 of the 1996 legislation and the power of the Home Secretary to publish ministerial objectives and performance targets, which was introduced in the 1994 Police and Magistrates' Courts Act, was now governed by sections 37 and 38 of the 1996 Police Act.

In addition, the 1996 measure developed earlier legislation by making incremental adjustments to changes that had already been introduced. The role of a police authority was redefined to make it responsible for the 'maintenance of an efficient and adequate police force for its area'. When devising its objectives for the policing of the area, it was required to consider views obtained under the consultative arrangements established by section 96 of the Act.

The powers of the Home Secretary were further enhanced in the 1996 legislation to include promoting the efficiency and effectiveness of the service, determining objectives for police authorities, issuing codes of practice for police authorities, setting minimum budgets and requiring reports to be written, giving directions to police authorities where inspection had found them to be inefficient or ineffective, and calling upon police authorities to require a chief constable to retire in the interest of the force (Loveday et al., 2007. 12).

Labour's reforms to policing, 1997-2005

Post-1997 Labour governments have pursued a number of reforms to policing. Many of them were built on earlier Conservative initiatives that were developed under the new public management agenda, although it is argued that the government's proposals went beyond managerialism to embrace the objective of modernisation that devoted attention to the impact of crime on society and sought to address its underlying causes through measures that included the involvement of local people and communities (Martin, 2003: 166–167). The main reforms that have affected the governance of the police service are considered in Box 6.3.

BOX 6.3

LABOUR'S REFORMS TO POLICING

The main features of Labour's reforms (discussed, for example, by Newman, 2000) were:

- *The retention of performance targets and indicators*: these have involved government departments other than the Home Office (for example, the Department of Communities and Local Government) and have considerably added to the control wielded by central government over policing.
- *A belief in the importance of long-term, strategic planning as opposed to a focus on short-term objectives*: this has entailed developments that include the introduction of national policing plans.

(Continued)

(Continued)

- *The introduction of best value as the key mechanism of performance management*: best value replaced the Conservative's attempts to create internal markets through the process of compulsory competitive tendering procedures and was a key reform of the 1997–2001 Labour government.
- *The promotion of joined-up government*: this approach considerably extended earlier initiatives in multi-agency working: and has had considerable implications for the autonomy of the police service.
- *The continuance (under the guise of workforce modernisation) of earlier developments concerned with 'hiving off' police functions to other service providers, coupled with a new emphasis on public–private partnerships and private finance initiatives to deliver public services*: these developments are of particular importance to contemporary police work since demands for higher levels of services cannot be matched with an enhanced level of central government finance (Loveday et al., 2007: 34–37).
- *The advancement of the empowerment agenda*: this sought to promote the enhanced involvement of local people in the policing of their own communities.

The 1998 Crime and Disorder Act

The 1998 Crime and Disorder Act had considerable implications for policing. The service ceased to have an exclusive claim to prevent crime and disorder and was compelled to enter into 'joint working and collective responsibility' arrangements with the community and other agencies to identify and respond to crime and disorder issues (Newburn, 2002: 107). The mechanism through which this was achieved was the crime and disorder reduction partnership (CDRP), which placed partnership work on a statutory footing, thereby placing formal and informal constraints over the future performance of police work.

Section 17 of the 1998 legislation also developed the process of collaboration by giving local government and police authorities a statutory duty to exercise their functions with due regard to their likely effect on preventing crime and disorder in their area and to do all that they reasonably could to prevent it. This principle was also advanced through the creation of multi-agency Youth Offending Teams.

These developments, which were latterly advanced through mechanisms that included Local Strategic Partnerships and Local Area Agreements (see Chapter 5), affected the existing system of police governance. Houghton (2000) has argued that the new role of local government in crime prevention changed the tripartite system of police control and accountability into a quadripartite structure. The legislation also impacted on the role of both police authorities and chief constables since it is potentially more difficult for a police authority to hold a chief constable accountable for his or her performance when key elements of crime and disorder policies are delivered by a partnership arrangement involving other agencies. It has thus been concluded that fragmented responsibility makes for blurred accountability (Newburn, 2002: 109).

The 1999 Local Government Act

Continued government concern with the efficiency and performance of the police service was justified by the large amount of public money expended on it, which totalled £9,117 million in 2002/03 (Home Office, 2002: 23). Although this expenditure had some desirable outcomes (in particular a fall in the overall levels of crime), other problems remained, in particular a decline in detection and conviction rates and variable standards of performance by police forces across the country (Home Affairs Committee, 2005: 1). In order to obtain further efficiency in the delivery of public services, a new approach to performance management was implemented. The principle of best value was introduced by the 1999 Local Government Act.

The best value approach required local authorities, police authorities and fire and rescue service authorities (termed best value authorities) to seek continuous improvement in the delivery of its services in order to achieve the objectives specified in the legislation, that is 'a combination of economy, efficiency and effectiveness'. Although many of the ideas embraced by best value had their origins in reforms associated with new public management, the approach was now underpinned by legislation. Spottiswoode (2000: 4) has described it as 'the central plank in the drive to improve police performance' by enabling efficiency to be measured.

Best value replaced the former policy of compulsory competitive tendering (CCT) as the main structure by which the public sector purchased services. Whereas CCT had placed priority on securing the cheapest form of service delivery, best value looked beyond cost to embrace other aspects of value for money, such as quality of service. It also imposed an obligation on best value authorities to consult with stakeholders (including service users), thus enabling services to be tailored to the needs of those living in the locality.

Best value aimed to ensure that services were performed in innovative ways that provided the consumer with good value for money. It provided public bodies with enhanced freedom as to how they achieved goals, and they were encouraged to pursue innovative ways to do this. Local service providers were required to demonstrate that they were providing best value through a process of independent audit, which in the case of the police service was the Audit Commission and Her Majesty's Inspectorate of Constabulary (HMIC). They were also required to consult to ensure that service delivery matched local needs. It was in this sense that it could be argued that best value provided 'a rigorous system for delivering high quality, responsive services based on locally determined objectives' (Cabinet Office, 1999).

In order to assess the attainment of best value, the government not only laid down standards that were required to be met but also set the indicators that would be used to assess attainment. The latter were termed best value performance indicators (BVPIs). Although best value increased the degree of central control over the police service, the introduction of BVPIs also enhanced the role of police authorities in the delivery of services. From 1 April 2000, police authorities were required to develop a five-year rolling programme of service reviews and summarise their findings and planned actions for improvement (accompanied by measures and targets) in an annual performance plan (Spottiswoode, 2000: 9). The aim was to ensure continuous improvements in their standards of service delivery.

To do this, their review took into account the 'four Cs': challenge (questioning how and why a service was provided), compare (judging their performance in comparison with other service providers, with a view to improving the services for which they were responsible), compete (ensuring that the service they provided was efficient) and consult (seeking the views of local taxpayers, service users and the business community (Martin, 2003: 168). A fifth 'C', collaboration, was subsequently incorporated into the review process.

BOX 6.4

HER MAJESTY'S INSPECTORATE OF CONSTABULARY

Changes introduced by both Conservative and Labour governments associated with performance measurement expanded the traditional role of the Her Majesty's Inspectorate of Constabulary (HMIC), providing an additional centralising influence over police affairs.

Following the 1994 Police and Magistrates' Courts Act, the role of HMIC was extended into the area of effectiveness as well as its traditional concern for efficiency. To expedite these changes, HMIC's role was subsequently (in 1994) separated into three functions: primary inspection, performance review inspection and thematic inspection (O'Dowd, 1998: 7).

Performance review inspection further increased the emphasis on the production and assessment of performance data, using a database called the HMIC Matrix of Indicators. The database, which is concerned with the assessment of a single function across a number of forces, typically involves areas of activity delivered by a multi-agency approach. Inspections may use experts from bodies such as the Commission for Racial Equality/Equalities Commission and the Crown Prosecution Service (CPS).

The adoption of best value further affected the role of the HMIC, requiring it to move into 'a prospective role of certification when historically the task has been *ex post facto* review' (O'Dowd, 1998: 7). In 2004, HMIC published its new baseline assessments. These set baselines for particular activities against which forces should be performing and enabled HMIC to focus on areas within a force that required improvement (Home Office, 2004: 155).

The 2002 Police Reform Act further extended the role of HMIC to include reviews of individual BCUs. Its role in connection with identifying bad performance and disseminating good practice envisaged a close working relationship with the Police Standards Unit (PSU), whose role is discussed on pages 136–137.

The process was subject to a system of independent audit conducted by the Audit Commission and Her Majesty's Inspectorate of Constabulary. An important aim of best value was to enable service providers to compare their performance with that of the best deliverers. It thus embraced a measurement of comparative efficiency. However, when the Home Office published comparative performance data about police forces in England and Wales for the first time in 2003, an attempt was made to avoid comparing the performance of individual police forces against a national average for a given performance measure, and instead to use specific comparison groups for each force, enabling the performance of 'most similar forces' to be compared. Subsequently, a new Policing Performance Assessment Framework (PPAF) was put forward by the Police Standards Unit to assess police performance (including cost) across the full range of policing responsibilities for all forces in England and Wales (Martin, 2003: 173).

To do so, PPAF divided policing responsibilities into six outcome areas (or domains): citizen focus, promoting safety and security, resource usage, investigating crime, reducing crime and helping the public. A seventh area, measuring force performance against local priorities, was also included in the PPAF. The attainment of these was measured by a number of key performance indicators and, commencing in 2004/05, the BVPIs were incorporated into the PPAF.

Although the full assessment schedule was intended to be in place by April 2005, measures that were compatible with its approach were introduced earlier. In April 2003, activity-based costing was introduced in all forces, and the first PPAF performance measures were introduced in April 2004. One difficulty with the approach adopted by PPAF was that it did not take into account the resourcing available to a force, which made comparisons between them difficult. However, it could help in the evaluation of the year-by-year performances of individual forces.

Further changes to this system of performance management were introduced in the 2007 Local Government and Public Involvement in Health Act. Here, best value performance indicators for local authorities working alone or in partnership were replaced by the new National Indicator Set (NIS), which would be measured by a new performance framework, the Comprehensive Area Assessment (CAA). The NIS was introduced alongside a new framework to manage police performance. This was the Assessments of Policing and Community Safety (APACS), which replaced the PPAF. One intention of the new performance management regime was to create greater scope for local flexibility in service delivery. Indicators shared by local authorities and police authorities are included in both the NIS and APACS.

Basic Command Units

Performance measurement extends beyond scrutiny of the activities performed by police forces as a whole and includes assessments of the operations of individual Basic Command Units (BCUs). In an attempt to enable BCU performance to be scrutinised, data relating to the performance of BCUs was initially published in 1999, and in 2001 measurements allowing comparative analysis of BCU performance were introduced. BCUs were grouped into 13 'families' that were defined on the basis of socio-economic and demographic characteristics. This enables a comparison to be drawn of the performance of BCUs in comparable areas. However, this approach may have implications for the relationship between BCUs and the police forces in which they are housed, if the assessment of their performance takes them beyond the organisational confines in which they operate.

The 1999 Greater London Assembly Act

Different governance arrangements applied to the Metropolitan Police, where the Home Secretary exercised the role of the police authority since the force's creation in 1829. This situation persisted until the enactment of the 1999 Greater London Assembly Act, which established the Greater London Assembly and an independent Metropolitan Police Authority (MPA) to oversee policing in London. This now comprises 23 people – 12 members of the Greater London Assembly (including the Mayor of London, who chaired the Authority between 2008 and 2010) and 11 independent members. One of these is appointed by the Home Secretary and 10 are chosen through an open recruitment campaign.

The role of the MPA is similar to that performed by police authorities elsewhere in England and Wales, incorporating changes to their functions which occurred after 1964 (discussed below). It was charged with maintaining an efficient and effective police force for the metropolitan police areas, securing best value in the delivery of police services, publishing an annual police plan, setting policy targets and monitoring the performance of the police against them, and in general terms with exercising general scrutiny over the work of the Metropolitan Police Service (MPS).

The MPA also has a role in appointing, disciplining and removing senior officers. The MPA and Mayor of London may make recommendations to the Home Secretary regarding the appointment of the Commissioner, although the final choice is made by the Minister on account of the Commissioner's national remit with regard to terrorism. However, informal pressures may also be exerted by the MPA, an important example of which was the announcement of the resignation of Commissioner Sir Ian Blair in October 2008 following a meeting with Mayor Boris Johnson. The MPA also approves the police budget, which is set by the Mayor of London (subject to reserve powers possessed by the Home Secretary to set a minimum budget). The Greater London Assembly performs a limited role in policing, its main power being the ability to summon members of the MPA to answer questions.

It has been argued, however, that the MPS remains subject to complicated lines of accountability, and the Home Secretary, the Home Office, the MPA and the Mayor of London all seek to influence the activities of the force. Other officials may also make demands on the MPS. They include the prime minister, who exercised an important role in connection with the 2002 Safer Streets' Campaign to combat street robberies and muggings. The result is that 'the Met is pulled one way then another. ... What often happens is that we don't deliver on anything' (Senior MPS officer, quoted in Loveday and Reid, 2003: 26).

The 2002 Police Reform Act

The 2002 Police Reform Act contains a number of important provisions that related to the performance culture of the service. It constituted what has been described as the first phase of the 2001–05 government's reform agenda, which served to further enhance central control over the police service. It included the requirement to produce a National Policing Plan (Home Affairs Committee, 2005: 1).

National Policing Plans

National Policing Plans draw on data prepared by HMIC and the Police Standards Unit (PSU) and have been described as 'the clearest expression of the policy of centralisation' (Bassett et al., 2009: 14). The Plans established the government's three-year strategic priorities for policing and how they were to be delivered, and were expressed through a range of targets, metrics or directives. A key concern of the Plans was to 'set out a clear national framework for raising the performance of all forces' (Blunkett, 2002: 2).

The National Plans provided a framework within which police authorities set their annual policing plans and their local three-year strategy plans (a development which was introduced by the 2002 legislation). This meant that the content of local policing plans became increasingly directed by central government. The first National Policing Plan listed 51 actions that chief officers and police authorities should take into account in their local policing plans. Some of these actions had specific targets attached to them, which included the requirement that local policing plans must include three-year targets for reducing vehicle crime, burglary and robbery (Home Office, 2002: 44–48). Police authorities set local targets against these indicators, and in this way the National Plan formed the basis for local plans drawn up by Chief Officers and police authorities to improve standards and ensure forces are responsive to the needs and priorities of their communities.

Following consultation with key stakeholders represented on the National Policing Forum (including ACPO and the Association of Police Authorities (APA)), the first National Policing Plan was published for the period 2003–06. The contents of this Plan included ministerial objectives and the performance indicators used to measure their attainment under the provisions of the 1996 Police Act and the Best Value Performance Indicators for police authorities. This Plan established four key national priorities: (1) tackling anti-social behaviour, (2) reducing crime volume, street, drug-related and violent and gun crime, (3) combating serious and organised crime operating across force boundaries, and (4) increasing the number of offences brought to justice. These priorities were linked to the Home Office public service agreements (Home Office, 2002: 3 and 6).

BOX 6.5

CENTRAL MECHANISMS OF CONTROL

In addition to the enhanced power that the 2002 legislation provided to the Home Secretary, additional central mechanisms of control were developed in the government's 2001–05 police reform agenda. These included the Police Standards Unit and the National Centre for Police Excellence.

The Police Standards Unit (PSU) was established in July 2002 within the Home Office. It directly reports to the Home Office and, in conjunction with HMIC, was designed to deliver the government's objectives of promoting improved standards and levels of operational performance by embedding a performance culture within the police service (Home Affairs Committee, 2005: 2). In particular, it seeks to identify best practice regarding the prevention, detection and apprehension of crime and focused on particular areas where variations had been identified. It provided support to BCUs and forces where it deemed that remedial action was required. A key aspect of its role was to supervise the development of new methodologies to assess police performance, with a view to reducing the performance gap between the best and the worst forces. These methodologies included the PPAF (see above).

Its work also included the preparation of a Police Standards Unit Management Guide, which set out a number of hallmarks (including clarity about the roles and responsibilities of the police authority, chief constable and managers at all levels for performance and the development of a framework linking performance to corporate planning, budgeting and resource management) that underpinned good organisation and the ability to drive and sustain high standards of performance (Home Office, 2004: 155). Its role had significant implications for the exercise of central control over policing at the expense of responsibilities discharged by police authorities and chief constables (Loveday et al., 2007: 13).

The National Centre for Police Excellence was established in 2003 to work with ACPO, HMIC, the PSU and the Association of Police Authorities (APA) in identifying, developing and spreading good practice in operational policing throughout the service. It was operated by the Central Policing Training and Development Authority (CENTREX). It also provided operational support to forces in the investigation of major and high-profile cases. The Police Reform Act enabled good practice, that had been identified to be enshrined in codes of practice to chief constables. These initially covered the use of firearms and less lethal weapons and the management of health and safety within the service (Home Office, 2002: 13).

The Home Secretary and police authorities

The 2002 Police Reform Act provided the Home Secretary with additional powers over police authorities. The Minister could direct police authorities to institute remedial measures when an HMIC inspection indicated that the force was not efficient or effective. The Home Secretary was also empowered to direct the police authority to submit an action plan as to how deficiencies of this nature would be addressed. The legislation further gave the Home Secretary the reserve power to compel police authorities to require their chief constable to retire or resign in the interests of force efficiency or effectiveness.

Labour's 1997–2005 police reforms: a conclusion

The reforms that were pursued by the 1997–2005 Labour governments created a police service that was increasingly subject to central direction in relation to its performance and management practices. This was secured through initiatives promoted by the Home Office and also from bodies within the police service that included ACPO and the National Policing Improvement Agency (NPIA) (see below). Targets imposed by central government have become a key tool of performance management and have constituted a major mechanism through which central government has increased its control over policing. They have developed considerably from the priorities that the 1994 Police and Magistrates' Courts Act authorised the Home Secretary to set for the police service. In recent years the police service has been subjected to a wide range of Home Office targets which take the form of statutory performance indicators (SPIs). Thirty-four of these were set for 2008/09 (Home Office, 2008a). Performance against these targets was measured by Her Majesty's Inspectorate of Constabulary through the Police Performance Assessment Framework between 2004 and 2008, and subsequently by the Assessment of Policing and Community Safety.

Targets have been imposed on the police service from sources other than the Home Office. Public Service Agreements (PSAs) were introduced in 1998 to promote clarity in service delivery. These were published as part of Comprehensive Spending Reviews to set performance targets for particular areas of activity. They consist of 'explicit agreements, targets and indicators established between the Treasury and individual government departments, which are subsequently cascaded throughout the entire public sector in an effort to ensure delivery alignment' (Micheli et al., 2006: 1).

PSAs have exerted considerable influence over policing. Three of the 2002 PSAs and 10 indicators applied to the police service. The Home Office then translated these into 49 separate indicators which were then further developed at the local level, resulting in 78 separate indicators (Micheli et al., 2006: 4). Central targets have also been set by the Department of Communities and Local Government, currently through its National Indicators for Local Authorities and Local Authority Partnerships.

Centrally-imposed targets have been subject to criticism. They tend to place central concerns over local needs and considerations, and exert an adverse effect on the accountability of the service to local communities. Targets have also been accused of producing perverse outcomes: centrally-determined targets 'tend to distort priorities, tempting officers into using their time in unproductive ways or into directly fiddling performance figures' (Loveday and Reid, 2003: 19). They have also been criticised for creating a 'counting culture' within the police service, where 'only what got measured got done' (Loveday and Reid, 2003: 22).

Targets have a particularly adverse effect on the ability of BCUs to address the needs and priorities of their areas. A survey of local commanders suggested that a large majority felt that centrally-directed targets had 'degraded their ability to provide high quality policing' (Loveday et al., 2007: 5). This led to the conclusion that performance management should be restructured with a bottom-up approach to incorporate the demands of local communities (Loveday et al., 2007: 18). In this way performance targets would reflect community safety concerns, including how safe the public felt (Loveday et al., 2007: 5).

Criticisms of this nature prompted the 2005–10 Labour government to initiate further reforms to policing, in which localism assumed a prominent position.

Labour's reforms to policing, 2005–10

Further reforms to policing were undertaken by the 2005–10 government. Although these reforms initially reflected the tendencies displayed in previous

Labour governments to place the police service under increased centralised control, exerted either by the Home Office or bodies set up within the police service, they subsequently moved in a different direction, underpinned by the empowerment agenda.

The 2006 Police and Justice Act

This legislation made a number of important changes to the governance of policing. It amended the composition of police authorities. Magistrates ceased to be a specific membership category, although the 2008 Police Authority Regulations stipulated that a police authority should contain at least one magistrate as an independent member. The 2008 Regulations required most police authorities to consist of 17 members (nine councillors and eight independent members) with five consisting of 19 members (10 councillors and nine independents). In addition, the 2006 legislation reduced the degree of central government involvement in the appointment of independent members.

The 2006 legislation extended the role of a police authority beyond that of 'securing the maintenance of an efficient and effective force' to that of additionally requiring the police authority to hold the chief constable to account for the exercise of his or her functions and those of the officers and staff under their control. The Act also removed the requirement for police authorities to conduct best value reviews and prepare best value plans, although they were still required to operate according to best value criteria.

The 2006 Act amended the Home Secretary's powers of intervention, provided for in the 2002 Police Reform Act, by extending the sources of information which the minister could employ in connection with allegations of a force's inefficiency or ineffectiveness. The Minister could also require a police authority to produce reports relating to the policing of its area. The Act removed the requirement to publish a National Policing Plan, but the Minister is required to determine and publish strategic priorities for police forces in England and Wales, following consultation with the APA and ACPO, in any format of his or her choosing. The non-statutory National Community Safety Plan has subsequently been used to disseminate information of this nature.

The National Policing Improvement Agency

One difficulty with the reforms associated with phase 1 of the 2001–05 Labour government's police reform agenda was that a variety of central bodies were given responsibility to oversee various aspects of policing, resulting in some overlapping of responsibilities. To remedy this, the 2006 legislation established a National Policing Improvement Agency (NPIA) that would provide for the continuous reform of the operations of the service. The NPIA works closely with ACPO and the Home Office and is a key agency in seeking to secure the adoption by the service of government plans and initiatives. It sits alongside the Police Standards Unit and the Home Office. Other central bodies, such as CENTREX (the Central Police Training and Development Authority) and the Police Information Technology Organisation (PITO), have been replaced by the NPIA.

It was intended that it would focus on three key areas: (1) the development of good policing practice, (2) the implementation of the support function, and (3) operational policing support. It would further be responsible for driving the delivery of a small number of 'mission critical priorities' that would be established in the National Policing Plan (Home Office, 2004: 112).

All the work undertaken by the NPIA is now covered in the newly developed (2009) National Improvement Strategy for Policing (NISP), which outlines key strategic plans for the next 10 years. One of their newest roles emerged from the Policing Green Paper (Home Office, 2008b), which proposed to reshape the police performance and inspection regime. A new capability support function has been formed to support those forces that have been subject to an adverse inspection report by HMIC.

The NPIA has been responsible for a number of innovations that have included the new Airwave radio to aid communication across forces, the IMPACT information-sharing programme and the development of the Police National Database. The NPIA lacks the power to compel forces to adopt its initiatives (Bassett et al., 2009: 15), although ownership by the service of this agency (which is headed by a chief constable) may help to secure the adoption of its initiatives by individual forces.

The National Policing Board

The National Policing Board was created in 2006. Its members represent key stakeholders, including the NPIA, ACPO, APA, HMIC, the Home Office and the Metropolitan Police Commissioner. Its main functions (Home Office, 2009a) are to:

- Agree the Home Secretary's annual national strategic priorities for policing and key priorities for the National Policing Improvement Agency;
- Set agreed priorities for the police reform programme;
- Enable ministers, the professional leaders of the service and police authorities to monitor progress in implementing the reform programme and identify and overcome barriers to delivery;
- Provide a regular forum for debate and three-way communication between the tripartite partners on the opportunities and challenges facing policing.

It has been argued that the National Policing Board has developed into the main national forum for tripartite discussions in policing. It 'has the potential to be a powerful leadership coalition and to help drive and support performance and capacity improvement' in policing throughout England and Wales (Home Office, 2008b: 66).

The creation of the National Policing Board indicated an attempt to base the future development of policing on a consensual approach, as opposed to one that was primarily based on various forms of central control. This approach was supplemented by a new emphasis on localism, a result of the empowerment agenda.

Community empowerment

The empowerment of communities has received considerable attention in the early years of the twenty-first century and is a key aspect of the 're-inventing government agenda' (Osborne and Gaebler, 1999). The principle of community empowerment in policing has been developed within the context of increased public involvement in a wide range of local affairs. This principle was promoted in the 2000 Local Government Act, which (as amended by the 2007 Sustainable Communities Act) extended the role of local authorities to promote or improve the economic, social or environmental well-being of their areas through the mechanism of a sustainable community strategy, and the 2007 Local Government and Public Involvement in Health Act, which introduced the 'duty to involve' local people in key decisions.

Empowerment: the key proposals relating to policing

According to Sergeant (2008: 2 and 11), in the UK 'the public ... lacks the power to get the policing they want'. This resulted in a gap between public expectations and the kind of policing people were getting. Empowerment is the means to address this deficiency and the key proposals to achieve this objective are considered below.

The Policing Pledge   The objective behind the Policing Pledge, which was introduced towards the end of 2008, was to improve the level of customer service provided by the police force. It established a set of national standards as to what the public could expect from the police service, covering issues such as the time taken to answer emergency and non-emergency calls and information to victims of crime regarding the progress of their case (Home Office, 2008b: 28–29).

These national standards were supplemented by a local component that contained a number of common elements, including the photographs and contact details of the neighbourhood policing team and the top three locally-identified crime and anti-social behaviour priorities to be tackled in the neighbourhood. In this way, communities were to be better informed regarding local policing arrangements and were able to exert a stronger role in influencing police activities.

The main problem with the Policing Pledge was that it was put forward in isolation, reflecting a form of 'silo-thinking' from the Home Office. The police service was viewed in isolation from all other agencies with which it worked in partnership to serve the needs of local communities.

The development of neighbourhood policing A second proposal to advance community empowerment is the development of neighbourhood policing to enhance the extent of police engagement with local communities. Neighbourhood policing seeks to secure the empowerment of local communities by involving them in setting priorities for police action. This task is carried out through a number of methods, including public meetings, surveys and internet communication. One prerequisite of public engagement with their neighbourhood team has been the provision of local crime information, which has been implemented by a national crime-mapping service, enabling anyone to type in their postcode and obtain information regarding crime in their area, what action the police are taking to counter it and what is happening to criminals who are caught.

Casey (2008: 22) proposed to reform neighbourhood policing through a greater degree of standardisation, ensuring that all 43 forces delivered to neighbourhoods on the issues that the public felt to be important (such as response times to 999 calls and the provision of named officers and their contact details). It was proposed that all forces should adopt a standardised approach to neighbourhood policing, using a common name to describe this approach and a single name for local public engagement meetings on crime, and the provision of 'common and comparable' local information on crime and neighbourhood problems (Casey, 2008: 32).

A second reform of neighbourhood policing sought to develop it into a broader neighbourhood management structure in which local partners would deliver on a wide range of issues affecting community safety and quality of life (Flanagan, 2008: 67). This joint approach would be based upon community involvement in identifying priorities, but to achieve this would require the formalised structures that Casey (2008: 43) proposed. These would consist of the appointment of strategic Neighbourhood Crime and Justice Coordinators in every CDRP area, and the nomination of a local authority officer as a Neighbourhood Policing Team Liaison person, working together to resolve neighbourhood policing problems and provide feedback to the public.

In addition, there should be local authority officers present at each Partnerships and Communities Together (PACT) meeting at which local residents are able to raise their concerns to neighbourhood policing teams. PACT meetings would then provide one forum for resolving a wide range of problems.

The 2008 Green Paper (Home Office, 2008b) endorsed the recommendations made by the Flanagan review on neighbourhood management and suggested that the neighbourhood structure should be composed of senior officers from the police service, local authority and other organisations, be headed by a neighbourhood manager or coordinator and underpinned by participatory budgeting. This structure, a Community Safety Partnership (CSP), would be piloted in a few police force areas during 2008 and be rolled out nationally in 2009.

However, it was evident that there were potential impediments to the progress of neighbourhood management that would need to be addressed. Middle managers in participating agencies could not be allowed to block progress in achieving the aims that had been agreed upon at neighbourhood level. Also, some changes in the working practices of key personnel would be required since staff employed by local government agencies, for example, often work 9–5 and may thus not be available at times when their services were needed to respond to neighbourhood problems.

Police authorities and local accountability Community empowerment can be advanced if police authorities act as effective mouthpieces to articulate local concerns about policing. However, this role has been difficult to achieve in practice and has been used to justify reforms to the composition of police authorities.

Perceptions that police authorities are remote from the general public have been voiced from a number of quarters. One study concluded that 'police authorities are invisible and irrelevant' (Loveday and Reid, 2003: 7) and another asserted that the 'vast majority' of participants to a research study on these bodies 'had not previously heard of police authorities. The few who had heard of them generally did not know what they were or what their role was' (Docking, 2003). This situation justified attempts to link these bodies more closely to local communities in order to remedy what was described as 'a serious imbalance of power and lack of accountability' (Blunkett, 2009: 24).

One way to achieve this reform would be to reform the composition of police authorities to make them more democratic and responsive to the community (Home Office, 2008b: 32). In 2008 the government proposed that the majority of members of police authorities should consist of directly elected Crime and Policing Representatives. These would have sat on the local CDRP/CSP (one of whom would chair it). In the case of areas with directly elected mayors, the mayor would have been the Crime and Policing Representative. Arrangements in London would not have been affected by these reform proposals.

The Home Affairs Committee was sceptical of the proposal for direct election (Home Affairs Committee, 2008: para 247) and in December 2008 the Home Secretary announced that this reform would not go ahead. One concern was that it might serve to politicise the police. The subsequent 2009 Policing and Crime Act substituted the proposal with an amendment to the 1996 Police Act, requiring police authorities to take on board the views of people in a police authority area. A further suggestion (Home Office, 2009b: 9) was that police authorities should nominate a lead member for each BCU and enable members of the public to sit on the local authority committees that held CDRPs to account.

The introduction of new structures of local accountability Proposals to increase the ability of local people to influence police affairs extend beyond reforming the composition of police authorities and have been directed at remedying the 'democratic deficit' at a more local level. A new relationship has been constructed between BCUs and local government through mechanisms such as CDRPs and Local Area Agreements (LAAs). A further reform to enhance the accountability of police actions to local communities would be to provide for a closer match between BCU and CDRP/local government boundaries, which would facilitate much closer links between the BCU commander and the local authority he or she was working with (Local Government Association, 2008: 23).

The 2006 Police and Justice Act subjected CDRPs to the oversight of relevant local authority Overview and Scrutiny Committees. These committees were responsible for scrutinising the functioning of the CDRPs' responsible authorities and thus enhanced the accountability of the BCU commander to local communities. Although the effectiveness of this procedure was affected by the various ways in which local government has traditionally discharged the scrutiny function and the status of these committees within the local authority, this approach could be built upon by providing for the routine examination of local police affairs. However, this would provoke resistance from the police service, fearing that this would subject policing to political constraints.

The accountability of the BCU commander to local government could be further developed by giving the local authority (exercised by the mayor or council leader) a role in the appointment of the BCU commander and in assessing his or her performance. The Local Government Association (2008: 23) proposed that in the case of a BCU commander who was not performing satisfactorily, the council would be able to pass a vote of no confidence in him or her which would require the chief constable to review that commander's suitability for the post.

A final reform affecting local accountability would be to remedy the existing democratic deficit at neighbourhood level and provide mechanisms where 'the local community ... set the local police's priorities, set out targets for tackling crime and question the chief constable if these are not delivered' (Local Government Association, 2008: 10). There are various ways this might be achieved. In Northern Ireland, neighbourhood policing has been supplemented by District Policing Partnerships. There are 29 of these and they act as a link between the District Council, councillors and representatives of the local community and enable local people to influence the way in which their community is policed.

Promoting the active community   An important consequence of empowering local communities is the active participation of local communities in police-related activities. This latter approach embraces the 'responsibilization strategy', which encourages widespread popular involvement in combating crime (Garland, 1996: 445; Hughes, 1998: 128). It is also compatible with what has been described as 'the self policing society', which involves the incorporation of 'the intermediate institutions which lie between the state and the individual' into tackling local crime and disorder issues (Leadbeater, 1996: 34).

Volunteering underpins community involvement in issues of this kind. Casey (2008: 72) referred to the strong tradition of volunteering in Britain, which was apparent in community-oriented initiatives such the Special Constabulary and Neighbourhood Watch. However, she argued that too little information was provided on the opportunities for volunteering, and that on occasions health and safety concerns stifled these sorts of initiatives (Casey, 2008: 77).

In order to stimulate volunteering, it was proposed (Home Office, 2008b) that a Community Crime Fighting Fund should be established to enable community groups to play a stronger role in tackling crime. This would increase the visibility and effectiveness of some community-oriented groups that were already in existence (such as Neighbourhood Watch) and also stimulate citizen involvement in new areas. This programme would be taken forward by Neighbourhood Crime and Justice Advisers.

Reversing centralising tendencies   It has been argued above that targets have become the driving force behind many of the activities performed by the police service. This development reduced the role performed by police authorities so that they have become 'much the weakest pillar in the tripartite structure. ... The consequence of the gradual weakening of police authorities over the 40-year period since the passing of the Police Act, is that the connection of the police to their local communities has been severely reduced' (Local Government Association, 2008: 6).

To redress this situation, a number of changes have been proposed to the current system of performance measurement. In future there should be less reliance on top-down targets and a greater role for local people and police authorities, a sharper role for the Inspectorate and a more strategic role for the Home Office (Home Office, 2008b). In addition, the amount of data collected from forces by the centre should be reduced – a target figure of a 50% reduction has been suggested.

In order to implement these aspects of the Green Paper proposals, the Home Secretary Jacqui Smith announced on 8 December 2008 that her strategic priorities for the police service for 2009/10 would be to move to a single, top-down numerical target for police forces in England and Wales, with the removal of all other targets set by central government. This new target required every force to focus on whether they had the public's confidence in identifying and addressing the crime and anti-social behaviour issues that mattered most to their local communities (Smith, 2008). It meant a fundamental rebalancing of the relationship between government and the police (Home Office, 2009b: 8). Related proposals were also put forward in the *Data Burden Review* (Normington, 2009) which 'significantly reduced' the amount of information that the Home Office required from forces.

In addition, the new Public Service Agreements for 2008–11 (which sought to ensure that a wide range of public institutions worked together to achieve a designated strategic outcome) provided more space to focus on serious and violent crime and also on local priorities (Home Office, 2008b: para 7.5). The performance management system for the police would be reshaped to reflect the approach embodied in the new PSAs and to move towards a more self-improving system. The role previously performed by centrally-imposed targets in police performance management would be replaced with an increased emphasis on localism and new functions for Her Majesty's Inspectorate of Constabulary.

QUESTION

To what extent is contemporary police work dominated by control exerted through central government?

The material that forms the basis of this answer is contained in this chapter and in Chapter 10. You should also consult work that is cited in the references. To answer this question you should:

- Briefly discuss the concept of the tripartite division of responsibility for police affairs contained in the 1964 Police Act as a context for your discussion;
- Analyse the rationale for an increased degree of central government control over policing;
- Evaluate the means by which central control has been imposed: you should discuss the 1994 Police and Magistrates' Courts Act, which was an important departure, and consider subsequent developments relating to central control imposed by the Home Office and by other central bodies, especially in relation to targets;
- Present a conclusion that assesses the arguments you have put forward relating to central control over police work but that also considers the ability of police authorities, chief constables and BCU commanders to ensure that local concerns are able to influence the local policing agenda.

REFERENCES

Alderson, J. (1994) 'Hark the Minister of Police Approaches', *The Independent*, 19 January.

Association of Chief Police Officers (ACPO) (1990) *Strategic Policy Document: Setting the Standards for Policing: Meeting Community Expectations*. London: ACPO.

Audit Commission (1990a) *Effective Policing: Performance Review in Police Forces.* London: Audit Commission.

Audit Commission (1990b) *Footing the Bill: Financing Provincial Police Forces.* Police Paper Number 6. London: Audit Commission.

Bassett, D., Haldenby, A., Thraves, L. and Truss, E. (2009) *A New Force.* London: Reform.

Blunkett, D. (2002) 'Home Secretary's Foreword', in Home Office, *The National Policing Plan, 2003–2006.* London: Home Office Communications Directorate.

Blunkett, D. (2009) *A People's Police Force: Police Accountability in the Modern Era.* [Online] www.davidblunkett.typepad.com/files/a-peoples-police-force.pdf [accessed on 11 November 2009].

Brake, M. and Hale, C. (1992) *Public Order and Private Lives: The Politics of Law and Order.* London: Routledge.

Cabinet Office (1999) *Modernising Government.* Cm 4310. London: HMSO.

Casey, L. (2008) *Engaging Communities in Fighting Crime – A Review by Louise Casey.* London: The Cabinet Office.

Docking, M. (2003) *Public Perceptions of Police Accountability and Decision-making.* Home Office Online Report 38/03. London: Home Office.

Dunleavy, P. and Hood, C. (1994) 'From Old Public Administration to New Public Management', *Public Money and Management,* 14 (3): 9–16.

Flanagan, Sir R. (2008) *The Review of Policing Final Report.* London: Review of Policing.

Garland, D. (1996) 'The Limits of the Sovereign State', *British Journal of Criminology,* 36 (4): 445–471.

Henig, R. (1998) 'Strengthening the Voice in Local Policing', *Criminal Justice Matters,* 32 (Summer): 8–9.

Home Affairs Committee, (2005) *Police Reform.* Fourth Report, Session 2004–05. House of Commons Paper 370. London: TSO.

Home Affairs Committee (2008) *Policing in the Twenty-first Century.* Seventh Report, Session 2007–08. House of Commons Paper 364. London: TSO.

Home Office (1981) *The Brixton Disorders, 10–12 April 1981: Report of an Inquiry by the Rt. Hon. The Lord Scarman, OBE.* Cmnd 8427. London: HMSO.

Home Office (1983) *Manpower, Effectiveness and Efficiency in the Police Service.* Circular 114/83. London: Home Office.

Home Office (1988a) *Civilian Staff in the Police Service.* Circular 105/88. London: Home Office.

Home Office (1988b) *The British Crime Survey, 1988.* London: Home Office.

Home Office (1993a) *Police Reform: A Police Service for the Twenty-First Century.* Cm 2281. London: HMSO.

Home Office (1993b) *Inquiry into Police Responsibilities and Rewards.* The Sheehy Report. Cm. 2280. London: HMSO.

Home Office (1995a) *Review of the Police Core and Ancillary Tasks: Final Report.* The Posen Report. London: HMSO.

Home Office, (1995b) *Performance Indicators for the Police and Core Statistics for Chief Officers' Annual Reports.* Circular 8/95. London: Home Office.

Home Office (2002) *The National Policing Plan 2003–2006.* London: Home Office Communications Directorate.

Home Office (2004) *Building Communities, Beating Crime: A Better Police Service for the 21st Century*. Cm 6360. London: Home Office.

Home Office (2008a) *Guidance on Statutory Performance Indicators for Police and Community Safety*. London: Home Office.

Home Office (2008b) *From the Neighbourhood to the National: Policing Our Communities Together*. Cm 7448. London: Home Office.

Home Office (2009a) Police Reform National Policing Board. [Online] www.police.homeoffice. gov.uk/police-reform/nat-policing-board/ [accessed 6 May 2009].

Home Office (2009b) *Protecting the Public: Supporting the Police to Succeed*. Cm 7749. London: TSO.

Houghton, J. (2000) 'The Wheel Turns for Local Government and Policing', *Local Government Studies*, 26 (2): 117–130.

Hughes, G. (1998) *Understanding Crime Prevention: Social Control, Risk and Late Modernity*. Buckingham: Open University Press.

Jefferson, T. and Grimshaw, R. (1984) *Controlling the Constable: Police Accountability in England and Wales*. London: The Cobden Trust.

Jones, T. (2003) 'The Governance and Accountability of Policing', in T. Newburn (ed.), *Handbook of Policing*. Cullompton, Devon: Willan Publishing.

Jones, T. and Newburn, T. (1997) *Policing after the Act: Police Governance after the Police and Magistrates' Courts Act 1994*. London: Policy Studies Institute.

Leadbeater, C. (1996) *The Self-Policing Society: Brit Pop*. London: Demos.

Local Government Association (2008) *Answering to You: Policing in the 21st Century*. London: Local Government Association.

Loveday, B. (1987) *Joint Boards for Police: The Impact of Structural Change on Police Governance in the Metropolitan Areas*. Occasional Paper, New Series No. 20. Birmingham: Department of Government and Economics, City of Birmingham Polytechnic.

Loveday, B. (1994) 'The Police and Magistrates' Court Act', *Policing*, 10 (4): 221–233.

Loveday, B. (1995) 'Reforming the Police: From Local Service to State Police?', *Political Quarterly*, 66 (2), April–June: 141–156.

Loveday, B., McClory, J. and Lockhart, G. (2007) *Fitting the Bill: Local Policing for the Twenty-first Century*. London: Policy Exchange.

Loveday, B. and Reid, A. (2003) *Going Local: Who Should Run Britain's Police?* London: Policy Exchange.

Martin, D. (2003) 'The Politics of Policing: Managerialism, Modernisation and Performance', in R. Matthews and J. Young (eds), *The New Politics of Crime and Punishment*. Cullompton, Devon: Willan Publishing.

Micheli, P., Neeli, A. and Kennerley, M. (2006) 'Performance Measurement in the English Public Sector: Searching for the Golden Thread'. *ESADE Public Newsletter*, 13 November. [Online] www2.sa.unibo.it/seminari/Papers/20080327%20Micheli.doc [accessed on 29 March 2009].

Morgan, R. (1989) 'Police Accountability: Current Developments and Future Prospects', in M. Weatheritt (ed.), *Police Research: Some Future Prospects*. Aldershot: Avebury.

Newburn, T. (2002) 'Community Safety and Policing: Some Implications of the Crime and Disorder Act', in G. Hughes, E. McLaughlin and J. Muncie (eds), *Crime Prevention and Community Safety*. London: Sage.

Newman, J. (2000) 'Beyond the New Public Management? Modernising Public Services', in J. Clarke, S. Gewirtz and E. McLaughlin (eds), *New Managerialism: New Welfare*. London: Sage.

Normington, Sir D. (2009) *Data Burden Review*. London: Home Office.

O'Dowd, D. (1998) 'Inspecting Constabularies', *Criminal Justice Matters*, 32 (Summer): 6–7.

Osborne, D. and Gaebler, T. (1999) *Re-inventing Government: How the Entrepreneurial Spirit is Transforming the Public Sector*. New York: Penguin.

Reiner, R. (1994) 'The Dialectics of Dixon: The Changing Image of the TV Cop', in M. Stephens and S. Becker (eds), *Police Force, Police Service*. Basingstoke: Macmillan.

Royal Commission on Criminal Procedure (1981) *The Royal Commission on Criminal Procedure Report*. Cmnd 8092. London: HMSO.

Savage, S. (1998) 'The Shape of the Future', *Criminal Justice Matters*, 32 (Summer): 4–6.

Sergeant, H. (2008) *The Public and the Police*. London: Civitas.

Smith, J. (2008) Speech in the House of Commons, 8 December, HC Debs, Vol 485, Col 38WS.

Spencer, S. (1985) *Called to Account*. London: National Council for Civil Liberties.

Spottiswoode, C. (2000) *Improving Police Performance: A New Approach to Measuring Police Efficiency*. London: Public Services Productivity Panel.

Weatheritt, M. (1986) *Innovations in Policing*. London: Croom Helm.

7

Diversity and the police service

CHAPTER AIMS

The aims of this chapter are:

- To evaluate the background to the 1999 Macpherson report;
- To examine the content of the reforms proposed in the Macpherson report on the police service and the impact made by the Macpherson report on the subsequent operations of the police service;
- To analyse the status of women in the police service;
- To examine the impact of equal opportunities legislation and policy on the position of women in the police service;
- To consider the role played by community contact in relationship to police relations with 'hard to reach' groups.

The police service and its relations with minority ethnic communities in the 1990s

There has been a long history of tension between minority ethnic communities and the police service. The belief that the police were biased against black people was an important factor in the riots that occurred in 1981, commencing in Brixton. A key source of antagonism was the disproportionate use of stop and search powers against black people (Smith and Gray, 1983: Vol. 4, 128), which came to a head in the attempted crackdown on street crime that was implemented in the police operation termed 'Swamp 81'. The issue of police–public relationships was the subject of an enquiry by Lord Scarman (Home Office, 1981). He identified a number of problems and put forward reforms to address them (discussed in Joyce, 2002: 123–126). However, these failed to make any significant improvements to the relationship between the police service and minority ethnic communities and the issue resurfaced on the police agenda in the 1990s.

During the 1990s, perceptions arose that the police service operated in a racist manner, discriminating against members of ethnic minority communities. It was argued that 'PACE stop/searches have important symbolic significance in the context of the "race" and crime debate' (Fitzgerald and Sibbitt, 1997: ix) and a number of studies suggested that these powers were used disproportionately against black people (Home Office, 1998; Statewatch 1999). Criticism was levelled at the arrest rates of people from minority ethnic communities (Statewatch, 1998, 1999). Concern was also expressed regarding the deaths that occurred either at the time of a police intervention or later in custody and the inadequate procedures through which those responsible could be called to account for their actions (Institute of Race Relations, 1991).

An important explanation for the issues discussed above is that some police officers believed black people (especially young black people) constituted a criminal element within society that needed to be controlled in a coercive manner. This has been described as the 'black-youth crime linkage' (Gutzmore, 1983: 27). An important corollary of this was that police officers often found it difficult to view black people as victims of crime and often failed to take appropriate action to protect them. On occasions they would prosecute victims who took actions to defend themselves while being attacked, thereby criminalising the right to self-defence (Wilson, 1983: 8).

A particular problem was the apparent inability of police officers to discern a racial motivation for attacks on members of minority ethnic communities. A report by the Crown Prosecution Service stated that in 1997/98 only 37% of incidents with a racial element were flagged up as such by the police (Kirkwood, 1998). This failing was endorsed by Her Majesty's Inspectorate of Constabulary (HMIC), which expressed a number of concerns in connection with this issue, stating that many officers remained unaware of the definition of a racial incident initially laid down by ACPO in 1985, and that those who did know of it adopted widely different interpretations of what it meant (HMIC, 1997: 30).

The Macpherson report (1999)

The murder of a black teenager, Stephen Lawrence, on 22 April 1993 was a major catalyst in changing in the way in which the police service, and especially the Metropolitan Police Service (MPS), related to members of minority ethnic communities, including their handling of racially motivated violence. The inability of the MPS to find those guilty of Stephen's murder prompted Home Secretary Jack Straw (who entered office in 1997) to appoint Sir William Macpherson to examine the manner in which the Metropolitan Police Service had conducted their inquiry into his murder.

His report was fiercely critical of the police handling of this matter. Sir William stated that the investigation had been fundamentally flawed and 'marred by a combination of professional incompetence, institutional racism, and a failure of leadership by senior officers' (Home Office, 1999: 317). He especially drew attention to 'the lost opportunities for full and proper searches and investigation during the first hours after Stephen Lawrence's murder' which he felt was 'to be deplored' (Home Office, 1999: 87).

BOX 7.1

INSTITUTIONAL RACISM

In 1981, Lord Scarman's report attributed racism in the police service to attitudes held by a small minority of officers (a few 'rotten apples in the barrel'). Macpherson, however, went further than this, effectively arguing that racism existed throughout the Metropolitan Police Service and was akin to a virus that infected the entire system. He put forward the concept of 'institutional racism', which his report defined as 'the collective failure of an organisation to provide an appropriate and professional service to people because of their colour, culture or ethnic origin. It can be seen or detected in processes, attitudes and behaviour which amount to discrimination through unwitting prejudice, ignorance, thoughtlessness and racist stereotyping which disadvantage minority ethnic people' (Home Office, 1999: 321).

It has been argued that this built on existing definitions of institutional racism by focusing on the 'processes' through which racism was constructed, and also by highlighting outcomes, thus accepting that unwitting or unintentional racism was as significant a problem as overt or intentional racism (Gilborn, 2008).

It has sometimes been argued within police circles that the police represent society and if society is racist, then this is inevitably reflected in the attitudes of police officers. This implies that the solution rests in reforming society (especially through the educational system) rather than reforming the practices of the police service. It is therefore important to draw a distinction between institutionalised racism, which refers to beliefs and attitudes which are prevalent in society, and institutional racism, which affects the conduct of particular organisations and can be reformed in order to eliminate racist practices.

Macpherson's report suggested a number of reforms (70 in total) which were designed to ensure that the criminal justice system in general and the police service in particular operated in a manner that was perceived to be fairer to ethnic minority communities. The key proposals relating to the police service are discussed below.

A drive to rebuild the confidence of the ethnic minority communities in policing Macpherson's proposal that a 'ministerial priority' should be established for the police service was his first recommendation. This required the government to take a leading role in repairing minority ethnic community confidence in the police service to guard against the bureaucratic inertia that often prevents organisations (when left to their own devices) from initiating reforms to their operational practices. It was proposed that the performance indicators to be used to monitor its implementation include strategies for the recording, investigation and prosecution of racist incidents, measures to encourage such incidents to be reported and an increase in multi-agency cooperation and information exchange.

Definition of racist incidents

Macpherson observed that a key shortcoming of the Metropolitan Police Service's investigation into Stephen Lawrence's murder was the failure of the first investigating team 'to recognise and accept racism and race relations as a central feature of their investigation … a substantial number of officers of junior rank would not accept that the murder of Stephen Lawrence was simply and solely "racially motivated"' (Home Office, 1999: 23).

One possible reason for this was that the definition of a racist incident put forward by ACPO in 1985 was confusing and not understood by many officers. Macpherson thus put forward a new, and far simpler, definition, suggesting that a racist incident is defined as 'any incident which is perceived to be racist by the victim or any other person'. The term should be understood to include actions that, in policing terms, are defined as both crimes and non-crimes. Macpherson argued that both should be recorded and investigated with equal commitment (Home Office, 1999: 328–329).

The significance of this recommendation was to ensure that police work in connection with hate crimes became more victim-oriented and that low-level racist incidents received an appropriate response from the police since official inaction emboldened racists to commit more serious criminal acts. However, Macpherson's definition was subsequently criticised for judging these incidents on the 'perception and articulation of individuals'. This raised the problem of subjectivity being the determining factor as to how such incidents were classified – 'clear procedures accompanied by rules of accountability in relation to any form of differential treatment of social categories are required' (Anthias, 1999: para 5.2).

The recruitment of more black and Asian police officers

In 1998 the ethnic minority population comprised 5.6% of the total population. However, there were only 2,483 black or Asian police officers in all English and Welsh police forces (below 2% of the total personnel of 124,798) (Home Office, 1998: 37). This was a particular problem in London where the ethnic minority community comprised 19.2% of the population but only 3.3% of the Metropolitan Police Service 28,000 officers were from such communities. In order to make the composition of police forces more reflective of the societies they policed, Macpherson proposed that the Home Secretary and police authorities' policing plans should include targets for recruitment, career progression and retention of minority ethnic staff (Home Office, 1999: 334).

Reform of the 1976 Race Relations Act

Macpherson proposed that the police service should be subject to the require-ments of race relations legislation. The main significance of this recommendation was to make the police service accountable to an outside agency for its actions in connection with race and diversity issues by enabling the Commission for Racial Equality to launch investigations into individual police forces.

Racial awareness training

The changes that Lord Scarman had proposed to police training programmes in order to prepare officers for policing a multi-racial society had been progressively scaled down in most forces so that they were primarily directed at officers who had regular dealings with minority ethnic organisations and communities. Macpherson pointed out that 'not a single officer questioned before us in 1998 had received any training of significance in racism awareness and race relations throughout the course of his career'. He proposed that there should be an immediate review and revision of racism awareness training within police forces, and that all officers, including detectives and civilian staff, should be trained in racism awareness and valuing cultural diversity (Home Office, 1999: 30).

Stop and search

Like Lord Scarman, Macpherson accepted the rationale for stop and search pow-ers to prevent and detect crime, but he wished to improve the level of protection of those who were subjected to them. He therefore proposed that records should be kept by police officers of all non-statutory (or voluntary) 'stops' in addition to 'stops and searches' made under any legislation. The aim of this reform was to more closely monitor the use made by officers of their discretionary powers in their dealings with members of minority ethnic communities.

The introduction of a tougher police disciplinary regime

Macpherson proposed that racist words or actions should lead to disciplinary proceedings, the ultimate sanction being an officer's dismissal from the service. This proposal sought to secure compliance to the principles of racial equality by compulsion if other initiatives to do this were unsuccessful.

The government's response to the Macpherson report

In March 1999 the Home Secretary announced the government's response to the proposals of the Macpherson report. These were contained in an 'action plan' that was presented to the House of Commons on 23 March 1999. The main elements of the government's response are considered below.

Recruitment, retention and promotion

In March 1999 the Home Secretary published his race equality employment targets (Straw, 1999c) relating to the recruitment, retention and progression of minority ethnic officers and staff. This required the police service to incrementally increase the proportion of staff from minority ethnic communities from the present 2% to 7% by 2009, with each force being set individual targets to attain by that date that reflected the proportion of persons from minority ethnic backgrounds living in the force area. It would amount to the recruitment of more than 8,000 officers from minority ethnic communities over the next ten years in order to kick-start 'the police service attaining a proper ethnic balance' (Straw, 1999c). Targets for retention and progression were set at parity with white officers, although progression targets were staged over time and by rank.

Recruitment – weeding out racists   The initial interview process is crucial to ensure that those with racist views and opinions do not enter the service in the first place. Prior to 2002 no national scheme existed for the recruitment and selection of constables by individual police forces, although general guidance was provided by the Home Office. In 2002, the Home Office commissioned CENTREX (the Central Police Training and Development Authority) to develop a method of selection, the National Recruitment Standards Assessment Centre (or 'assessment centre', also known as SEARCH [Selection Entrance Assessment for Recruiting Constables Holistically]), based on job-related exercises, for the use of all police forces.

The centre (which was designed in line with British Psychological Society Guidance) use a combination of interviews, tests and role-plays to assess seven competences. These are: teamwork, personal responsibility, community and customer focus, effective communication, problem solving, resilience, and respect for diversity. In each SEARCH process the candidate was required to undergo four role-playing exercises, two written exercises, two psychometric ability tests and one structured interview (Calvert-Smith, 2005: 51).

A candidate's attitude towards race and diversity was tested across all exercises in the new assessment centre, including the interview. In addition, assessors were trained to be alert for any inappropriate speech or behaviour by candidates, 'for example swearing, disrespect, aggression or the expression of racist, sexist or homophobic sentiments, whether within the exercises or without them'. If behaviour of this nature arose, it was noted and the quality assurers then decided if it warranted a reduction in the marks awarded for the respect for diversity competence (Calvert-Smith, 2005: 52).

Racist incidents

Macpherson's definition of a racist incident was accepted by the government in 1999. It was subsequently incorporated into the Home Office Code of Practice for the Reporting and Recording of Racist Incidents, which highlighted the need for police investigations to consider fully the possibility of a racist element. However, this would only be used in the initial reporting of an incident and not to determine the issue of racial motivation when someone was charged and tried.

Amendment of the Race Relations Act

The 2000 Race Relations (Amendment) Act placed a duty on the entire public sector (including the police, prisons and immigration service) to promote race equality. In order to help public authorities achieve this goal, the Home Secretary was empowered to impose specific duties upon them. The 2000 legislation enabled chief constables to be found liable for the discriminatory acts of one officer against another – a situation that the Court of Appeal had previously ruled (in the case of *Chief Constable of Bedfordshire v Liversidge* [2002]) was not possible under the 1976 legislation.

Racism awareness and diversity training

In 1994 the Police Training Council had put forward proposals for the delivery of community and race relations training. These proposals had not been fully or effectively implemented by all forces. The government therefore required all forces to positively respond to the 1994 proposals. In October 1999 new training courses were introduced by the Metropolitan Police, and the Home Office set a target date of December 2002 for all 'front line' staff to received training in race and diversity issues.

A key development in connection with training was the implementation, overseen by the Home Office, ACPO, the Association of Police Authorities (APA) and CENTREX, of National Occupational Standards on race equality and cultural diversity. They not only provided a framework within which training took place but also specified the learning outcomes to be achieved. This new approach was set out in ACPO, APA and Home Office (2004). It covered all diversity areas and the training was adjusted to the requirements of individual officers. The National Occupational Standards (NOS) will eventually be incorporated into the Equalities Standards developed by the National Policing Improvement Agency (NPIA) (Rollock, 2009: 49–50).

Police discipline

In April 1999 the Police Disciplinary Code was replaced by a Code of Conduct. This set out standards of behaviour that were expected from officers and included the requirement of politeness and tolerance and the need to avoid 'unreasonable discrimination' (a term which was not, however, defined in the Code). The absence of a specific offence of racially discriminatory behaviour meant that statistics dealing with racial discrimination were not automatically generated. Although each case is dealt with on its merits, it was anticipated that racist behaviour by officers would normally result in their dismissal. Under the new procedure, officers lost their right of silence in connection with disciplinary hearings, and the standard of proof was lowered to the civil law test of the balance of probabilities (Calvert-Smith, 2004: 40).

Stops and stop and search

The Home Secretary agreed to consider whether a written record of reasons for all stops should be given to those searched. It was subsequently agreed that in order to ensure this reform did not place an unacceptable burden on police officers, the introduction of the recording of 'stops' would be phased in and the results monitored (Home Office, 2002: 22).

An independent complaints system

The government conducted a feasibility study into the costs of an independent complaints system and proposals were subsequently put forward by the Home Secretary to introduce a stronger independent element into the system of investigating complaints against the police (Home Office, 2000a). This reform was introduced in the 2002 Police Reform Act.

Although a formal complaint by one officer against a fellow officer is normally referred to the force's grievance procedure, the Independent Police Complaints Commission (IPCC) has a broader role than that of the Police Complaints Authority (PCA) in examining internal disciplinary matters. This opened the possibility that most allegations of racism brought by serving police officers could be investigated by the new body.

The elimination of racism – the progress of reform

No reforms proposed by Macpherson or endorsed by the government were specifically designed to eliminate institutional racism from the police service, although it was central in placing this issue 'at the forefront of political and public consciousness' (Rollock, 2009: 4). Rather, it was assumed that progress in tackling the issues that were identified in the Macpherson report would achieve this objective. Some of the key indicators that might be used to assess the success of reforms designed to eradicate racism from police forces are considered below.

Racial violence

One aspect of the police response to the Macpherson report was the formation in 1999 of specialist victim-oriented community safety units throughout the MPS area. Aided by changes spearheaded by these units, the reporting and arrests for racial crime increased, as did intelligence on crimes of this nature. In addition, the Metropolitan Police established an 'understanding and responding to race hate crime' project whose role was to analyse and review data to give the force a clearer understanding of the issue. In 2005, ACPO and the Home Office published guidance to forces on how to deal with hate crime. Some forces, most notably the Metropolitan Police, secured success in achieving convictions in a number of high-profile cases of this nature.

Statistics suggested that racial violence was on the increase following the publication of the Macpherson report. In England and Wales there were 47,814 racist incidents reported to and recorded by the police in 1999/2000, compared to 23,049 in the previous year. This included 21,750 offences created by the 1998 Crime and Disorder Act (Home Office, 2000a: 49). Subsequent figures indicated that the number of racist incidents recorded by police in England and Wales rose from 59,000 in 2005/06 to 61,000 in 2006/07 (Jones and Singer, 2008:10). In 2006/07, 42,551 people were charged with racial or religious aggravated offences. Most (65%) were for harassment and many were disposed of using the Penalty Notice for Disorder (PND) procedure where police issue an on-the-spot fine. In 2006/07, 13,544 charges were forwarded by the police to the Crown Prosecution Service, of which around 75% were prosecuted and 25% dropped by the CPS (Crown Prosecution Service, 2007; Rollock, 2009: 31).

These figures suggest a significant rise in racial crimes that may have been affected by the adoption of Macpherson's suggestion to record offences as race crimes when the victim used this designation. However, recording methods (whereby one incident may generate several offences or several incidents one offence) have also influenced these statistics. These figures may also reflect aspects of 'perverse reporting', where an increased number of white victims have reported crimes as racially motivated – an 'absurdity' when 'anyone can make a complaint about another person and apply a racist label' (Chahal, 1999: para 1:6). Police officers themselves have aggravated this situation by labelling insults directed at themselves as a racist incident when made by a person of different racial origin (Fitzgerald, 2001). The consequence of such reporting was to overload community safety units with casework.

In addition, the effectiveness of changes to police procedures to deal with racial violence in London was questioned in a report by Her Majesty's Inspectorate of Constabulary (HMIC, 2000). This praised the role performed by officers in specialist units but argued that more needed to be done to win over the hearts and minds of non-specialist police officers. Reference was made to 'a pervasive feeling … among some staff that what is seen as special treatment to the victims of racial attacks can only be delivered by prejudicing service to the broader community. The report thus urged that this issue should be addressed in community and race relations training courses (HMIC, 2000: 6).

Recruitment issues

Weeding out the racists

A survey conducted by *The Guardian* that was published in 24 February 2000 revealed that 20 forces had no tests in place to measure whether officers had racist attitudes.

Targets

Progress in recruiting more police officers drawn from African-Caribbean and Asian communities was initially slow. By early 2002, the Metropolitan Police Service had 1,205 officers drawn from minority ethnic communities, 4.42% of the total (Hopkins, 2002) and the global figure for England and Wales stood at 3,386 (2.6% of the total) (Home Office, 2002: 27). This meant that in order to attain the Home Secretary's target for the Metropolitan Police Service up to 80% of new recruits would have to be black or Asian from 2004 onwards, a situation that the president of the National Black Police Association described as 'ridiculous' (Powell, quoted in *The Observer*, 22 August 2004)

Retention

Research revealed that rates of resignation and dismissal from the police service were higher for minority ethnic officers than for white officers (Bland et al., 1999) and that in March 1999 only 14% of minority ethnic officers had been promoted compared to 23% of white officers (Bowling and Phillips, 2002: 218). The seriousness of this problem was noted by the then Home Secretary, Jack Straw, who drew critical attention to a Home Office report that indicated that black and Asian police officers were twice as likely to resign and three times more likely to be dismissed as their white peers. He argued that ways had to be found to stop this 'exodus' (Straw, 1999c).

However, attempts to deal with this problem caused dissention within the police service. The promotion of minority ethnic officers led to resentment from their white colleagues and resulted in a record number of white officers resorting to employment tribunals alleging that their prospects had been hindered by racial discrimination (Hinsliff, 2004).

Discipline

A new Standards of Professional Behaviour was introduced in 2008, following the publication of the Morris and Taylor reports in 2004 and 2005 respectively. These new standards included a specific reference to equality and diversity that required officers to act with fairness and impartiality and to not discriminate unlawfully or unfairly. Police officers were also expected to report, challenge or take action against colleagues whose conduct was contrary to the standards of professional behaviour. Misconduct hearings were held before a panel of independent members (Home Office, 2008a).

Diversity training

The race equality duty imposed on forces by the 2000 Race Relations (Amendment) Act required all forces to train their staff on the general duty to promote race equality. The diversity element of the initial residential Probationer Constable Training Programme (which was delivered at Hendon for recruits into the Metropolitan Police Service and at a CENTREX centre for recruits to other forces) was extended into a module lasting from three to five days. All forces introduced a post-probationary programme that was composed of compulsory 'Community and Race Relations' workshops, and most officers and staff had attended these programmes by the end of 2003 (Calvert-Smith, 2004: 25). Diversity issues were incorporated into specialist training that included stop and search courses and senior command courses. In addition, a three-day Personal Leadership Programme was developed by CENTREX, in partnership with the National Black Police Association, and by the middle of 2004 around 700 minority ethnic staff had attended (Calvert-Smith, 2004: 25). Individual force initiatives (such as 'Community and Race Relations' workshops delivered in 24 of London's 32 boroughs in 2001–02) were also pursued following the Macpherson report.

Stop and search and stop and account

The Home Secretary's commitment to consider the recommendations made by the Macpherson report regarding stop and search led to a 'scoping' study (prior to the introduction of national pilots) being mounted by the Home Office Policing and Reducing Crime Unit. This study revealed several problems with existing procedures, including the use made of 'voluntary' searches, the monitoring by officers of the use of stop and search powers (which in all forces that participated in the study had been developed relatively recently), the issue of 'how best to manage officers suspected, through improved monitoring, of using stop and search unlawfully or unfairly' (Quinton and Bland, 1999: 2), and the definition that should be accorded to 'stops' (as distinct, for example, from exploratory questioning).

Changes to stop and search procedures were introduced by the 2003 Criminal Justice Act. This extended police powers to stop and search to cover situations where a constable reasonably suspected that a person was carrying an article that he/she intended to use to cause criminal damage (such as graffiti). The Codes of Practice of the Police and Criminal Evidence Act (PACE), introduced in 2004, placed a new responsibility on supervisors to monitor and detect what was referred to as 'disproportionality' in the searches conducted by officers. Disproportionality regarding the use of stop and search powers would also be measured within the Police Performance Assessment Framework (PPAF). The Police Federation, however, was critical of this development concerning disproportionality, arguing that 'the Home Office and Chief Officers readily admit they do not understand the term and yet are determined to judge police officers by it' (Police Federation, 2008).

Reasons for lack of progress

In the early years of the twenty-first century, the perception arose that the momentum in achieving the objectives contained in the Macpherson report was slowing down. A study published in 2003 suggested that some participants from minority ethnic groups 'thought that the police were still "institutionally racist", had negative attitudes towards minority communities and were slow in responding to them' (Docking, 2003). Perceptions of this nature seemed substantiated in a BBC television programme, *The Secret Policeman*, which was screened on 21 October 2003.

This programme used covert observation of officers in the early stages of their careers when they were undergoing training at the Police National Training Centre at Bruche, Warrington, which was used by ten forces in the North of England and Wales. Some of these recruits articulated racist language and sentiments that, in the wake of the Macpherson report, beggared belief and called into question the extent to which the police service had meaningfully taken Macpherson's recommendations on board.

Various explanations can be put forward to explain the persistence of problems that questioned the commitment of the police service to diversity. These include resistance by rank-and-file police officers to this objective. Opposition took a number of forms, one of which was to deny the validity of Macpherson's claims that the service was institutionally racist. This view is underpinned by an assertion that it is difficult to discern '*collective* failure' based on the behaviour of a *few* officers involved in the investigation of Stephen Lawrence's murder (Lea, 2003: 50–51).

It has also been asserted that the reform agenda contained in the Macpherson report was inadequate as a basis of effective reform. In particular, it 'fails to locate with sufficient precision' the roots of institutional racism 'within the structure of operational policing and in the relationship between police and minority communities' (Lea, 2003: 48). That is, it is necessary to identify precisely what it is about day-to-day police work that generates and sustains an occupational culture that supports racism (Lea, 2003: 51). Allied to this view is a suggestion that institutional racism was not the key problem and should not be regarded as the sole, or perhaps even the major, factor that characterised the Lawrence murder investigation. Instead, it has been argued that the practices revealed in this investigation reflected the poor quality of service affecting working-class communities in general as opposed to police racism (Skidelsky, 2000: 2). Police practices might also be governed by a complex interrelationship of class and racial factors: 'racisms are forms of subordination and exclusion and work in tandem with class-related and gender-related forms of subordination and exclusion'. This view led to the conclusion that racism and struggle against it should be treated 'within a broader ideological and political framework and as a catalyst for thinking about social democratisation, equality and citizenship' (Anthias, 1999: para 7.1).

A further obstacle hindering the progress of Macpherson's reforms has been the perception that the government began to lose interest in the subject. In 2003, during David Blunkett's tenure as Home Secretary (2001–04), the ministerial priority to 'increase trust and confidence in policing amongst minority ethnic communities' was revoked and replaced by a more generalised commitment contained in the 2004 National Policing Plan to 'inspire confidence in the police, particularly amongst minority ethnic communities'. It was argued that the goal of inspiration would be hard to assess in practice (Rollock, 2009: 4 and 16). Subsequently, the Lawrence Steering Group, which had been established to oversee the implementation of Macpherson's recommendations, was disbanded in 2005 and replaced by a Racist Incident Group to scrutinise the delivery of local, regional and national policy to tackle racial crime.

A final problem related to the failure of the police service to put its own house in order. Attempts to eradicate racism within police forces have been traditionally directed at the external issue of police–public relationships. Accordingly, 'absolutely no critical attention is given to the features of the occupational culture that redefine what … are "good" and desirable features of a work environment … but exclude minority ethnic officers from full and active membership' (Holdaway, 1996: 171). This view suggests that changing police culture is integral to tackling institutional racism within the police service. It is, however, a difficult goal to achieve since 'not only is the police culture responsible for racist attitudes and abusive behaviour, but it also forms part the basis of secrecy and solidarity among police officers, so that deviant practices are covered up and rationalised' (Chan, 1997: 225).

A reform agenda whose objective was to promote the need for the police service to put its own house in order was put forward in reports written by David Calvert-Smith (in 2004 and 2005) and Bill Morris (in 2004), a common theme of which was the need to ensure that police officers from minority ethnic communities were not subject to racial discrimination within the service.

In September 2005 the Home Office, ACPO and the APA produced the *Race Equality Programme for the Police Service* (ACPO, APA and Home Office, 2005) that was based upon findings contained in a report by the Commission for Racial Equality (2005). These three bodies formed an Equality and Diversity Board to advance the implementation of the recommendations contained in the report. The reforms that were initiated included a new national programme of police training and post-entry race and diversity training, a more streamlined and simpler disciplinary and grievance procedure for alleged racist behaviour of officers, race and diversity training for members and staff of the APA, and new National Operating Standards. The latter stipulated the performance required of officers regarding race and diversity that underpinned the selection, appraisal and training objectives, revised training for trainers, established new procedures and guidance on staff appraisals and offered advice on 'positive action' (as opposed to 'positive discrimination', which is unlawful) to boost the recruitment of minority ethnic recruits (Bennetto, 2009: 15).

Progress in eradicating institutional racism in the twenty-first century

The minister who had been responsible for initiating the implementation of reforms to policing proposed by the Macpherson report in 1999 declared 10 years later that the MPS was not institutionally racist (Straw, 2009). He admitted, however, that pockets of racism remained. And yet, his views were not universally accepted. It was argued that 'continued failings by the police service in relation to Black and minority ethnic recruitment, retention and progression and the disproportionate number of Black people being stopped and searched' made it 'difficult to conclude that the charge of institutional racism no longer applies' (Rollock, 2009: 3). This view was more starkly expressed by Alfred John, chair of the MPS Black Police Association, who asserted to the Home Affairs Committee on 28 April 2009 that the MPS was 'without a doubt' institutionally racist.

From April 2007, the National Policing Improvement Agency (NPIA) assumed responsibility for the attainment of the Race Equality Programme objective of securing a representative police workforce. The minister with responsibility for policing stated his intention to establish a Ministerial Steering Group to oversee his recommendations for improvement in the recruitment, retention and progression of black and minority ethnic officers (Coaker, 2008: 8). Diversity policies would also be incorporated into a three-year Equality, Diversity and Human Rights Strategy that was being developed by ACPO and the APA, and supported by the NPIA and HMIC. This strategy would embrace equality standards that were developed by the NPIA.

The internal operations of the police service

This section examines whether the contemporary police service has succeeded in remedying institutional racism through the reforms that were directed at putting its own house in order.

Recruitment

Although the number of people from black and minority ethnic (BME) communities joining the police service has risen since 1999, statistics suggested that the service would struggle to attain the 7% of BME police officers by 2009 (Rollock, 2009: 6). This situation may have been one factor affecting the government's decision to discontinue the national equality targets and to replace them with locally determined race and gender targets set by each police authority. National oversight would be maintained by HMIC inspections of workforce issues in 2010 (Coaker, 2008: 9).

One suggestion to improve the recruitment of officers from BME backgrounds was to encourage minority ethnic Police Community Support Officers (PCSOs) and Special Constables to become fully-sworn officers. The Equality and Human Rights Commission suggested that the police service should investigate whether their probation period could be shortened in recognition of the policing experience they had obtained from working in these capacities (Bennetto, 2009: 7).

Retention

A particular issue undermining attempts by the police service to alter its racial composition has been the high wastage rate from recruits from minority ethnic backgrounds.

It was observed that minority ethnic officers had a higher resignation rate that white officers, especially in the first six months of service. In 2006/07, for officers with under six months service, 6.1% of those who resigned or who were dismissed in 2007 were from minority ethnic groups. The corresponding rate for white officers was 3.1% (Bennetto, 2009: 14). However, the gap had considerably narrowed in the following year to 3.5% and 3.2% respectively (Coaker, 2008: 15).

Additional data suggested that retention of BME officers was worse than retention of white officers at all lengths of service, but was most notable for officers with below five years' service (Coaker, 2008: 3). Overall, 46.6% of voluntary resignations came from BME officers compared with 25.9% of white officers (Jones and Singer, 2008: 104).

Promotion

In 2008, 83.2% of the 5,793 BME officers were at the rank of constable and 0.12% were of ACPO rank (Coaker, 2008: 15). Denial of promotion is a key aspect of what is perceived to be discriminatory practices. As a result, too few officers from BME backgrounds are in high ranking positions. Although it was argued that 'minority ethnic officer progression is very close to the white officer progression for all length of service bands assessed' (Coaker, 2008: 4), the Home Affairs Committee stated that during its inquiry there were a number of high-profile allegations of racism during promotion processes, particularly within the Metropolitan Police (Home Affairs Committee, 2008: para 351).

The promotion of BME staff is a particular problem for the senior ranks of the service, where progression targets have not been met (Bennetto, 2009: 3). In 2008 it was reported that only two minority ethnic officers had been passed by the Senior Police National Assessment Centre (SPNAC) in the past four years. There was a perception among minority ethnic officers that chief constables tended to endorse white officers to progress to this Centre, which was responsible for selecting future chief police officers (Coaker, 2008: 8).

A number of measures have been taken to remedy this imbalance. The NPIA collaborated with the National Black Police Association to promote the High Potential Development scheme (a national leadership development programme to train officers for leadership roles). It runs a four-day Positive Action Leadership Programme for officers or staff from under-represented groups in the service and is designed to encourage staff from such backgrounds to remain in the police service and apply for development opportunities and progression. ACPO formed a BME Progression Group and, in cooperation with the NPIA, established a BME Senior Staff Network (Home Affairs Committee, 2008: para 349). ACPO and the NPIA also set up a Tripartite Oversight Group to monitor the retention and progression of BME officers (Coaker, 2008: 9).

However, progress remained limited at the higher levels of the service. Dr Ranjit Manghnani, a Development Adviser at the National Senior Careers Advisory Service of the NPIA, indicated that only 4.6% of the 388 people currently in the High Potential Development Scheme were from a BME background. During the last assessments for senior positions (2007) 5% were from BME backgrounds and none achieved promotion (Home Affairs Committee, 2008: para 350).

Discipline

Figures suggest that BME officers were more likely to have been dismissed or required to resign than their white counterparts (8.5% compared with 1.7%) (Jones and Singer, 2008: 104). In December 2008, derived from the Morris Inquiry (Morris, 2004), a new Code – the Standards of Professional Behaviour – was introduced. It sought to make the complaints and disciplinary process more transparent. Police officer disciplinary and unsatisfactory performance procedures, which were based on the ACAS Code of Practice on Disciplinary and Grievance Procedures, were introduced.

However, the threat to allege racist treatment may be used as a mechanism to prevent genuine complaints against minority ethnic officers from being investigated. This issue was raised in the trial of Commander Ali Dizaei, who received a four-year prison sentence in 2010 for misconduct in a public office and perverting the course of justice.

Racist conduct

It is important that the police service develops appropriate responses to use against those members found guilty of racial misconduct. This is especially relevant when dealing with problems derived from unwitting racism, where, as the Police Complaints Authority's guidelines for investigating complaints of racism stated (Travis, 2003), the sanction of dismissal may not be appropriate. Adequate retraining should be available so that officers who are guilty of racial misconduct have the opportunity to understand why their actions were wrong and become aware of how they should conduct themselves in the future.

Ultimately, however, coercive means have an important role to play in influencing the culture of the service. Accordingly, the penalty of dismissal for severe cases of racial misconduct should be consistently applied. It was only in response to the BBC programme *The Secret Policeman* that the sanction of loss of employment was utilised, and in all cases those who stood accused of racist misconduct were allowed to resign from the service rather than being dismissed from it.

Training

Diversity training is delivered through the Initial Police Learning and Development Programme and the Race and Diversity Learning and Development Programme, 'in which race and diversity are embedded throughout the full suite of learning materials and underpinned by a fundamental "business case" that recognises the critical importance of improved and sustained performance in all diversity matters and the internal and external benefits of establishing a culturally diverse workforce' (Coaker, 2008: 5).

The Equality and Human Rights Commission proposed that diversity training should be incorporated into every part of police training rather than being seen as a separate part of the course (Bennetto, 2009: 7). To make an impact on the behaviour of officers, the purpose of such courses must be spelled out to participants at the outset to secure their support (including, but extending beyond, the pragmatic considerations set out in HMIC (2003: 13)), and effective ways must also be devised to monitor their subsequent impact by devising measurable outcomes.

Conclusion

Allegations of racial discrimination lay at the heart of many of the arguments that the police service has failed to eradicate institutional racism. In the period November 2005–November 2007 police forces received more than 700 complaints of discrimination from police officers and staff. When forces lost cases, the person responsible often went unpunished (Home Affairs Committee, 2008: para 351).

Evidence from the Metropolitan Police Service suggested that BME officers were overrepresented in Fairness at Work (FAW) procedures. In the period April 2007–March 2008 a total of 192 FAW cases were lodged in the MPS, with BME officers accounting for 10% of these cases (compared with BME officers comprising 8.2% of the MPS workforce), an increase of 1% over the previous year (Rollock, 2009: 53).

BME officers also lodged claims at employment tribunals, although not all of these cases related to racial discrimination *per se* (Rollock, 2009: 6). In 2007/08, 58% of the 117 cases lodged were from white officers, 12% by black officers and 13% by Asian officers: black and minority ethnic officers were three and a half times more likely to lodge a claim compared to their number in the MPS workforce. Race discrimination as the sole element of a complaint accounted for 18% of all on-going claims. Race as both a sole and a joint element (where the claim included allegations of additional forms of discrimination such as sex or age discrimination) accounted for 45% of all claims in the year ending March 2008. However, around a third of claimants submitting race-based claims were white (Rollock, 2009: 53–54).

A number of high-profile disciplinary cases involving senior officers from BME backgrounds led the Metropolitan Black Police Association in 2008 to actively discourage members of BME groups from joining the police service because it was a racist organisation (Rollock, 2009: 12). In 2008, a BBC *Panorama* documentary, *The Secret Policeman Returns*, argued that racism remained a persistent problem for many BME officers throughout England and Wales. Kent's chief constable, Mike Fuller, argued that black officers had to work twice as hard as their white counterparts to achieve advancement within the service (Bennetto, 2009: 17). Issues of this nature prompted the suggestion that the service should focus its efforts on tackling issues of discrimination within the workforce (Home Affairs Committee, 2009).

The external relations of the police service

Evidence that institutional racism has been eradicated from the police service also requires an examination of its relationships with the general public, in particular with minority ethnic communities. Although confidence in the police has risen in minority ethnic communities (Coaker, 2008: 1), a number of problems remain. These are considered in the following sections.

Stop and search

It has been suggested that 'while searches play some role in tackling crime and lead to about a tenth of arrests nationally, they appear to have only a small impact on the detection and prevention of recorded or reported crime' (Willis, 2000: iii). Nonetheless, there was evidence to suggest that searches made a substantial contribution to arrests for certain classes of offences, such as carrying offensive weapons (Miller et at., 2000: 11). However, any contribution that they make towards combating crime has to be considered in the context that 'searches have a negative impact on public confidence in the police' (Willis, 2000: iii), and that 'the disproportionate use of searches against people from minority ethnic communities appears to contribute directly to a reduced confidence in the police among these groups' (Miller et al, 2000: vi).

The 2005 London bombings initiated new trends affecting the use of stop and search powers, in particular their increased use against persons of Asian heritage under the 2000 Terrorism Act (Rollock, 2009: 6). Although the bulk of those stopped and searched under these powers were white (rising from 14,429 in 2002/03 to 20,637 in 2003/04, a 43% increase), the number of black people stopped and searched increased in the same period by 55% (from 1,745 to 2,704) and the number of Asian people rose by 22% (from 2,989 to 3,668) (Dodd and Travis, 2005). Further statistics revealed that in 2006/07 Asian people were almost twice as likely to be stopped as white persons, a similar figure to that in 1998/99 (Jones and Singer, 2008: 34).

Disproportionality is 'a major impediment to good race relations' (Bennetto, 2009: 21). Although there were examples of effective monitoring to address this (Miller et al., 2000: 55), the Equality and Human Rights Commission noted 'a lack of rigour and interest' among the police service and other agencies in connection with stop and search disproportionality (Bennetto, 2009: 6).

An amended version of PACE Code A, which became operative on 1 January 2009, specifically stated that reasonable grounds for suspicion for stopping and searching anyone 'cannot be based on generalizations or stereotypical images of certain groups or categories of people as more likely to be involved in criminal activity' (Home Office, 2008b: 4). In addition, supervising officers who monitored the use of stop and search powers were specifically instructed to 'consider … whether there is any evidence that they are being exercised on the basis of stereotyped images or inappropriate generalisations' (Home Office, 2008b: 16).

Stop and account

Figures for stop and account in 2006/07 suggested that black people were almost two and a half times more likely to be stopped and asked to account than white people, although Asians were only slightly more likely to be subject to this procedure than white persons (Rollock, 2009: 58).

From 1 April 2005, all police forces were required to have mechanisms in place to ensure that anyone who was asked by an officer to account for themselves in a public place regarding their actions, behaviour, presence or items in their possession was provided with a record of the encounter. This form of police intervention was now referred to as a 'stop and account' as opposed to 'stop'.

However, following the Flanagan review, the government amended the recording process for stop and account. A revised version of PACE Code A, which became operative on 1 January 2009, amended stop and account documentation so that a receipt rather than a record of the encounter was provided and the officer conducting the encounter was required only to record the person's self-defined ethnic background (Home Office, 2008b: 15). In addition, stop and account recording would include only race and location. The officer conducting the exercise could refuse to issue a receipt if he or she 'reasonably believes that the purpose of the request is deliberately aimed at frustrating or delaying legitimate police activity (Home Office, 2008b: 15–16).

Changes affecting stop and account documentation were designed to reduce the bureaucratic burden on police officers, thus allowing them to devote more of their time to frontline duties. The 2010 Crime and Security legislation also proposes to streamline the recording of stop and searches. However, the Equality and Human Rights Commission expressed its concern regarding these reforms, arguing that the government 'appear to put cutting bureaucracy before accountability in an area that is key to race equality' (Bennetto, 2009: 5).

Racial incidents

The Equality and Human Rights Commission believed that there had been 'significant progress' in the past 10 years in how the police dealt with racial incidents (Bennetto, 2009: 32) and this view was echoed in an unpublished HMIC report that concluded, in connection with hate crime, that 'forces had much of the necessary infrastructure in place, were demonstrating effective leadership in many areas, and were using third party reporting practices effectively. Overall performance and satisfaction levels were up to standard' (HMIC, 2008: 1).

Figures from the British Crime Survey suggested that the number of racially motivated incidents had declined from 390,000 in 1995 to 184,000 in 2006/07. It was argued that initiatives such as multi-agency panels (which were based on a report from the Racial Attacks Group in 1989 and whose role was to enable the police and other statutory and voluntary agencies to share information on cases reported to them and coordinate a response) and ACPO's Hate Crime Guide (launched in 2000 and amended in 2004) had contributed to improvements in reducing the number of incidents of this nature. The detection rate for hate crimes had risen to 44% (Home Affairs Committee, 2009).

The National DNA Database

A relatively new aspect of alleged racial discrimination by the police service in its dealings with ethnic minority communities arose in connection with the National DNA Database (NDNAD) (see Chapter 2).

A parliamentary debate on the NDNAD, initiated by Lib Dem MP Sarah Teather, drew attention to the 'disproportionate number of black people' on this database. Overall, 27% of the entire black population, 42% of the male black population, 77% of young black men and 9% of all Asians were on the database compared with 6% of the white population (Teather, 2008).

Although the government denied the existence of any bias (Hillier, 2008), the Equality and Human Rights Commission supported this argument, stating that 'for the past ten years the police service has failed to properly acknowledge or address the race equality impact of the database', which it believed was 'considerable'

(Bennetto, 2009: 28). It was argued that potential threats posed by this disproportionality included ethnic profiling (whereby black men were regarded as the
prime suspects for particular offence types because of their over-representation on
the database) and that samples or DNA records could be sold to commercial
companies for research into issues such as trying to establish criminogenic genes
in certain races. In addition, the stigma of 'extreme' representation for one racial
group had potential social consequences (Bennetto, 2009: 29).

The chair of the Equality and Human Rights Commission, Trevor Phillips,
informed the Home Affairs Committee on 28 April 2009 that NDNAD was 'mas-
sively and hugely discriminatory'. The Commission thus proposed that a race
equality impact assessment should be carried out in relation to this database and
full ethnic monitoring data should be published for those on the NDNAD
(Bennetto, 2009: 8).

BOX 7.2

DIVERSITY IN THE POLICE SERVICE

In the year ending 31 March 2007 there were 141,892 police officers employed in the
43 police forces in England and Wales (142,374 including those seconded to central
units such as SOCA). Of these:

- 33,177 (23%) were female, although female officers in the year ending 31 March
  2007 constituted 35% of the intake;
- 5,540 (3.9%) were from minority ethnic communities.

Overall, the wastage rate was 6%, but 15% of those choosing to leave the police service
in the year ending 31 March 2007 were women.

The total number of police support staff (including PCSOs) employed in the year
ending 31 March 2007 was 91,056. Of these, 58% were female and 7% were from
minority ethnic communities (Bullock and Gunning, 2007).

By 2008, 8% of Special Constables were from BME communities (Rollock, 2009: 6).

Women and the police service

This section examines a further issue relating to diversity by examining the
stance of the police service towards the recruitment of women officers and the
treatment subsequently accorded to them. These issues are crucial underpin-
nings to the manner in which the service responds to women who are victims
of crime since 'genuine and long-standing improvements in service delivery' in
this area first requires the service to put its own house in order (Gregory and
Lees, 1999: 200–201).

Recruitment and conditions of work – the historical position

The police service was historically an occupation for males. In the nineteenth century some forces employed women to supervise female prisoners while in police custody, but the employment of women as police officers did not occur until the First World War. After 1914 a number of independent organisations (such as the Women's Auxiliary Service) were set up, performing functions such as protecting girls from the 'brutal and licentious soldiery' (Ascoli, 1975: 207). At the end of the war women police patrols were established by the Metropolitan Police Commissioner, although the women were not sworn in as constables. An attempt to regularise the employment of women was subsequently made when a select committee argued that women should be fully attested and trained and become an integral element of police forces in England and Wales (Baird, 1920). However, opposition to the implementation of these proposals meant that only a few women were sworn in as constables and even this limited progress was halted in 1922 when the Home Secretary met the Joint Central Committee of the Police Federation and agreed to remove all female officers.

Further pressures to secure the employment of women officers included the Bridgeman Committee (1924), which asserted that police efficiency had been strengthened by the employment of police women but argued that their appointment should not be seen as a substitute for the employment of men (Bridgeman, 1924), and the Royal Commission on Police Powers and Procedure (1929). In 1930 the Home Secretary standardised the pay and conditions of service for women officers and specified that their main purpose was to perform police functions concerned with children and women. The 1933 Children and Young Persons Act gave legal recognition to the status of female officers by requiring them to be available to deal with juveniles. However, their numbers remained low: by 1971 only 3,884 were employed throughout England and Wales. They were organised in their own departments, had their own rank and promotion structures and their actions were supervised by their own inspectorate. Their pay was only nine-tenths of that of their male counterparts.

The recruitment and conditions of work of female police officers was improved by the 1970 Equal Pay Act and the 1975 Sex Discrimination Act. These measures (and other related reforms undertaken by individual forces) were designed to boost the recruitment of female officers and secure their full integration into police forces. Separate women's police departments were abolished and female officers received the same pay as their male counterparts. However, although the number of women police officers increased, most were in the lower ranks.

It was argued that the progress of female officers was impeded by the entrenched nature of 'cop culture' that made the service resistant to any changes conflicting with long-established practices and attitudes (Gregory and Lees, 1999: 199). It has also been argued that that policing is dominated by men and male values (Heidensohn, 1992) and that the police occupational culture is characterised by 'an almost pure form of hegemonic masculinity' that emphasises 'aggressive physical action, competitiveness, preoccupation with the imagery of conflict, exaggerated heterosexual orientation and the operation of patriarchal misogynistic attitudes' (Fielding, 1994: 47). This has given rise to suggestions within the service that 'women as police officers are physically and emotionally inferior to men, police work is not women's work and is unfeminine, and that they do not stay in the job for any length of time' (Jones, 1986: 11).

One aspect of this problem is that women officers may suffer from discrimination. During the 1990s, there were several well-publicised cases of female officers alleging sexual discrimination. These included Alison Halford, who in 1992 took the Merseyside Police Authority to an industrial tribunal alleging that sexual discrimination accounted for her failure to secure promotion to the rank of deputy chief constable. She settled the dispute for a large payment and secured a further £10,000 in 1997 for the breach of her right to privacy arising from her office telephone being tapped when she communicated with her lawyers over the sexual discrimination case. The 'serious problem' of sexual harassment within the police service was officially recognised in 1993 (HMIC, 1993: 16) and evidence was later found of 'high levels of sexist … banter' (HMIC, 1995: 10).

Recruitment – the contemporary situation

The proportion of female police officers has risen considerably in recent years and women represent 24% of police officers, 44% of PCSOs and 60% of police staff. In some forces women formed a higher percentage of the intake. In Thames Valley Police, for example, they comprised 40% or 45% of recruits (Home Affairs Committee, 2008: para 339). However, the overall figure of female police recruitment fell considerably short of the Home Office target of 35% representation and it has been estimated that it will take another 15 years for women to reach this target unless some form of affirmative action is introduced (Home Affairs Committee, 2008: para 340).

There are, however, significant issues that need to be addressed regarding the recruitment of female police officers. The proportion of female officers in the senior ranks of the service is a cause for concern. Twelve per cent of senior police officers (chief inspector level and above) are women and only five forces in England and Wales are led by female chief constables. This situation has been attributed in part to the length of time it takes to progress through the ranks, which means that the increased intakes of female officers in recent years will take a while to penetrate the highest echelons. Cultural reasons might also account for the relative failure of women to progress even though structural barriers have been removed. Chief Constable Thornton informed the Home Affairs Committee that it was necessary to challenge the idea that leadership in the service entailed being white and male. She argued for more networks and mentoring schemes for female officers (Home Affairs Committee, 2008: para 342).

Reforms affecting women's employment in the police service

A number of reforms have been pursued to improve the status of women in the police service. In 1987 the British Association for Women in Policing was set up. This was open to all ranks and aimed to enhance the role and understanding of the specific needs of women employed in the police service.

One problem concerns the resignation rates of female police officers, which is twice as high as for their male counterparts. One woman in four cites domestic responsibilities as the reason for their leaving the service (Home Affairs Committee, 2008: para 341). One reform to ameliorate this situation is for part-time working and job-sharing to be available to all ranks and grades in order to make employment practices consistent with the requirements of family life (HMIC, 1995: 14).

Career breaks may also help to retain female police officers. A national policy on police career breaks was agreed by the Secretary of State in 2000. This aimed to support the personal needs of staff by providing an extended break from work and ensuring a subsequent return, while maintaining an effective operational capability. Police officers can apply for unpaid career breaks of up to five years. The Home Affairs Committee reported that as at October 2004, 776 police officers were on career breaks. The vast majority of these were police constables, and only one was of the rank of chief superintendent or above. Chief constables are responsible for ensuring that officers on career breaks receive appropriate refresher training and induction into new technology so that they were not disadvantaged on their return to police duties (Home Affairs Committee, 2005: para 150).

Further progress affecting the status of women in the police service will derive from the 2006 Equality Act. This required all public authorities, including the police service, to eliminate unlawful discrimination and harassment and to promote equality of opportunity between men and women in areas such as policy-making, service delivery and employment. The mechanism used by police forces to achieve this is the Gender Equality Scheme.

The treatment of female victims of crime

Discriminatory behaviour towards female police officers by their male colleagues may create a perception of injustice towards female members of the public, especially when they are victims of crime. Crime of this nature is a significant problem, embracing rape, domestic violence and people trafficking. This section examines the manner in which the police service has responded to violence against women.

One of the unintended consequences of the abolition of separate women's police departments was the loss of an orientation that was favourable towards female victims of crime. Serious crimes, such as rape, became routinely investigated by male officers who sometimes lacked the empathy with victims that female officers might have more readily displayed. Evidence for this assertion included the number of instances of domestic violence and sexual assault that were either 'no-crimed' by the police (Gregory and Lees, 1999: 60–66) or, if accepted as a crime, not transmitted to the Crown Prosecution Service (Gregory and Lees, 1999: 68–71).

In 1982 a fly-on-the-wall television documentary, *Police*, publicised the insensitive and inappropriate manner in which officers from the Thames Valley force responded to a complaint of rape. Public outcry arising from this programme resulted in guidance being provided to chief constables concerning the handling of rape cases and the treatment of victims (Home Office, 1983). One practical consequence was the establishment of rape suites.

Individual forces also introduced reforms to the way in which rape investigations were undertaken, including the establishment in 2001 of specialist rape centres (called Sapphire Units) in each of London's 32 boroughs by the Metropolitan Police. These were designed to ensure that any person making an allegation of rape was sympathetically treated. The 2002 Rape Action Plan required all forces to review their facilities for examining victims and specialist training was developed for officers. In addition, Sexual Assault Referral Centres were set up across England and Wales by the police and health services.

Domestic violence is another crime where the victims are frequently women. The response to domestic violence required effective training to foster a greater level of understanding of the needs of victims and to develop the skills and sensitivities necessary to encourage the confidence and cooperation of victims of domestic violence. (Home Office, 1986).

In 1995, it was estimated that there had been 3.29 million incidents of domestic violence against women, 1.86 million of which resulted in physical injury. Women were estimated to have received over 5 million frightening threats in that year. Although it was estimated that men had been the subject of a similar number of assaults (3.25 million), they received far fewer frightening threats (1.98 million) than women (Mirrlees Black, 1999: 22). Pressure on the police service to act robustly with regard to domestic violence was subsequently exerted by government programmes such as the 1998 Crime Reduction Programme. This included the Reducing Violence Against Women Initiative, which focused on domestic violence, rape and sexual assault by perpetrators known to their victims.

Domestic Violence Units became an important aspect of the police's response to this crime. The first of these had been set up by the Metropolitan Police in Tottenham in 1987. The 1990 circular urged chief officers to consider establishing dedicated Domestic Violence Units (Home Office, 1990: 9) and by the end of 1992, 62 of the Metropolitan Police's 69 divisions had set up such units. They were also established in 20 of the remaining 42 police forces (Home Affairs Committee, 1993: para 23). Officers from these units were responsible for cooperating with other agencies, such as Women's Aid, and reflected the need for the police service to become victim-oriented in the sense of accepting women's experiences and understandings of domestic violence (Morley and Mullender, 1994: 26). One difficulty with this approach, however, was that it amounted to hiving off the responsibility for tackling domestic violence on to the specialist units, and this had the effect of marginalising the work, and the officers who performed it, from mainstream policing (Home Affairs Committee, 1993: para 27).

A further report noted that there were wide variations in the scope and content of force policies on domestic violence. The definition of domestic violence was subject to wide variation and standards of performance monitoring were generally poor. A range of organisational models for dealing with domestic violence was found, and it was argued that the line management of domestic violence officers was blurred and that some of these officers felt themselves to be isolated from force structures. Other difficulties that were identified included the frequent lack of accessibility of the records of domestic violence officers (thus undermining their general intelligence potential) and the need to improve the training given to both junior and senior officers on domestic violence (Plotnikoff and Woolfson, 1998: 5–7). It was recommended that the role of domestic violence officers should be more clearly integrated into force structures and that HMIC inspections should continue to assess the quality of forces' arrangements for dealing with this crime (Plotnikoff and Woolfson, 1998: 58).

Findings of this nature prompted the Home Office to revise its 1990 circular on the subject of domestic violence. The new guidance stated that domestic violence was 'a serious crime which is not acceptable, and should be treated as seriously as any other such crime' (Home Office, 2000b: 1). Accordingly, it was stated that the duty of officers attending a domestic incident was to protect the victims and (if applicable) any children from further acts of violence. It was anticipated that the perpetrator would normally be arrested. The Home Office further required a force policy on domestic violence to be drawn up to give guidance to officers regarding how the force prioritised the issue, what standards of investigation were expected and the procedures that should be followed. The police service was also urged to maintain regular contact with victims and keep them informed of developments regarding the case (Home Office, 2000b). Further changes occurred in 2002 when all forces were required to review their facilities for examining victims.

The effectiveness of changes

The above account has argued that during the 1990s the police service made several important changes in the manner in which they responded to female victims of sexual assault and violence. The inclusion of domestic violence in the annual plans of local crime and disorder reduction partnerships might also help to tackle this problem, by providing enhanced police accountability to local communities, and contribute to offsetting the present imbalance of power which is alleged to be prejudiced against women and children (Gregory and Lees, 1999: 216). But problems, nonetheless, remain.

One important omission has been the failure to appreciate that meaningful changes in the orientation of policing towards viewing issues such as rape and domestic violence as key concerns first require the deep-rooted gender assumptions on which policing is based to be addressed (Silvestri, 2003: 184), thereby providing 'a redefined conception of what policing is about' (Walklate, 2004: 171). The failure to embark upon this examination is likely to mean that crimes such as rape and domestic violence will remain on the margins of the police agenda.

Community contact with 'hard to reach' groups

Community contact forms an important role within the police diversity agenda. It typically entails the police establishing mechanisms through which they can liaise with representatives of groups traditionally seen by the service as hard to reach. Community contact has a long history in connection with the police and minority ethnic groups, but more recently the approach has been extended to other groups, including faith communities and gay and lesbian communities.

Faith groups meet regularly to pray in churches, mosques, synagogues, temples and other places of worship and police contact with them is necessary both as a source of information on crimes committed by members of the community within which the faith group is located and also to secure a more effective police response to crimes committed against members of this community. Faith groups may also play an important role in undertaking initiatives (including those involving some form of direct action) that are designed to combat crime and disorder and improve the environmental features within localities. Examples of this include City Links (Manchester), in which a number of different churches have become involved in a range of social action projects associated with the 'redeeming our communities' programme. Another example is that of street pastors. This approach was initiated in 2003 and involves pastors going out in the evenings to try to combat gangs, drugs and gun crime.

The role performed by faith groups has assumed considerable importance in connection with combating terrorism. The Prevent Strategy (the fourth strand of the CONTEST counter-terrorism strategy) emphasises the importance of engagement with Muslim communities, in particular to support those who challenge extremist views, to disrupt those who advocate extremism and to support those who are vulnerable to the extremist message. Faith and community leaders can play an important role in activities of this nature, although one potential danger is that those who perform such a role may lose credibility within their own communities if they are seen to be a part of a police surveillance network.

Community contact was traditionally conducted at force or divisional level but neighbourhood policing teams now often form an important link between faith groups and the police service. However, the practice adopted by individual forces is subject to considerable variation. In Leicestershire, multi-agency Joint Action Forums have been set up at neighbourhood level.

Contact with lesbian, gay, bisexual and transgender (LGBT) communities is a responsibility placed on crime and disorder reduction partnerships. Contact is conducted in a number of different ways. Liaison officers, typically at divisional level, may perform work of this nature, establishing links with relevant LGBT groups. Formalised consultative arrangements (such as the Greater Manchester Lesbian and Gay Police Initiative) may also be used as a means of establishing contact with LGBT communities. Such consultations can aid the formulation of local policing plans and, as such, play a vital role in partnership mechanisms. In the West Country, for example, Intercom is an LGBT community resource that provides help against homophobic and transphobic prejudice, crime and discrimination. It works in partnership with agencies that include the police, local government and health authorities.

QUESTION

Why did the Macpherson report fail to eradicate institutional racism within the police service?

To answer this question you should:

- Identify what Macpherson understood by the term 'institutional racism' as it applied to the police service and the problems that arose as a consequence of this;
- Evaluate the key reforms proposed in the Macpherson report that were designed to tackle this problem;
- Discuss the impact of these reforms on the subsequent operations of the police service, including an assessment of evidence that suggested that progress in eliminating institutional racism was limited;
- Analyse why Macpherson's reforms failed to completely eradicate the problem of institutional racism in the police service;
- Evaluate what further reforms or approaches are needed to solve this problem.

REFERENCES

Anthias, F. (1999) 'Institutional Racism, Power and Accountability', *Sociological Research Online* 4 (1) www.socresonline.org.uk/4/lawrence/anthias.html [accessed on 2 March 2009].

Ascoli, D. (1975) *The Queen's Peace*. London: Hamish Hamilton.

Association of Chief Police officers, Association of Police Authorities and Home Office (2004) *A Strategy for Improving Performance in Race and Diversity 2004–2009*. London: Home Office.

Association of Chief Police Officers, Association of Police Authorities and Home Office (2005) *Race Equality Programme for the Police Service*. London: Home Office.

Baird, L. (1920) *Report of the Committee on the Employment of Women in Police Dutie*. Cm 877. London: HMSO.

Bennetto, J. (2009) *Police and Racism: What has been Achieved 10 Years after the Stephen Lawrence Inquiry Report?* London: Equality and Human Rights Commission.

Bland, N., Mundy, G., Russell, J. and Tuffin, R. (1999) *Career Progression of Ethnic Minority Police Officers*. Home Office Police Research Series Paper 107. London: Home Office Research, Development and Statistics Directorate.

Bowling, B. and Phillips, C. (2002) *Racism, Crime and Justice*. Harlow: Longman.

Bridgeman, W. (1924) *Report of the Departmental Committee on the Employment of Police Women*. Cm 2224. London: HMSO.

Bullock, S. and Gunning, N. (2007) *Police Service Strength England and Wales, 31 March 2007*. Research Development and Statistics Bulletin 13/07. London: Home Office.

Calvert-Smith, D. (2004) *A Formal Investigation of the Police Service in England and Wales: An Interim Report*. London: Commission for Racial Equality.

Calvert-Smith, D. (2005) *A Formal Investigation of the Police Service in England and Wales: Final Report*. London: Commission for Racial Equality.

Chahal, K. (1999) 'The Stephen Lawrence Inquiry Report, Racist Harassment, Racist Incidents: Changing Definitions, Clarifying Meaning?' *Sociological Research Online* 4 (1), www.socresonline.org.uk/4/lawrence/chahal.html [accessed on 2 March 2009].

Chan, J. (1997) *Changing Police Culture: Policing in a Multicultural Society*. Cambridge: Cambridge University Press.

Coaker, V. (2008) *Policing Minister's Assessment of Minority Ethnic Recruitment, Retention and Progression in the Police Service: A Paper for the Home Secretary*. London: Home Office, Research, Development and Statistics Directorate.

Commission for Racial Equality (2005) *Formal Investigation into the Police Service in England and Wales*. London: Commission for Racial Equality.

Crown Prosecution Service (2007) *Racist and Religious Incident Monitoring*. London: Crown Prosecution Service.

Docking, M. (2003) *Public Perceptions of Police Accountability and Decision-making*. Home Office Online Report 38/03. London: Home Office.

Dodd, V. and Travis, A. (2005) 'Muslims Face Increased Stop and Search', *The Guardian*, 2 March.

Fielding, N. (1994) 'Cop Canteen Culture', in T. Newburn and E. Stanko (eds), *Just Boys Doing Business: Masculinity and Crime*. London: Routledge.

Fitzgerald, M. (2001) 'Ethnic Minorities and Community Safety', in R. Matthews and J. Pitts (eds), *Crime, Disorder and Community Safety: A New Agenda*. London: Routledge.

Fitzgerald, M. and Sibbitt, R. (1997) *Ethnic Monitoring in Police Forces: A Beginning*. Home Office Research Study 173. London: Home Office Research and Statistics Directorate.

Gilborn, D. (2008) *Racism and Education: Coincidence or Conspiracy?* London: Routledge.

Gregory, J. and Lees, S. (1999) *Policing Sexual Assault.* London: Routledge.

Gutzmore, C. (1983) 'Capital, Black Youth and Crime', *Race and Class*, XXV (2), Autumn: 13–30.

Heidensohn, F. (1992) *Women in Control? The Role of Women in Law Enforcement.* Oxford: Clarendon Press.

Her Majesty's Inspectorate of Constabulary (1993) *Equal Opportunities in the Police Service.* London: Home Office.

Her Majesty's Inspectorate of Constabulary (1995) *Developing Diversity in the Police Service: Equal Opportunities: Thematic Report.* London: Home Office.

Her Majesty's Inspectorate of Constabulary, (1997) *Winning the Race: Policing Plural Communities, HMIC Thematic Report on Police Community and Race Relations 1996/97.* London: Home Office.

Her Majesty's Inspectorate of Constabulary (2000) *Winning the Race: Policing Plural Communities Revisited. A Follow up to the Thematic Inspection Report on Police Community and Race Relations 1998/99.* London: Home Office.

Her Majesty's Inspectorate of Constabulary (2003) *Diversity Matters: HM Inspectorate of Constabulary Thematic Inspection, Executive Summary.* London: Home Office.

Her Majesty's Inspectorate of Constabulary (2008) *Duty Calls: Race Equality Inspection – Closing Commentary.* London: HMIC.

Hillier, M. (2008) Speech in the House of Commons, 29 February, HC Debs, Vol 472, Col 1429–30.

Hinsliff, G. (2004) 'White Police Claim Racism', *The Observer*, 22 August.

Holdaway, S. (1996) *The Racialisation of British Policing.* Basingstoke: Macmillan.

Home Affairs Committee (1993) *Domestic Violence.* Third Report, Session 1992–03. House of Commons Paper 245. London: HMSO.

Home Affairs Committee (2005) *Police Reform.* Fourth Report, Session 2004–05. House of Commons Paper 370. London: TSO.

Home Affairs Committee (2008) *Policing in the Twenty-first Century.* Seventh Report, Session 2007–08. House of Commons Paper 364. London: TSO.

Home Affairs Committee (2009) *The Macpherson Report – Ten Years On.* Twelfth Report, Session 2008–09. House of Commons Paper 427. London: TSO.

Home Office (1981) *The Brixton Disorders, 10–12 April 1981: Report of an Inquiry by the Rt. Hon. The Lord Scarman*, OBE. Cmnd 8427. London: HMSO.

Home Office (1983) *Investigation of Offences of Rape.* Circular 25/83. London: Home Office.

Home Office (1986) *Violence Against Women: Treatment of Victims of Rape and Domestic Violence.* Circular 69/86. London: Home Office.

Home Office (1990) *Domestic Violence.* Circular 60/90. London: Home Office.

Home Office (1998) *Statistics on Race and the Criminal Justice System.* London: Home Office, Research and Statistics Directorate.

Home Office (1999) *The Stephen Lawrence Inquiry: Report of an Inquiry by Sir William Macpherson of Cluny.* Cm 4262. London: TSO.

Home Office (2000a) *Complaints Against the Police: A Consultative Paper.* London: Home Office Police Operational Unit.

Home Office (2000b) *Domestic Violence*. Circular 19/2000. London: Home Office.

Home Office (2002) *The National Policing Plan 2003–2006*. London: Home Office Communications Directorate.

Home Office (2008a) *The Police (Conduct) Regulations 2008: Standards of Professional Behaviour*. London: Home Office.

Home Office (2008b) *Police and Criminal Evidence Act 1984 CODE A*. London: Home Office. [Online] www.police.homeoffice.gov.uk/publications/operational-policing/pace-code-a-amended-jan-2009?view=Binary [accessed on 22 March 2009].

Hopkins, N. (2002) 'Met Winning the Battle Against Prejudice', *The Guardian*, 22 February.

Institute of Race Relations (1991) *Deadly Silence: Black Deaths in Custody*. London: Institute of Race Relations.

Jones, A. and Singer, L. (2008) *Statistics on Race and the Criminal Justice System, 2006/7*. London: Ministry of Justice.

Jones, S. (1986) *Policewomen and Equality, Formal Policy versus Informal Practice*. Basingstoke: Macmillan.

Joyce, P. (2002) *The Politics of Protest: Extra-parliamentary Politics in Britain since 1970*. Basingstoke: Palgrave.

Kirkwood, A. (1998) *Crown Prosecution Service: Racial Incident Monitoring, Annual Report 1997–1998* (amended version). York: Crown Prosecution Service.

Lea, J. (2003) 'Institutional Racism in Policing: The Macpherson Report and its Consequences', in R. Matthews and J. Young (eds), *The New Politics of Crime and Punishment*. Collumpton, Devon: Willan Publishing.

Miller, J., Bland, N. and Quinton, P. (2000) *The Impact of Stops and Searches on Crime and the Community*. Police Research Series Paper 127. London: Home Office.

Mirrlees Black, C. (1999) *Domestic Violence*. Research, Development and Statistics Directorate Report, Home Office Research Study 191. London: Home Office.

Morley, R. and Mullender, A. (1994) *Preventing Domestic Violence*. Police Research Group, Crime Prevention Unit Series, Paper 48. London: Home Office.

Morris, Sir W. (2004) *The Case for Change: People in the Metropolitan Police Service – The Report of the Morris Inquiry*. London: TSO.

Plotnikoff, J. and Woolfson, R. (1998) *Policing Domestic Violence: Effective Organisational Structures*. London: Home Office, Research, Development and Statistics Directorate, Policing and Reducing Crime Unit.

Police Federation (2008) *Stop and Search*. Police Federation. [Online] www.polfed.org/federationpolicy/AB450E0CE3204B528A180C4BCE922FE3.htm [accessed 2 March 2009].

Powell, R. (2004) quoted in *The Observer*, 22 August.

Quinton, P. and Bland, N. (1999) *Modernising the Tactic: Improving the Use of Stop and Search*. Briefing Note Number 2/99. London: Home Office Research, Development and Statistics Directorate, Police and Reducing Crime Unit.

Rollock, N. (2009) *The Stephen Lawrence Inquiry 10 Years On: An Analysis of the Literature*. London: The Runnymede Trust.

Royal Commission on Police Powers and Procedure (1929) *Report of the Royal Commission on Police Powers and Procedure*. Cm 3297. London: HMSO.

Silvestri, M. (2003) *Women in Charge: Policing, Gender and Leadership*. Cullompton, Devon: Willan Publishing.

Skidelsky, R. (2000) 'The Age of Inequality', in D. Green (ed.), *Institutional Racism and the Police: Fact or Fiction?* London: Institute for the Study of Civil Society.

Smith, D. and Gray, J. (1983) *Police and People in London.* London: Policy Studies Institute.

Statewatch (1998) 'UK: Stop and Search and Arrest and Racism', 8 (3/4), May–August.

Statewatch (1999) 'The Cycle of UK Racism – Stop, Search, Arrest and Imprisonment', 9 (1), January–February.

Straw, J. (1999a) Speech at Gloucester, 1 March, quoted in *The Guardian*, 2 March.

Straw, J. (1999b) Speech to a conference of chief constables, Southampton, 14 April.

Straw, J. (1999c) *Race Equality – the Home Secretary's Employment Targets.* London: Home Office.

Straw, J. (2009) BBC TV *Politics Show*, cited in A. Topping, 'Met Police No Longer Institutionally Racist, says Straw', *The Guardian*, 23 February, p. 8.

Taylor, B. (2005) *Review of Police Disciplinary Arrangements Report.* London: Home Office.

Teather, S. (2008) Speech in the House of Commons, 29 February, HC Debs, Vol 472, Col 1430.

Travis, A. (2003) 'Police Racism Need Not Lead to Dismissal', *The Guardian,* 11 August.

Walklate, S. (2004) *Gender, Crime and Criminal Justice* (2nd edition). Cullompton, Devon: Willan Publishing.

Willis, C. (2000) 'Foreword', in J. Miller, N. Bland and P. Quinton, *The Impact of Stops and Searches on Crime and the Community.* Police Research Series Paper 127. London: Home Office.

Wilson, A. (1983) 'Conspiracies to Assault', *New Statesman*, 105 (2/10), 22 February.

8

The police and politics

████████████████ CHAPTER AIMS ████████████████

The aims of this chapter are:

- To examine the transition of the police as servants of local elites to becoming state functionaries;
- To identify the police as defenders of the state against those who pose a threat to it, specifically considering the policing of protest;
- To evaluate the concept of paramilitary policing;
- To discuss the role of the police as political actors and to consider the role of the key police staff associations in this context.

The police service and the state

It was argued in Chapter 1 that the police performed an array of functions during the nineteenth century that were concerned with providing services to the communities in which they operated. These activities might on occasions assume political significance, for example in policing demonstrations on political reform or in dealing with industrial disputes. However, in order to avoid the impression that the new policing system was similar to the 'Bourbon' style of activity, in which civil and political liberties were undermined by a complex system of spying, police interventions of this nature were traditionally justified by the need to preserve public order in the interests of all citizens.

Local police involvement in such activities was extended during the twentieth century. Functions performed in the interests of (and sometimes at the behest of) local elites now became activities carried out on behalf of the state. The extent to which this departed from the principle of serving the community is flavoured by political opinion concerning the nature of the state – whether it reflects the interests of all (or the majority of) its members (a view held by liberals), or whether it serves the interests of those who wield power and who use the state to further their own economic and political interests (an opinion held by Marxists).

Marxists assert that the distancing of the police and the working class following the end of the First World War was achieved through the enactment of the 1919 Police Act, which was responsible for transforming the police into state functionaries, the coercive arm of the state. This view argued that in order to cope with the economic and political unrest of the inter-war years, 'state influence on the police institution became more pronounced' (Brogden, 1982: 102). It resulted in the police service becoming part of the state's weaponry to defeat those whose actions threatened to bring about its downfall and institute a new social order.

Subsequently, this opinion argues that the police have performed a number of activities in connection with acting as guardians of the state, taking offensive action against those who threaten to undermine it through political activities such as industrial disputes, direct action and demonstrations. It has also been alleged that the police 'have consistently assumed responsibility for enforcing moral conformity' (Bowden, 1978: 72). This stance is justified since 'history shows that the loosening of moral bonds is often the first stage of disintegration, so that society is justified in taking the same steps to preserve its moral code as it does to preserve its government and other essential institutions' (Bowden, 1978: 76).

Liberals contend that when the police intervene in activities such as political events or industrial disputes they do so in the interests of the majority of citizens, seeking to uphold the law and maintain order against those who seek to impose their will, often through coercive means, on the majority.

The policing of protest

The policing of protest is a specialist area of police work. It is especially associated with dealing with all forms of extra-parliamentary political activity, including industrial disputes, riots, demonstrations, civil disobedience and direct action, or what has been referred to as 'the politics of contention' (Waddington, 2003: 415).

Legislative changes

The key piece of legislation shaping police powers to combat public disorder was the 1936 Public Order Act. Deficiencies in this legislation (for example, it dealt with a limited range of extra-parliamentary political activities and the organisers were not compelled to give the police advance warning of their intentions to protest) prompted post-1979 Conservative governments to pass the 1986 Public Order Act and the 1994 Criminal Justice and Public Order Act. These increased police powers in relation to public order events.

The main powers currently possessed by the police in connection with protests (derived from information adapted from Joint Committee on Human Rights, 2009: 8–30) are:

- *The 1986 Public Order Act*: this outlined the procedures that must be followed by the organisers of a march or procession and the powers possessed by the police in relation to both mobile and static protests (such as a counter-demonstration). Protest organisers are normally required to give advance notice to the police of a march (but not a static protest or assembly). The police may impose conditions on processions either before or during the event.
- *The 1994 Criminal Justice and Public Order Act*: this measure was especially directed at the activities of hunt saboteurs, new age travellers and youth subcultures. The police were given new powers to regulate 'collective trespass or nuisance on land'. The new offences were *aggravated trespass, trespass on land* and *trespassory assembly* and they applied to common or privately-owned land and scheduled monuments. Bans on trespassory assemblies could be imposed for a period of up to four days (provided the local authority agreed) and persons whom the police suspected of seeking to attend such a banned event could be directed not to proceed. The police were also given powers to regulate 'raves'.
- *The 2005 Serious Organised Crime and Police Act*: this criminalised protests, whether static or moving, that took place within the vicinity of Parliament or other designated areas without prior notification to, and authorisation by, the police. The measure also made it an offence to trespass on certain designated sites (such as nuclear facilities) where the Home Secretary felt this action would threaten national security.
- *Stop and search powers* contained in the 1984 Police and Criminal Evidence Act and section 44 of the 2000 Terrorism Act.
- *Breach of the peace*: this derives from common law and provides the police with the power of arrest which, on occasions (such as the intercept policy employed during the miners' dispute) had been used pre-emptively. However, this is now less likely to occur following the House of Lords judgment (*R. Laporte*) *V. Chief Constable of Gloucestershire Constabulary*) in 2007 when it was ruled that a breach of the peace had to be imminent in order to invoke breach of the peace powers.
- *Civil injunctions obtained under the 1997 Protection from Harassment Act*: this may be used, for example, to restrict protest outside company premises. Conservative industrial relations legislation also contained a number of civil remedies for those threatened with industrial action.

Although it has been suggested that formal powers that include imposing conditions on protest are not widely used (Joint Committee on Human Rights, 2009: 12), organisations such as the National Union of Journalists have argued that police actions in the early years of the twenty-first century displayed a concern to control and prevent demonstrations through other measures, including the filming of both protesters and journalists and the over-zealous use of stop and search powers (Dear, 2009; Joint Committee on Human Rights, 2009: 13). Informal methods that include the use of the 'ways and means act' have also been employed to prevent demonstrators from reaching their destinations.

Mutual aid

Mutual aid entails one chief constable calling on another for assistance. Requests of this nature are usually made in connection with public order events. Mutual aid was initially organised on an *ad hoc* basis until the 1890 Police Act formalised the practice, enabling police forces voluntarily to enter into standing arrangements to supply officers to each other in the event of major disorder. The arrangements governing mutual aid were not significantly altered until 1964, when section 14(2) of the 1964 Police Act effectively made it obligatory for forces to come to the aid of another to provide an effective response to public disorder.

The decision to apply for mutual aid, and from where to seek it, was initially in the hands of a chief constable faced with disorder. However, following the success of the National Union of Miners in forcing the closure of Saltley Coke Depot during the 1972 miners' dispute, when the local City of Birmingham police force was over-whelmed by the number of pickets, these matters have been determined centrally.

In that year, ACPO established a mechanism that was initially known as the National Reporting Centre (NRC) and later termed the Mutual Aid Coordination Centre (or MACC). This body operated from New Scotland Yard, was operationally under the control of ACPO's president and was acti-vated when an event that posed major implications for public order. Its role was to coordinate the deployment of police officers from across the country to the area affected by disorder. This arrangement was utilised in the 1984–85 miners' dispute, where it was viewed as a key aspect of a centralised system of policing (Bunyan, 1985: 298–299).

A related body, the National Information Centre (NIC), was available to coor-dinate and disseminate information between police forces in connection with events that posed the potential for public disorder, but where it was thought the widespread use of mutual aid was not required. An example of this occurred when the Pope's visited Britain in 1982.

The coordination of policing public order events was further developed with the 1999 millennium celebrations, the 2000 fuel protests and the responses to post-9/11 events in 2001. A new body, the Police National Information and Coordination Centre (PNICC) was created. This was initially formed on a tempo-rary, *ad hoc* basis under the control of the president of ACPO but later became a permanent body responsible for the coordination of mutual aid in connection with public disorder or other incidents such as a major disaster.

Public order specialism in the police service

In addition to reforms associated with mutual aid, developments have also occurred in the way in which the police service is trained and equipped to deal with such incidents and to implement the powers with which they have been provided.

Specialist public order units

Since the 1960s a number of police forces developed units that were not tied to a specific division or involved with implementing routine police functions but that operated anywhere within a force's boundaries. These units have been extensively utilised in public order situations in addition to dealing with crime-related matters. An early example of this was the Metropolitan Police's Special Patrol Group, which was initially established as the Special Patrol Group Unit in 1961 and renamed the Special Patrol Group in 1965. The SPG played a leading role in policing demonstrations during the 1970s (for example, at Red Lion Square in 1974 and at Southall in 1979).

These units posed a number of difficulties: they lacked local knowledge and sensitivity to the people of an area in which they were deployed; they were frequently associated with heavy-handed and aggressive policing (National Council for Civil Liberties, 1980: 169); and by virtue of possessing their own command structure they operated independently of the main policing operation that was being conducted, resulting in confusion. Criticisms of this nature ,and events in Southall in 1979, led to the replacement of the Metropolitan Police's SPG with District Support Units and later with Territorial Support Groups. These were located within each of the Metropolitan Police districts and were thus more locally oriented than their predecessors. Other forces, however, have retained a centralised specialist unit, such as the Tactical Aid Unit of the Greater Manchester Police.

Police Support Units

Specialist public order units have been augmented by Police Support Units (PSUs). These consist of uniformed police officers (organised at divisional level) whose main role is to perform routine police duties but who receive public order training on a regular basis. They train together as a unit and are available for deployment in public order situations when the need arises. Training is delivered according to ACPO national standards and embraces three levels. Officers trained to level 1 standards receive public order training every five weeks whereas those trained to level 2 standards receive training twice each year. Level 3 training embraces a basic introduction to public order methods and is delivered at training schools.

Equipment and weaponry

Initially, police forces were ill-equipped to handle the public order problems that surfaced during the 1970s and 1980s. This deficiency was apparent at Notting Hill in 1976 when officers were attacked by missiles thrown by a hostile crowd and were forced to improvise their own defence using items such as dustbin lids and traffic cones. Three hundred and twenty-five police officers suffered injuries (Thackrah, 1985: 149). This event led to the issue of riot shields, which were first deployed in a demonstration against a National Front procession at Lewisham the following year (P. Waddington, 1987: 39).

The 1981 riots prompted further developments in equipment, including protective helmets. The use of petrol bombs in 1981 also resulted in the future availability of flameproof overalls to police officers (Reiner, 1991: 171), following pressure from ACPO and the Police Federation. Other developments affecting equipment during the 1980s included the provision of shin guards and longer truncheons that could be used with short shields. The 1983 ACPO Training Manual listed nine items of protective clothing that officers should wear when dealing with serious disorders. These included riot helmet and visor, fire resistant overalls and any additional body protection that forces considered necessary. The murder of PC Keith Blakelock in the 1985 Broadwater Farm Estate riot prompted a consideration of issuing body armour to the police for protection against knife attack, although this was not adopted at that time. Baton rounds were also made available in that year (P. Waddington, 1987: 39).

Key developments affecting weaponry included the use of CS gas against rioters (in Toxteth, 1981), baton charges (at the National Graphical Association–*Warrington Messenger* dispute in 1983) and the deployment of police horses against crowds (at Orgreave in 1984).

An important issue with weaponry and equipment concerns when the decision to use them is taken. Their availability may prompt a premature decision to deploy them, that is before an incident occurs to justify their use. This may result in a more confrontational police response than was required which may in turn adversely affect the mood of the crowd and prompt further disorder.

However, judgements as to whether police actions at a particular event were proportionate to the behaviour of the participants are frequently based upon hindsight analysis rather than an evaluation of circumstances as they were unfolding. Police commanders at public order events are fully aware that Health and Safety legislation applies to their own officers as well as to members of the public and this may influence decisions relating to equipment, weaponry and tactics that may later be regarded as unwarranted and depicted as measures designed to deter protest.

Tactics

Changes affecting weaponry and equipment had implications for the tactics used by the police at crowd situations. Initially, the tactics deployed by the police at public order events were non-confrontational. The post-war period was epitomised by a style of public order policing that aimed at 'winning by appearing to lose' (a policy that was based upon securing public sympathy for the police). It entailed activities such as gently picking up demonstrators who had mounted a 'sit down' protest or using the time honoured tactic of 'push and shove' (especially at industrial disputes), in which officers linked together (in either a straight line or a wedge formation) in the 'butcher's grip'.

The mounting violence experienced at public order events, commencing at the Grosvenor Square demonstration in 1968, prompted significant changes to the way in which the police responded to these events. A key deficiency was the absence of any defined police strategy to deal with disorder, especially if this was spontaneous disorder. Officers on the scene had to improvise and formulate tactics without any master plan to guide their conduct. This deficiency was tackled with the publication in 1983 of ACPO's *Public Order Manual of Tactical Operations and Related Matters*.

Each force was issued with a binder that contained 'a detailed analysis of the stages of a riot and the police responses appropriate to them'. A total of 238 tactics and manoeuvres were set out in its 30 sections 'arranged in order of escalating force, from normal policing up to plastic bullets, CS gas and live firearms' (Northam, 1989: 42). These new tactics included the deployment of static lines of officers behind large shields (5'5" high and 24" wide) and snatch squads composed of officers carrying smaller shields who would go into crowds to arrest offenders.

The publication of the *Public Order Manual* in 1983 was preceded by the formation of an ACPO body, the Public Order Forward Planning Group, to review all new developments and emerging tactics. Other centralised developments followed this ACPO initiative, including the formation of a Central Intelligence Unit during the miners' dispute, 1984–85, to analyse intelligence gathered by officers on the ground. The ACPO manual has subsequently been replaced by the 2007 *ACPO Manual of Guidance on Keeping the Peace*.

Improved managerial control

A key problem associated with public order events during the early part of the 1980s was that senior commanders lacked training in managing the large numbers of police officers that were placed under their command in public order events. How could police commanders relay instructions to their officers and enforce their directions?

One development affecting managerial control over public order events has been the introduction (in the wake of the 1984 Libyan Embassy siege) of the Gold/Silver/Bronze hierarchy of command. This sought to provide an effective chain of command and improve the control and coordination of police resources at public order events.

The Gold commander is responsible for setting the overall policing strategy for the event, the Silver commander is charged with implementing this strategy on the ground and the Bronze commanders exercise responsibility for specific territorial areas and authority over the officers who were allocated to policing them. One aim of this system was to exert more effective supervision over police officers and guard against undisciplined actions at these events. Technology such as close-circuit television has also been increasingly used to police public order events, enabling commanders to secure an overall view of an event and respond to problems wherever these arise. Improved organisation underpinned by technology has greatly improved the ability of the police commanders to control crowd situations.

Intelligence

A number of initiatives have been undertaken that seek to pre-empt problems before they erupt into disorder. These include the use of tension indicators.

The 1983 ACPO *Training Manual* listed eight tension indicators which included the increase in disturbances between groups or gangs and racial attacks, and enjoined officers to keep their ears to the ground to gather intelligence related to public order situations. Observations relating to heightened tensions would form the basis for pre-emptive police action, which might take the form of 'saturation policing' and involved techniques to ensure that the police enjoyed numerical and physical supremacy in the affected area. It was hoped that the spectre of well-trained, disciplined police officers would exert a profound psychological impact to deter disorder. Saturation policing might be accompanied by a range of other tactics, such as the use of cordons and interception tactics to prevent crowds from converging on a hot spot.

However, this form of policing may be seen as a form of harassment or provocation by those on the receiving end of it and could result in a violent response. As a result, more recent developments include the use of rumour management and various forms of community engagement. These activities may be conducted by the police in partnership with other agencies, such as local government, and seek to defuse tensions that have in the past resulted in violent confrontations between the police and public.

Intelligence may also be derived from other sources. The unwillingness of some groups who utilise extra-parliamentary forms of political activity to enter into consultation with the police regarding specific events may justify the use of informants to provide information of this nature. Although such activities reflect the 'spying' that early nineteenth-century police reform sought to avoid, it may enable the police to differentiate between various groups who jointly participate in contemporary forms of protest and adjust their methods of policing accordingly.

The style of public order policing

The nature of the police response to various forms of protest has undergone a number of changes in the period since 1979. The main trends affecting this are discussed below.

The Thatcher years (1979–1990) and 'escalated force'

The 1980s have been depicted as the 'decade of disorder' (Joyce, 1992: 232). Changes affecting the policing of protest occurred within a political context that favoured a more aggressive response, to which the term 'escalated force' has been applied (D. Waddington, 2007: 10). A Marxist view refers to the emergence of the 'strong state', which was depicted as the inevitable consequence of the introduction of the free market economic policies after the Conservative 1979 general election victory. This entailed the state and agencies such as the police developing the capacity to counter the opposition mounted by those who were adversely affected by economic policies or who sought to orchestrate challenges to them

(Hall, 1980; Gamble, 1988). These were the working class who bore the brunt of the fall in living standards through inflation and who were the first to experience unemployment (Bunyan, 1977: 277).

Their reaction to the loss of established rights was mounted through 'a whole panoply of public order challenges' (Brewer et al., 1996: xiv), including demonstrations, direct action, industrial disputes and riots (see Joyce, 2002). Their challenge to the authority of the government was depicted as a challenge to the legitimacy of the state, and the police were able to utilise the additional powers with which they had been provided and the new tactics and methods of crowd control that they had developed in the knowledge that aggressive actions to quell dissent would be endorsed by the government.

Changes in the 1990s – 'negotiated management'

The 1990s were characterised by a more sensitive form of policing protest, underpinned by an approach that has been described as 'a negotiated management style'. This involved 'a greater respect for the "rights" of protesters, a more tolerant approach to community disruption, closer communication and cooperation with the public, a reduced tendency to make arrests (particularly as a tactic of first resort) and application of only the minimum force required in order to control a situation' (D. Waddington, 2007: 10).

There were several reasons that explained the shift away from escalated force, in particular a perception that what public opinion deemed to be an overly aggressive response by the police service at public order events did the image, and ultimately the legitimacy, of the service harm. Changes to public order legislation (especially the advance notice requirement that was contained in the 1986 Public Order Act) also encouraged police and protesters to meet and negotiate issues such as the route of an event. The absence of discussions on matters of this nature had previously contributed to disorder.

A differentiated response

Although the introduction of negotiated management during the 1990s characterised the future police response to protest, there have been variations to this approach, resulting in a differentiated police response to protest. This situation has led to the conclusion that the 'nature of contemporary public order policing is too variable and complicated to lend itself to trite or superficial analysis' (D. Waddington, 2007: 5).

The anti-capitalist movement in particular remained on the receiving end of aggressive forms of policing that entailed the use of new tactics such as 'kettling' or corralling (whereby crowds were cordoned off into confined spaces and retained there for long periods of time with attempts sometimes being made by the police to collect the names and addresses of the protesters) in conjunction with the use of batons and snatch squads (D. Waddington, 2007: 3). The G20 protests in 2009, for example, were aggressively handled by the police, some of whom removed their identification numbers and indulged in acts of gratuitous violence towards protesters, including women.

It might thus be concluded that the stance of the police towards protest is influenced by a range of factors which exert a positive or negative view being taken towards specific events. These include the willingness of protesters to obey police instructions or requests and the track record of an organisation that has been involved in previous protests. In this respect, a distinction has been drawn between contained and transgressive protests (Noakes, et al., 2005: 247–248). The former embraces groups that are willing to abide by the rules of the game. They are likely to be treated differently from protesters whose attitudes are perceived as less cooperative and antagonistic towards the police, and who are unwilling to enter into a dialogue with them regarding a specific event. Episodes that the police were unable to control, such as the 1999 Stop the City demonstration, exerted an important influence on the policing of subsequent events associated with the anti-capitalist movement.

A range of other factors may also influence the way in which protest is policed (D. Waddington, 2007: 15). These include the influence of politicians over police actions (an issue that is considered more fully below in connection with politicisation) and the influence of public opinion, as reflected in the media.

The media's interpretation of an event may have a considerable impact on how the police handle it. Media portrayals of the fuel protesters in 2000 being widely supported, coupled with the absence of pressure being placed upon the police service by the government in the early days of the protest, were important factors in explaining the laid-back nature of the initial police response. Conversely, later media arguments that this protest posed a threat to the operations of the NHS and government pressure on the petrol companies to commence the delivery of fuel contributed to the public's acceptance of a more robust police action, including the police escorting tankers to forecourt points of delivery.

Paramilitary policing

Paramilitary policing has been described as 'the application of (quasi)military training, equipment and organisation to questions of policing (whether under central control or not)' (Jefferson, 1990: 16). This section evaluates the key aspects of this style of policing.

Aggressive police behaviour

Paramilitary policing has sometimes been equated with aggressive policing in which protesters are subjected to a violent police response. This view of paramilitary policing suggests the use of coercive means that are designed to quell manifestations of dissent: 'armed with new powers, possessing new equipment and coordinated on a national basis ... they appear unfamiliar and discomfiting: less a part of society: more apart from it' (Brewer et al,1996: 6). In 1984 the methods used by the police at Orgreave (during the 1984–5 miners' dispute) were alleged to have witnessed 'the unveiling of colonial policing tactics in mainland Britain' (Northam, 1989: 59) following the adoption of methods used by the Hong Kong police (Northam, 1989: 39–40). It has been alleged that the presence at a specific incident of police officers who are dressed and equipped as if they are 'looking for trouble' has the potential to exacerbate violence (Jefferson, 1987: 51–53) and may actually provoke it or legitimise the use of violence by a crowd (Saunders, 1996: 118).

The above opinion thus suggests that paramilitary policing set aside the historic principle of minimum force (Brewer et al.,1996: 22), which was characterised by 'conventionally uniformed officers tolerantly pushing and shoving in defensive formation against lines of pickets or demonstrators (D. Waddington, 1996: 1). However, this opinion has been challenged by arguments that suggest that the changes to police methods introduced in the latter decades of the twentieth century were reactive in nature, and were prompted as a response to the violence to which police officers were often subjected. These changes did not undermine the concept of minimum force, but the baseline was altered so that what constitutes a 'minimum' level of force was pushed upwards in response to the violence associated with protest. Police actions continued to be based upon the under-enforcement of the law and the use of discretion (Reiner, 1998: 46).

It has further been argued that aggression did not become a universal feature of the policing of all public order events during the 1980s. Similar events (for example, the policing of picket lines during the 1984–85 miners' dispute) frequently witnessed a different outcome in terms of disorder. Explanations for this situation included the interaction between protesters and the police at what the flashpoint model referred to as the 'interactional' level (D. Waddington et al., 1989). This was heavily reliant on the calibre of leadership displayed by both police and protesters at these sorts of events.

Improved command and control

Arguments that equate paramilitary policing with an aggressive police response at public order events emphasise weaponry, tactics and training as the key aspects of this style of policing. This view, however, presents an incomplete account of the range of developments with which paramilitary policing is associated (P. Waddington, 1987; King and Brearley, 1996: 87–93).

Particular attention has been drawn to the importance to paramilitary policing of command and control systems that enable 'a more disciplined approach to disorderly and violent situations than is possible by traditional methods (P. Waddington, 1993: 353; see also P. Waddington,1987). The improved central planning and supervision of public order events by police forces using trained personnel acting 'under hierarchical command in accordance with a formulated strategy and tactics' (P. Waddington, 1993: 366) enhance the degree of control that senior officers are able to exert over officers deployed in public order situations, suppress the discretion of individual officers and undermine the influence that subcultural values might otherwise exert over their actions (P. Waddington, 1993: 357).

Why might aggressive policing occur?

The above view has suggested that aggressive police behaviour is not an inherent feature of paramilitary policing. Nonetheless, violence and confrontation sometimes arise at public order events. This section seeks to explain why aggressive police behaviour may arise if it is not an indispensable aspect of paramilitary policing.

A desire based on professional pride not to be overwhelmed and defeated by protesters may make for aggressive tactics, especially if aggression or violence is displayed towards the police by protesters with an anti-authoritarian disposition who view them as the embodiment of a state they wish to overthrow. A tendency by the police to act aggressively may be exacerbated when large numbers of officers are deployed at a specific event. This may result in 'excessive aggression' if police officers become emboldened by a sense of power derived from their weight of numbers (Alderson, 1979: 25).

Aggressive actions are further influenced by ineffective mechanisms of accountability governing the actions of rank-and-file police officers when deployed in public order situations. This is especially likely to arise if centralised command and control breaks down, releasing officers from the constraints imposed upon their behaviour by their senior commanders and leaving their actions subject only to the gaze of public scrutiny.

The uniform donned by officers at public order events of this nature makes officers more anonymous, and hence less accountable for their actions, than is the case when they operate within their communities. The sense of anonymity has sometimes been increased by practices such as removing identification numbers. In the an absence of evidence on which to bring charges, even in cases where severe problems have arisen resulting in the death of members of the public, complaints against the behaviour of officers engaged in dealing with protests are unlikely to be upheld. In 2004, for example, the IPCC and CPS concluded that six officers had committed criminal offences against demonstrators involved in the Countryside Alliance demonstration. One officer was acquitted at a magistrates' court, two by juries at Crown Courts and the CPS discontinued the remaining cases (Hardwick, 2009). The apparent weaknesses of legal accountability may help to fuel instances of unwarranted violence towards protesters.

However, the traditional anonymity that police officers have possessed when handling protest has been eroded by contemporary developments. Many of the images of police violence towards protesters at the G20 Summit event in London in 2009 were derived from pictures and videos taken from mobile telephones, and the knowledge that the action taken by any officer can be recorded and subsequently made available for viewing is likely to influence future police actions at events of this nature.

The police, protest and civil liberties

The ability to protest is an indispensable aspect of a liberal democratic political system, which implies that the police service should uphold the civil and political liberties of those who wish to engage in activities of this nature. However, this duty has not been consistently discharged in the contemporary period. Accusations that police tactics undermined civil and political liberties were levelled against the intercept policy used in the miners' dispute (which contravened freedom of movement) and also the 'zero tolerance' approach adopted by the police at the May Day anti-capitalist protest in London in 2001, in which demonstrators were heavily outnumbered by police officers. As has been noted above, the tactics of corralling (or kettling) demonstrators (or perceived demonstrators), whereby they are penned in and prevented from leaving an area, has become a feature of police actions towards anti-capitalist protesters.

The argument that associates paramilitary policing with aggression and confrontation also suggests that this approach is designed to deter protesters from taking to the streets. It promotes a concern that the police would use the pretext of the imminent breakdown of public order as a justification for deploying the range of coercive resources at their disposal against those wishing to protest, whether sanctioned by the law or not and regardless of their impact on civil liberties. For this reason, paramilitary policing that entails the use of aggressive tactics has been depicted as being incompatible with the fundamental freedoms traditionally associated with liberal democratic political systems and as more appropriate to the treatment of subjugated populations under colonial regimes (Northam, 1989; Jefferson, 1990).

Arguments that allege that police actions have sought to limit the ability to protest often emphasise the service as being subject to the political direction of central government.

The accusation that policing had become less consensual and more politicised (Reiner, 1985: 4) viewed the police as acting as 'partisan enforcers of minority needs' and as 'agents of political control' (Brewer et al., 1996: 214). Regarding protest, this situation asserts that the role of the police is to defend the government against any threats that are posed to it through the use of extra-parliamentary activities.

This situation contributes to aggressive policing since the police service operates on the assumption that the government will support any actions to quell protests which threaten the government's interests. This was a key issue in the policing of the miners' dispute in 1984–85, when the importance attached by the government to defeating the action effectively gave the police service a free hand to deploy any tactics it wished in the sure knowledge the government would support it and condemn those who were engaged in the protest. Margaret Thatcher's robust defence of the actions taken by the police at Orgreave (when she blamed the violence on the miners, whom, she argued, wished to substitute the rule of law for the rule of the mob) was evidence of this.

The ability of the government to communicate with the police service has been facilitated by the formation of a new body. With specific reference to the handling of protest, the NRC/MACC (now the Police National Information and Coordination Centre (PNICC)) provided senior ministers with one police body with which they could liaise on an informal basis and to which they could indicate government concerns in connection with specific events (Kettle, 1985: 30-31). The main problem associated with a close relationship between the police and a political party is that it exerts an adverse effect on the image of the police and its relationship with the general public (Brewer et al., 1996: xiv–xv). This may undermine public trust and confidence in the police as an independent organisation. (Bassett et al., 2009: 10). The perception that the police were used in industrial disputes during the 1980s as 'Maggie's Boot Boys' (Smith, 1994: 101) in order to crush the dissent of trade unions arising from Conservative economic policies had an adverse effect on the image of the police in working-class communities and on the legitimacy they were accorded there. It also had repercussions for the consent accorded to the police when performing routine duties (Alderson, 1979: 12).

However, accusations that the police service does not respect the ability of citizens to engage in protest is not without challenge. Police forces rarely use their powers to ban events such as demonstrations and the police defence of the 'right to peaceful protest' (based upon the right to 'peaceful assembly' that is guaranteed by Article 11 of the European Convention on Human Rights) was at the forefront of their explanations regarding their actions during the 2000 petrol crisis. They do, however, take a more critical view of protest which breaks the law. Organisations that carry out 'criminal acts of direct action in furtherance of a campaign' have been officially labelled as 'domestic extremism' (NETCU, 2009) and have come under the scrutiny of the National Extremism Tactical Coordination Unit which was established by ACPO in 2004 to 'prevent, reduce and disrupt criminal activity associated with domestic extremism and single issue campaigning' (NETCU, 2009).

The role performed by the police when dealing with protest often requires an elaborate balancing act to ensure that one person's right to protest does not have an adverse effect on another's right to conduct their lives as they wish to do so, within the law. Protest may often constitute an attempt to secure a political outcome by coercion, and the police may act in order to defend the rights of those subject to this form of behaviour.

Improvements affecting the central planning and supervision of public order events associated with the Gold–Silver–Bronze hierarchy of command may result in an improved level of protection to demonstrators who are not subject to *ad hoc* and contradictory police managerial decisions (which was a major problem at the protest held in London, Red Lion Square in 1974 when a demonstrator died) and are less likely to experience undisciplined actions by junior police officers. (P. Waddington, 1996: 124–125). Further, improved management, new tactics and the availability of weaponry may give the police confidence to let events go ahead which they might previously have sought to prevent because of uncertainties as to whether public order could be maintained (P. Waddington, 1994: 201).

The aftermath of the G20 protests in London, 2009

The policing of the G20 protests that took place in London in April 2009 resulted in an investigation being conducted by Her Majesty's Chief Inspector of Constabulary (HMCIC) into public order policing. The investigation made a number of observations relating to the contemporary policing of protest and put forward several recommendations to guide future actions (HMCIC, 2009).

The report was concerned that the policing of protest reflected the core values of British policing. It identified the core values of British policing as being 'an approachable, impartial, accountable style of policing based on minimal force and anchored in public consent', whose key purpose was 'to ensure the safety of the public and the preservation of the peace within a tolerant, plural society' (HMCIC, 2009: 11–12). This model could be eroded by factors that included the 'premature displays of formidable public order protective uniform and equipment', which might give the perception 'of a hardening of the character of British policing' (HMCIC, 2009: 12). The model was further jeopardised 'by poor police communication, uncontrolled instances of force and the confused and inappropriate use of police powers' (HMCIC, 2009: 12).

The report discussed the difficulties of contemporary public order policing (which had been made more complex by factors that included the different legal frameworks that applied to protests conducted in public and private spaces) and identified a number of issues relating to the contemporary policing of protest. These included the absence of clear standards governing the use of force by individual officers involved in events of this nature, variations between forces concerning the interpretation of public order law and the use of public order powers (which sometimes resulted at specific events in the inappropriate use of powers such as stop and search and obtaining the names and addresses of demonstrators) and the inability of some forces to provide even a minimal public order command structure (HMCIC, 2009: 6–8).

The report also indentified a number of problems that related to the effectiveness of mutual aid arrangements that included inconsistencies in the approaches and tactics used by individual forces in public order training programmes (some forces, for example, training officers to use shields in an offensive as well as a defensive manner) and variations in the equipment made available by forces to their officers engaged in public order situations, a problem partly explained by the existence of two separate procurement processes for the purchase of body armour (HMCIC, 2009: 6–7).

Several recommendations were put forward to ensure that the future policing of protest strengthened and reinforced the core values of the British model of policing. These included the adoption of a set of fundamental principles governing the use of force; the codification of public order policing to ensure consistency in training and the use of equipment, tactics and powers (in particular the human rights obligations imposed on the police service by the 1998 Human Rights Act); clarification of the legal framework for the use of overt photography by the police during public order operations and the subsequent collation and retention of photographic images; and the adoption of a 'no surprises' communication philosophy with protesters, the media and the wider public in order that protesters and the public were aware of likely police actions and can then make informed choices and decisions (HMCIC, 2009: 7–8 and 14).

Political policing

The state's response to protest goes beyond the physical policing of crowds engaged in extra-parliamentary activities and embraces the monitoring of individuals and groups who participate in them. This is termed 'political policing' and embraces the official scrutiny of ideas and opinions. Although activities of this nature may provide intelligence which will guide public order operations, the main rationale for undertaking them is to defend the state against subversion.

The term 'subversion' has no fixed definition and became the pretext for state monitoring of activities which were not illegal but which were deemed to possess the potential to pose some form of threat to the political, social or economic *status quo* in the UK and/or to the well-being of its citizens. The key difficulty posed by monitoring subversion is that it threatens to undermine key liberal democratic freedoms, in particular the freedom of expression and the ability to protest. It has been argued that subversion has been used to justify state intervention on a scale that involved redrawing the boundaries of the liberal democratic tradition 'by declaring to be illegitimate political and industrial activities which had been thought to have distinguished a liberal democracy from an authoritarian or fascist society' (State Research, 1979).

Agencies undertaking action to combat subversion

Police officers may perform a number of activities related to subversion which are frequently cloaked under the heading of 'public order'. A specific arm of the police service, Special Branch, pays particular attention to activities of this nature. The origins of Special Branch date to 1883 when it was established to monitor political violence associated with Ireland. Historically, Special Branch was based in London, but all police forces formed special branches that were technically answerable to individual chief constables. Special Branch has engaged in the surveillance of foreign communities living in Britain and in the enforcement of anti-terrorist legislation. In London, the Metropolitan Police Special Branch was merged with the anti-terrorist squad in 2006 to form the Counter Terrorism Command.

The major responsibility for combating subversion has been performed by the Security Service (or MI5). This agency was established in the early years of the twentieth century to foil the spying activities of foreign governments within Britain. It is controlled by a director general appointed by the prime minister and is operationally accountable to the Home Secretary.

MI5 is primarily an intelligence-gathering body. Historically, it has collected information on subversive organisations and individuals through a number of methods, including:

- Mail interception;
- Interception ('tapping') of telephone calls and other forms of electronic communication;
- Placing bugs in a target's home or premises;
- Planting informants or agents in organisations.

Specific powers to do this were granted by the 1989 Security Service Act, which placed MI5 on a statutory basis and defined its sphere of operations. This Act authorised the issuance of 'property warrants' by ministers to enable the agency to 'bug and burgle' in order to gather intelligence. The 1997 Police Act gave the police service similar powers in connection with combating serious crime. The methods used by MI5 (which also apply to the police service) to obtain information are governed by the 2000 Regulation of Investigatory Powers Act.

This Act developed existing safeguards relating to *intrusive surveillance* (covering surveillance conducted in a private location, such as a person's home or property, such as a car, where a presumption of privacy would normally apply). It enabled a range of agencies, including MI5, to obtain warrants from a Secretary of State to intercept telephone calls and other forms of electronic communication such as emails and the internet.

Covert intelligence-gathering, or *directed surveillance*, was also authorised by the Act. This includes the use of informants. Covert intelligence typically takes place in a public place to obtain private information about a person. Permission to do this is not founded on warrants but is authorised by police officers whose actions are subject to a Code of Practice.

The role of MI5 has subsequently extended beyond intelligence-gathering to embrace other activities. Accusations have been made that the agency conducts operations (referred to as 'dirty tricks') that are designed to sabotage or destabilise an organisation that has been targeted as subversive. It has been alleged that MI5 played an important role in seeking to undermine public support for the National Union of Miners during its 1984–85 strike. One of the ways through which this was done was to plant a mole in the union's headquarters (Milne, 1994).

The police service as political actors

In addition to policing political issues, the police service itself operates as an important political actor in influencing the police agenda. This role is performed by the police staff associations – the Association of Chief Police Officers (ACPO), the Police Federation, the Police Superintendents' Association and a number of single-issue organisations, the most important of which are embraced under the umbrella of Diversity Staff Support Organisations (DSSOs).

The Association of Chief Police Officers

The origins of the Association of Chief Police Officers date from the formation of the County Chief Constables' Club in 1858 and the Chief Constables' Association of England and Wales in 1896, which represented the chief officers of urban forces. These two bodies amalgamated in 1948 to form ACPO, and the Royal Ulster Constabulary was incorporated in 1970. The organisation adopted company status in 1997. It consists of the most senior ranks of the police service (assistant chief constable and above) and its membership numbered 349 in 2010.

During the nineteenth century the chief constables' organisations did little more than facilitate social contact between their members. However, the role of ACPO in the twentieth century became broader, seeking to promote the effectiveness, efficiency and professional interests of the police service and to safeguard the individual and collective interests of its members. In 1996 these two functions were separated, with the newly-formed Chief Police Officers' Staff Association becoming responsible for negotiating with the Police Negotiation Board on issues relating to members' salaries and conditions of service. This meant that henceforth ACPO could concentrate on the development of police policy, both in the sense of influencing the activities pursued by individual forces (a role that had formerly been hindered by the doctrine of constabulary independence) and in seeking to influence the content of centrally-directed police policy (a function that was aided by its position as an 'insider' group within the Whitehall corridors of power).

Key changes to the position of ACPO in policy-making occurred during the 1990s when it was argued that its previous 'sporadic' influence over the police agenda was developed as the consequence of the emergence of a 'corporacy' (or cohesiveness) among ACPO members (Savage et al., 2000). This has been attributed to a number of circumstances but in particular the negative views of senior officers to government's reform agenda of the 1990s – the Sheehy report (Home Office, 1993), the Police and Magistrates' Courts Act (1994) and the Posen Inquiry into police core and ancillary functions (Home Office, 1995) – which enhanced the level of ACPO campaigning.

The acceptance by Home Secretaries of ACPO's ability to influence forces to adopt policy that government wished to promote induced Home Secretaries to seek a closer working relationship with ACPO and to strike bargains with it the organisation over the direction of policy (Bassett et al., 2009: 12). Money was made available to enable ACPO to extend its central secretariat and to facilitate policy development which in more recent years has aided the formation of several influential subgroups. ACPO has subsequently become extremely influential in formulating decisions regarding policing strategy and in advising the government on the future direction of policy. Initiatives such as the introduction of tasers and the automatic number plate recognition camera network have been said to have emanated from ACPO initiatives (Bassett et al., 2009: 12).

In addition, ACPO has played an important role in reforms to the performance culture of policing. At the behest of ACPO, activity-based costing was introduced in all forces to raise awareness of the cost of services and to guide more effective decision-making at force level. ACPO also piloted Business Process Analysis to promote understanding of the differences in processes, costs and effectiveness between forces (Spottiswoode, 2000: 10). Its role in both policy and performance evaluation has resulted in ACPO having a key centralising influence on the police service (Jones, 2003: 615).

Members of ACPO also operate in an individual capacity through personal involvement in campaigning, in particular in relationship to police powers and responsibilities. One example of this was the paper presented by Richard Brunstrom to his North Wales Police Authority in October 2007. He argued that current drug legislation was out of date and that the police were engaged in a battle they could not win. He advocated the replacement of the 1971 Misuse of Drugs Act with a new Substance Misuse Act to provide a new legal system of regulation and control of potentially dangerous drugs.

The Police Federation

The concerns of rank-and-file police officers are voiced by the Police Federation. This body emerged as the consequence of the police strikes of 1918 and 1919 that were organised by the National Union of Police and Prison Officers. The resultant 1919 Police Act forbade police officers from joining trade unions but set up the Police Federation as a statutory advisory body to represent the views of police officers (now up to the rank of chief inspector) on all matters relating to their welfare and efficiency. The Federation negotiates on pay and conditions of service and it is consulted on the formulation of police regulations.

The Police Federation (like ACPO) has evolved from a staff association into an organisation that seeks to exert influence on the police service and criminal justice policy. Unlike ACPO, it mainly performs this role from outside the corridors of power. It is a role that was developed after 1955 when it was granted the ability to levy a subscription from its members in order to campaign on different issues.

Initial Federation campaigns were concerned with issues such as police pay and support for the death penalty, but a watershed in its political role occurred during the 1970s when factors that included the increase of crime and the negative views held by some left-wing politicians towards the police prompted the Federation to more vigorously seek to influence public opinion. These campaigns used lobbying techniques and press advertising to appeal directly to the public over the heads of senior police officers and the government (McLaughlin and Murji, 1998: 371).

The Federation's 1975 law and order campaign has been described as 'the crucial moment of overt politicisation' (McLaughlin and Murji, 1998: 379). The targets of this campaign were liberal reforms promoted during the 1960s which it depicted as the root of the contemporary crime problem. It aimed to mobilise the silent majority in favour of tougher law and order policies. This campaign ran alongside a further one designed to increase police pay, which challenged the government's incomes policy.

The Conservative party enthusiastically endorsed many of the Federation's demands. Although there were some differences of opinion (on issues such as the 1984 Police and Criminal Evidence Act), a good relationship was struck between the police service and government during the 1980s. However, it led to the perception of the service being politicised in the sense of acting to further the government's objectives rather than serving society. This perception reached a climax during the 1984–85 miners' dispute as a result of the robust policing utilised during that strike.

However, the relationship between the Federation and the Conservative government was adversely affected by the Conservative reform agenda of the 1990s. It prompted the Federation to adopt aggressive lobbying and campaigning techniques and become willing to work with other groups to oppose these initiatives. This led to the Federation becoming more influential, one early product of which was the virtual abandonment of Sheehy's proposals affecting rank-and-file policing.

Campaigning also takes the form of rallies and demonstrations. One example of the latter was the procession of police officers through central London in 2008 to voice opposition to the Home Secretary's decision not to backdate a pay award. However, this event also demonstrated the relative weakness of the Police Federation as an 'outsider' group since the government refused to accede to the demands of the Police Federation on this issue.

The Police Superintendents' Association

A third body seeking to influence the policing agenda is the Police Superintendents' Association (PSA). This was set up in 1920 to represent superintendents and chief superintendents. It currently performs two key roles: it provides advice and support to its members and contributes and influences police policy and practice at a national level.

Initially, the PSA was seen as little more than a senior officers' dining club, but it subsequently pursued a more significant (if intermittent) role on policing and criminal justice policy on issues that included the imposition of gun controls in the wake of the 1996 Dunblane shootings (Savage et al., 2000).

The PSA serves as the main mouthpiece for BCU commanders and its influence over police policy may increase should the position occupied by these officers in delivering the local police agenda increase in future years.

Diversity Staff Support Organisations

The police service contains a number of single-issue organisations. Diversity Staff Support Organisations (DSSOs), which are responsible for promoting the principle of diversity within the police service, are especially important. This has raised the question as to the extent to which their existence 'affect[s] the provision of a unified police service where all staff are treated equally regardless of race, colour, creed, religion, gender or sexual orientation' (Stoddart, 2009). The government's view was that these (DSSOs) helped the Home Office and key policing partners 'to deliver equality and diversity outcome for the service' (West, 2009a).

Some DSSOs benefit from government funding, others do not. In 2008/09 the British Association for Women in Policing received £100,000 and the National Association of Muslim Police, £45,000 (West, 2009b).

The National Black Police Association

In 1994 a Black Police Association was launched within the Metropolitan Police to serve as a means to tackle aspects of the occupational subculture of the police service that marginalised minority ethnic officers (Rowe, 2004: 43–44). It became a national organisation in 1998. The organisation's vision is to 'ensure equitable service for all and for the Black and Minority Ethnic (BME) staff' who they represent, and to 'advocate the needs and expectations of BME communities by delivering and supporting strategies and initiatives which have a positive impact on all' (National Black Police Association, 2010).

The role of this body was initially concerned with internal operational aspects of the police service (especially in connection with racial discrimination and the high wastage rate of minority ethnic officers), but its activities have subsequently extended into community relations. Its aim is to ensure that all receive fair treatment from the police service. The Association therefore adopts a campaigning role, which was evident in 2006 when the National Black Police Associations of the UK and USA hosted the first International Education and Training Conference in Manchester. Delegates marched through Moss Side with the aim of reaching out to local communities.

Although this organisation 'may strengthen the racialised identity of its members and, realising their collective strength, unite them through both a shared experience of social exclusion ... and ... a positive commitment to policing' (Holdaway, 1996: 196), critics believe that this might have divisive consequences, diverting energy into internal police affairs perhaps to the detriment of the provision of a service to the public (Broughton and Bennett, 1994), or by aggravating conflict between this organisation and the Police Federation.

The National Association of Muslim Police

The National Association of Muslim Police was launched in July 2007 as a national representative body of Muslim police officers and police staff within the UK. It replaced a number of Muslim police associations that were then in existence. Its specific aims are to promote the recruitment, retention and progression of Muslim police officers and staff within the service and to support the welfare and religious needs of its members. Its role also extends beyond the service to promote an understanding of Islam within the police service and the wider community, thereby contributing to community cohesion. It performs its roles in several ways but especially in meetings with the Home Office and the NPIA and with staff associations that include ACPO and the Police Federation.

The British Association for Women in Policing

This association was set up in 1987 and exists to promote awareness of issues that specifically affect women in the police service and to contribute to debates on issues of concern to all officers by providing the female perspective. It performs these functions by organising events and meetings and through liaison with the Home Office. It also operates in conjunction with other staff associations, such as the Police Federation and the National Black Police Association, on issues that are of mutual concern.

The police, the media and public opinion

The relationship between the police and the media constitutes a further mechanism through which the service can carry out a task that is essentially political, that of seeking to influence public opinion. This issue was examined by the Home Affairs Committee (2009).

Most members of the general public lack first-hand knowledge of crime and thus rely on the media for this sort of information. As such, the media can play an important role in contemporary police work.

An important source of information from the police to the media is provided through on-the-record briefings. These are attributable sources of information given to journalists by police officers whose statements are usually in connection with individual crimes. Such information is usually provided in press conferences which are often televised. In addition, all police forces have media departments and internet sites through which they convey information to the general public regarding crime.

The information relayed by the police to the public is selective. Sometimes there are valid operational reasons for adopting this course of action. It may be supplemented by off-the-record briefings to journalists, in which journalists are given information on the understanding that they do not report it. This course of action may be justified on grounds of public interest, or perhaps to induce journalists not to report information they have uncovered as the police believe it would prejudice the investigation they are mounting.

Both parties may seek to use the other to their own advantage. Journalists may use contacts they have with police officers to obtain confidential information in order to secure a 'scoop'. On the other hand, police officers may tip the media off regarding actions such as an intended arrest or a search, perhaps to ensure that the public are aware that the police are treating a problem seriously or to document that their actions with regard to a delicate situation are being conducted with scrupulous fairness and professionalism. The main problem with actions of this nature is that people suspected of a crime are identified before they are charged, which undermines their civil liberties (especially if the police do not prefer a charge) and the publicity may also have an adverse effect on the fairness of a future trial.

The role performed by the media in contemporary police work may lead to the police engaging in activities that are overtly political. This is most apparent when the police service seeks to secure the presentation of its view in relation to a particular incident so that it flavours any subsequent debate on this topic. Accusations of this nature arose in connection with the death of Ian Tomlinson, whose route home took him through the the midst of the G20 protests in London in April 2009. He was shown on national television being thrown to the ground by a police officer and was alleged to have died of a heart attack. A subsequent *post mortem* suggested that he died from bleeding in his abdomen. It was subsequently argued that the Metropolitan Police Service and the and City of London Police may have either misinformed the public regarding the circumstances of Mr Tomlinson's death or failed to correct inaccurate information as to how he died (Lewis, 2009). This episode implied that the police service may occasionally use media manipulation to secure a desired official outcome. This point was made by the General Secretary of the National Union of Journalists, who argued that 'the police rely very heavily on the media in order to get their message out … and … there is a common interest between the police and the media in having a good working relationship' (Dear, 2009).

To what extent have changes in the policing of protest that have been introduced since the early 1970s restricted citizens' ability to engage in such activity?

In order to answer this question you should refer to the material contained in this chapter and consult some of the key references that are cited. You should address the following issues:

- Identify the main changes that have been introduced to the policing of protest (which includes weaponry, tactics, structure and organisation);
- Evaluate why these changes were introduced;
- Analyse these changes within the concept of paramilitary policing and the main developments with which this term has been associated;
- Present a conclusion in which you will assess whether these changes have served to restrict or to facilitate protest.

REFERENCES

Alderson, J. (1979) *Policing Freedom*. London: MacDonald and Evans.

Association of Chief Police Officers (1983) *Public Order Manual of Tactical Operations and Related Matters*. London: ACPO.

Association of Chief Police Officers (2007) *ACPO Manual of Guidance on Keeping the Peace*. London: National Policing Improvement Agency.

Bassett, D., Haldenby, A., Thraves, L. and Truss, E. (2009) *A New Force*. London: Reform.

Bowden, T. (1978) *Beyond the Limits of the Law*. Harmondsworth: Penguin.

Brewer, J., Guelke, A., Hume, I., Moxon-Browne, E. and Wilford, R. (1996) *The Police, Public Order and the State* (2nd edition). Basingstoke. Palgrave Macmillan.

Brogden, M. (1982) *The Police: Autonomy and Consent*. London: Academic Press.

Broughton, F. and Bennett, M. (1994) Statement, in *The Guardian*, 27 September.

Bunyan, T. (1977) *The History and Practice of the Political Police in Britain*. London: Quarter Books

Bunyan, T. (1985) 'From Saltley to Orgreave via Brixton', *Journal of Law and Society*, 12 (3): 293–303.

Dear, J. (2009) Oral Evidence to the Home Affairs Committee, 5 May, *Policing of Protests*. [Online] ww.publications.parliament.uk/pa/cm200809/cmselect/cmhaff/uc418-ii/uc418 [accessed on 5 June 2009].

Gamble, T. (1988) *The Free Market and the Strong State*. Basingstoke: Palgrave Macmillan.

Hall, S. (1980) *Drifting into a Law and Order Society*. London: The Cobden Trust.

Hardwick, N. (2009) Oral Evidence to the Home Affairs Committee, 21 April, *Policing of the G 20 Protests*. [Online] www.publications.parliament.uk/pa/cm200809/cmselect/cmhaff/uc418-i/uc418 [accessed on 23 May 2009].

Her Majesty's Chief Inspector of Constabulary (HMCIC) (2009) *Adapting to Protest – Nurturing the British Model of Policing*. London: HMIC.

Holdaway, S. (1996) *The Racialisation of British Policing*. Basingstoke: Macmillan.

Home Affairs Committee (2009) *Police and the Media*. Second Report, Session 2008–09. House of Commons Paper 75. London: TSO.

Home Office (1993) *Inquiry into Police Responsibilities and Rewards*. The Sheehy Report. Cm. 2280. London: HMSO.

Home Office (1995) *Review of the Police Core and Ancillary Tasks: Final Report*. The Posen Report. London: HMSO.

Jefferson, T. (1987) 'Beyond Paramilitarism', *British Journal of Criminology*, 27: 47–53.

Jefferson, T. (1990) *The Case against Paramilitary Policing*. Buckingham: Open University Press.

Joint Committee on Human Rights (2009) *Demonstrating Respect for Rights? A Human Rights Approach to Protest*. Seventh Report, Session 2008–09. House of Lords Paper 47 and House of Commons Paper 320. London: TSO.

Jones, T. (2003) 'The Governance and Accountability of Policing', in T. Newburn (ed.), *Handbook of Policing*. Cullompton, Devon: Willan Publishing.

Joyce, P. (1992) 'Decade of Disorder', *Policing*, 8 (3): 232–248.

Joyce, P. (2002) *The Politics of Protest: Extra-Parliamentary Politics in Britain since 1970*. Basingstoke: Palgrave/Macmillan.

Kettle, M. (1985) 'The National Reporting Centre and 1984 Miners' Strike', in B. Fine and R. Millar (eds), *Policing the Miners' Strike*. London: Lawrence and Wishart.

King, M. and Brearley, N. (1996) *Public Order Policing: Contemporary Perspectives in Strategy and Tactics*. Crime and Security Shorter Studies Series, No. 2. Leicester: Perpetuity Press.

Lewis, P. (2009) 'IPCC Begins Inquiry into Statements by Police over Ian Tomlinson Death', *The Guardian*, 16 May.

McLaughlin, E. and Murji, K. (1998) 'Resistance through Representation: "Storylines", advertising and Police Federation Campaigns', *Policing and Society*, 8: 367–399.

Milne, S. (1994) *The Enemy Within: The Secret War Against the Miners*. London: Pan Books.

National Black Police Association (2010) *The NPBA vision* [online] www.nationalbpa.com [accessed on 5 May 2010].

National Council for Civil Liberties (NCCL) (1980) *Southall 23 April 1979: The Report of the Unofficial Committee of Enquiry*. London: NCCL.

NETCU (2009) *About NETCU*. [Online] www.netcu.org.uk/de/default.jsp [accessed 28 May 2009].

Noakes, J., Klocke, B. and Gillham, P. (2005) 'Whose Streets? Police and Protester Struggles over Space in Washington DC, September 2001', *Police and Society*, 15 (3): 235–254.

Northam, G. (1989) *Shooting in the Dark: Riot Police in Britain*. London: Faber & Faber.

Reiner, R. (1985) *The Politics of the Police*. Brighton: Wheatsheaf.

Reiner, R. (1991) *Chief Constables: Bobbies, Bosses or Bureaucrats?* Oxford: Oxford University Press.

Reiner, R. (1998) 'Policing Protest and Disorder in Britain', in D. della Porta and H. Reiter (eds), *The Control of Mass Demonstrations in Western Democracies*. Minneapolis, MN: University of Minnesota Press.

Rowe, M. (2004) *Policing, Race and Racism*. Cullompton, Devon: Willan Publishing.

Saunders, P. (1996) 'A Preventive Approach to Public Order', in C. Critcher and D. Waddington (eds), *Policing Public Order: Theoretical and Practical Issues*. Aldershot: Avebury.

Savage, S., Charman, S. and Cope, S. (2000) *Policing and the Power of Persuasion*. London: Blackstone Press.

Smith, Sir J. (1994) 'Police Reforms', *Police Journal*, LXV11 (2), April–June: 99–104.

Spottiswoode, C. (2000) *Improving Police Performance: A New Approach to Measuring Police Efficiency.* London: Public Services Productivity Panel.

State Research (1979) 'Introduction', in E.P. Thompson, *The Secret State.* State Research Pamphlet No. 1. London: Independent Research Publications.

Stoddart, Lord (2009) 5 March, HL Debs, Vol 708, Col WA (Written answer) 185.

Thackrah, J. (ed.) (1985) *Contemporary Policing: An Examination of Society in the 1980s.* London: Sphere.

Waddington, D. (1996) 'Key Issues and Controversies', in C. Critcher and D. Waddington (eds), *Policing Public Order: Theoretical and Practical Issues.* Aldershot: Avebury.

Waddington, D. (2007) *Policing Public Disorder: Theory and Practice.* Cullompton, Devon: Willan Publishing.

Waddington, D., Jones, K. and Critcher, C. (1989) *Flashpoints: Studies in Public Disorder.* London: Routledge.

Waddington, P. (1987) 'Towards Paramilitarism? Dilemma in the Policing of Public Disorder', *British Journal of Criminology*, 27: 37–46.

Waddington, P. (1993) 'The Case against Paramilitary Policing Considered', *British Journal of Criminology*, 33 (3): 353–373.

Waddington, P. (1994) *Liberty and Order: Public Order Policing in a Capital City.* London: UCL Press.

Waddington, P. (1996) 'Public Order Policing: Citizenship and Moral Ambiguity', in F. Leishman, B. Loveday and S. Savage (eds), *Core Issues in Policing.* Harlow: Longman.

Waddington, P. (2003) 'Policing Public Order and Political Contention', in T. Newburn (ed.), *Handbook of Policing.* Cullompton, Devon: Willan Publishing.

West, Lord (2009a) House of Lords, 5 March, HL Debs, Vol 708, Col WA 185.

West, Lord (2009b) House of Lords, 26 January, HL Debs, Vol 707, Col WA19.

9

The global dimension to policing

═══════════════ CHAPTER AIMS ═══════════════

The aims of this chapter are:

- To consider the global aspects of contemporary crime;
- To evaluate cross-border initiatives to tackle organised crime and international terrorism;
- To analyse the impact of a number of key developments put forward within the EU to tackle cross-border crime;
- To analyse the impact made by global developments to tackle cross-border crime on UK policing arrangements;
- To consider the impediments to enhanced global policing and security initiatives.

The global dimension to crime

The end of the cold war and the opening of the previously sealed borders of central and Eastern Europe aggravated existing crime problems. It also created new ones, especially in connection with refugees fleeing the war in the former state of Yugoslavia. Subsequently, new problems emerged on an international scale which required nation states to coordinate their efforts. These include the need to combat crimes such as drug trafficking, commercial fraud, money laundering, illegal immigration and 'people trafficking'.

A further reason to justify individual nation states pooling their efforts has been the emergence of terrorism on a global scale. Terrorism utilises violence (or the threat of violence) to achieve political objectives and employs a diverse range of tactics, although a key distinction separates selective (or targeted) tactics and violence that is directed against the general public in an indiscriminate manner. The aim of violence is to create a sense of disorientation which 'erodes the relatively stable patterns of expectations required by social organisms' (Bowden, 1977: 284). Terrorists typically seek to achieve their aims by a prolonged campaign of attrition – the purpose of terrorism 'is not military victory, it is to terrorise, to change your behaviour if you're the victim by making you afraid of today, afraid of tomorrow and in diverse societies ... afraid of each other (Clinton, 2001).

Terrorism is not a new phenomenon to Britain. Campaigns involving violence have periodically occurred since 1970. However, in more recent years terrorism has progressed beyond attempts to influence the politics of individual nation states and has embraced an international dimension. This has especially been associated with the militant Islamic organisation, al-Qaeda. This organisation aims to remove American influence from Muslim nations and secure the removal of pro-western governments in the Middle East. Its activities frequently focus on the suffering endured by Palestinian Arabs as an alleged consequence of their treatment by the state of Israel. Action by western nations to counter what is depicted as a holy war or jidad served to further campaigns of violence associated with al-Qaeda, whose activities became increasingly decentralised following the overthrow of the Taliban government of Afghanistan by a coalition of western nations in 2001 and the invasion of Iraq in 2003. This has meant that an attack directed or inspired by this organisation may occur anywhere in the world and it has emphasised the need for international cooperation to combat the problem. Al-Qaeda has been held responsible for a number of attacks that include the 11 September 2001 attacks in the USA, the 2004 Madrid train bombings, the July 2005 London bombings and the attack mounted on Glasgow airport in 2007.

The cross-border response to organised crime

The global response to organised crime is delivered through a wide range of mechanisms. Of particular importance to UK policing has been arrangements put forward within the European Union (EU) to combat this problem. The concern of the EU to provide structural arrangements to combat organised crime was initially voiced at the 1996 Stockholm Conference in connection with activities arising from European economic integration and social exclusion. However, the main development concerned with organised crime occurred in April 1997 when the European Council approved an *Action Plan to Combat Organised Crime* (European Council, 1997).

It put forward a number of recommendations that were designed to prevent organised crime by focusing on the circumstances that facilitated its development rather than on those who carried out these activities. The recommendations included the development of an anti-corruption policy within government apparatus, banning persons convicted of offences related to organised crime from tendering procedures, devoting financial resources to prevent larger cities in the EU from becoming breeding grounds for organised crime, and developing closer cooperation between EU member states and the European Commission on combating fraud where the financial interests of the EU were concerned. The *Action Plan* also reiterated the desirability of promoting effective cooperation of the judicial and police services across national boundaries.

Subsequent positive action to foster knowledge on preventing organised crime and improving the exchange of information among member states included the Falcone and Hippocrates programmes, which were carried out under the auspices of the European Council within the Programme for Police and Judicial Cooperation in Criminal Matters (AGIS).

In May 2000 the Justice and Home Affairs Council published a new plan to combat organised crime. This followed the direction of the 1997 *Action Plan*, but incorporated some new ideas that included proposals to improve the sharing of information between member states and the European Commission. Since the 11 September 2001 attacks in America, tackling organised crime has been increasingly viewed within the EU as an aspect of combating terrorism (van de Bunt and van der Schoot, 2003: 18–20), a topic that is discussed in greater detail below. The UK's 2003 Crime (International Cooperation) Act implemented EU arrangements that were designed to simplify the procedures for Mutual Legal Assistance and in particular provided an enhanced level of police and judicial cooperation directed at terrorist activities.

People trafficking

People trafficking has been a long-standing concern of the EU. These concerns have been expressed in various forums, including the July 2002 Framework Decision of the EU Council on combating trafficking in human beings, and by a number of recommendations made by the Council of Ministers and European Parliament in connection with the trafficking of women, forced prostitution and violence and against women. Individual member states pursued their own actions to combat this issue. In the UK, such actions included a police-led anti-trafficking operation termed Pentameter 2.

In 2005 the EU Council drew up the European Convention on Action against Trafficking in Human Beings. This sought to prevent and combat trafficking in humans, to protect the human rights of the victims of trafficking and to promote international cooperation on action against trafficking in human beings. The Convention applied to all forms of trafficking in human beings, whether national or transnational and whether or not it was connected with organised crime. Signatories were required to strengthen their border controls to prevent and detect trafficking, to adopt legislation and other measures to prevent commercial carriers being used to commit offences created by the Convention, and to introduce measures in their national law to sanction people traffickers.

Cross-border response to terrorism

International cooperation to combat terrorism assumes a number of forms. An important aspect of a cross-border response to this problem is provided by the EU.

Following the 2001 attacks in America, the EU established an anti-terrorist policy which initially took the form of an anti-terrorism action plan. This is updated every six months and the implementation of measures contained in the action plan is monitored by the EU Commission. The action plan was followed by a Framework Decision in 2001 that defined terrorist offences and equalised the sanctions applied by member states.

A special meeting of the European Council was held in March 2004 following the Madrid train bombings. It issued a Declaration on Combating Terrorism. This updated the anti-terrorism action plan and suggested a number of measures that should be pursued, especially in relation to the exchange of information. One measure was the Legal Enforcement Network (LEN). It also proposed measures to coordinate policies to combat terrorism across the EU, including the appointment of a new post of Counter-terrorism Coordinator within the Council. These measures supplemented the work performed by both Europol and Eurojust in connection with terrorism.

The Commission made proposals in May 2004 to enhance the level of police and customs cooperation between member states through measures that included the interoperability of different databases. In June 2004 it put forward concrete proposals to achieve the aims of the European Council's Declaration, setting out measures to enhance the exchange of information between law enforcement authorities on the basis of the principle of 'equivalent access of data' between them. This meant that law enforcement and police authorities would be given access to data held in another member state on comparable conditions to those that applied to the authorities of the member state that possessed the data (House of Lords European Union Committee, 2005b: para 10). There were, however, problems in implementing this suggestion, including linguistic difficulties and the absence of a common format for storing such data (House of Lords European Union Committee, 2005b: paras 22–23).

Further communications were issued by the Commission later in 2004, proposing additional measures to combat terrorism. These measures over contingency planning, civil protection and the financing of terrorist organisations, which sought to promote 'a more hostile environment for terrorist financing' (House of Lords European Committee, 2005b: paras 2 and 81). The latter concern was pursued by the European Council in December 2004 when it urged the Commission to present proposals to prevent the misuse of charities to finance terrorist activities and called for the adoption of best practices in implementing financial sanctions and agreement on the third money-laundering Directive (House of Lords European Union Committee, 2005b: para 83).

The Hague Programme (2004)

The Tampere Programme, which was drawn up at a special meeting of the European Council in 1999, sought to develop the EU as an 'area of freedom, security and justice'. This gave rise to discussion as to how the Tampere Programme should be followed up, the outcome of which was the adoption by the European Council of the Hague Programme in 2004.

The Hague Programme reaffirmed the priority that EU citizens attached to justice and home affairs and emphasised areas that included asylum and mutual recognition in criminal and civil matters. It also aimed to advance the development of a Common European Asylum System and advocated the establishment of a European Asylum Office to facilitate practical cooperation between the national asylum services of the member states. The Hague Programme further emphasised that future action in the area of justice and home affairs must respect the principles of subsidiarity and proportionality as well as the different legal traditions of the member states (House of Lords European Union Committee, 2005a: paras 9 and 11).

A key role performed by the EU is to facilitate the exchange of information between member states (House of Lords European Committee, 2005b: abstract). The Hague Programme sought to advance this objective by promoting the 'principle of availability' (as opposed to the Council's proposed 'principle of equivalent access') regarding the sharing of data between 'competent authorities' in all member states to combat a wide range of cross-border criminal activities, especially terrorism (House of Lords European Union Committee, 2005a: para 35). Judicial cooperation in criminal matters was to be advanced by the Tampere principle of 'mutual recognition' and the Hague Programme envisaged accompanying this principle with some approximation of the criminal laws of member states, provided that this facilitated mutual recognition (House of Lords European Union Committee, 2005a: para 38).

Proposals to implement data-sharing were put forward by the EU Commission in 2005 (covering data sharing of DNA, fingerprints, ballistics, vehicle registration information and telephone numbers) (Home Affairs Committee, 2007a: para 15), but implementation was delayed on the grounds that the 2005 Prum Convention concerned with cross-border crime, terrorism and illegal immigration also covered some of these issues. In 2007 this problem was resolved when an amended version of Prum became part of EU law. This advanced the principle of availability by allowing member states to access 'reference checks' in the DNA files of other member states in connection with serious crime suspects and terrorists groups.

The aftermath of the London bombings (2005)

Following terrorist attacks in London in July 2005, a meeting of EU interior ministers was held, at which it was agreed to implement a package of measures. In addition to measures to combat the financing of terrorist groups and steps to address recruitment and radicalisation, new initiatives included the strengthening of the Schengen and visa information systems, the initiation of a European evidence warrant, the inclusion of biometric details on passports, the imposition of greater controls over trade, storage and the transport of explosives, and a proposal for a directive to require telephone companies and internet providers to store details of phone calls, emails and websites visited.

In September 2005 the issues of recruitment and radicalisation (that were initially raised in the 2004 action plan) were addressed by the EU Commission. It published a communication analysing the ways in which the radicalisation of individuals could be deterred through measures such as education, inter-faith dialogue and integration policies. A sum of 7 million euros was provided to prevent, prepare and respond to terrorist attacks.

Also in September 2005, the EU Council adopted a new directive designed to prevent money laundering and terrorist financing and it also adopted a decision which obliged member states to provide Europol with information relating to investigations in terrorist cases that involved two or more member states. However, member states have been tardy in supplying this sort of information (House of Lords European Union Committee, 2008: para 115).

In December 2005, the Justice and Home Affairs Council approved a new strategy whose objectives were to prevent, protect, pursue and respond. This strategy sought a joined-up response at state, EU and international levels. The Council put forward a communication on terrorist financing that sought to develop a common code of practice among member states for producing and exchanging information that could cut off terrorist funding.

In November 2007, the EU Commission put forward a further package of proposals to combat terrorism. It proposed to amend the 2001 Framework Decision to introduce new offences that included the criminalisation of terrorist training, recruitment and provocation to commit a terrorist offence, which would include material that was available in the internet. It proposed that Passenger Name Records should be made available on all flights arriving or leaving the EU. The Commission also proposed to update the action plan to improve the security placed on items such as explosives and detonators by measures that included EU-wide warning systems regarding lost and stolen explosives and suspicious transactions.

Contingency planning

In 2006, a report from the ESSTRT consortium was received by the European Commission. This viewed international terrorism as 'an acknowledged threat facing Europe', although the extent of this threat was not easy to quantify (ESSTRT Consortium, 2006: 15). It recommended that individual nations should conduct risk-based assessments of Critical National Infrastructures (assets or activities which, if damaged or destroyed, would affect a country's ability to conduct normal life. These included water, energy, transport and food supplies) (ESSTRT Consortium, 2006: 6). It also proposed the 'Four Plus Three Package' that embraced actions intended (1) to prevent terrorist action, (2) to pursue those responsible, (3) to protect against attacks (4) and to make preparations to develop resilience against them (the four Ps – an approach that was developed in the UK). These actions should be backed by a set of enabling capabilities, including enhanced intelligence information, a strong policy of public communication and robust relationships with international partners (ESSTRT Consortium, 2006: 6).

The report further proposed that the EU should develop a comprehensive strategy and a stronger tactical operational structure through methods that included the appointment of a High Representative for internal security and the establishment of a Crisis Management Centre in Brussels to act as the central institution for the exchange and coordination of information (ESSTRT Consortium, 2006: 8). This would communicate with the crisis management structures of the individual member states.

BOX 9.1

THE EU AND TERRORISM – A RECIPE FOR CONFUSION?

A particular problem affecting the EU's response to terrorism is the proliferation of bodies that exercise some degree of responsibility for this area of activity. It has been observed that 'there is a multiplicity of groups, some within the Second Pillar, some within the Third Pillar, some outside the pillared structure altogether. Some have a policy focus, some an intelligence focus and others an operational focus' (House of Lords European Union Committee, 2005b, para 61). This situation was in part attributed to the failure of Europol to perform a central role in implementing the EU's response to international terrorism.

It was anticipated that proposal I, the Constitutional Treaty for a Standing Committee within the Council to promote operational cooperation on internal security, would improve the position, replacing the role currently performed by COREPER (the Committee of Member States' Permanent Representatives), which did not have sufficient time to devote to this specialised area of work (House of Lords European Union Committee, 2005b: paras 61 and 63).

The EU, organised crime and terrorism – practical measures

The main practical measures that have emanated from the initiatives and proposals outlined above are discussed below.

European Police Chiefs Task Force

The formation of the European Police Chiefs Task Force was proposed by the Tampere meeting of the European Council in 1999 and operates outside the formal Council structures. Its role is to coordinate high-level operational cooperation to combat serious organised crime, including terrorism. The establishment of this Task Force (and the European Police Training College by a Council decision in 2005 to facilitate cross-border training for senior police officers in the EU) provide the potential for further enhanced cooperation between all police forces across Europe.

Counter-terrorism coordinator

A counter-terrorism coordinator was appointed within the Secretariat of the EU Council in 2004 to oversee EU anti-terrorist activity. The counter-terrorism coordinator acts as the key link between the EU Commission and the Justice and Home Affairs Council. The latter is an informal council with no decision-making powers whose role extends to countering terrorism. The function of this official is to coordinate the work of the Council in combating terrorism and to maintain an overview of all the instruments at the EU's disposal, but not to coordinate counter-terrorism operations. The coordinator reports to the Council and seeks to ensure that its decisions are followed up by monitoring the level of compliance by member states (House of Lords European Union Committee, 2005b: paras 55-56).

Eurojust

The formation of Eurojust supplements Europol's work concerning police cooperation with judicial cooperation. The origins of Eurojust stemmed from the proposal made by the 1999 Tampere European Council for the formation of an EU Judicial Cooperation Unit to reinforce the fight against serious organised crime, although there were earlier developments providing for mutual legal assistance that stemmed from the 1959 Council of Europe Convention on Mutual Assistance in Criminal Matters.

Eurojust was formally established by a Council decision in 2002 (it had been functioning on a provisional basis since 2001). It was established under the Maastricht Treaty's Third Pillar and is responsible for coordinating (rather than seeking to harmonise) judicial cooperation in criminal matters in the EU. Its work entails facilitating cooperation between the relevant authorities of member states and improving the coordination of investigations and prosecutions of member states in connection with serious crime concerning two or more member states, 'particularly when it is organised' (Article 3(1) 2002 Council Decision, cited in House of Lords European Union Committee, 2004: para 13).

The governing body of Eurojust is termed the 'College' and consists of one member for each state who may be a prosecutor, judge or a police officer. The powers given to these members are subject to considerable variation, the UK member possessing the full powers of a Crown Prosecutor (House of Lords European Union Committee, 2004: paras 35–36). Eurojust is based in The Hague and is directly accountable to the Council of Ministers (House of Lords European Union Committee, 2004: para 5). Its finance is mainly derived from the EU budget, unlike Europol which is funded through contributions of member states. It may be the basis from which other developments, most notably the establishment of a European Public Prosecutor's Office, will stem.

A key role of Eurojust is to secure mutual legal assistance between prosecution authorities in member states. It embraces activities such as extradition and serving judgments and witness orders (House of Lords European Union Committee, 2004: paras 26–27). It also performs a number of tasks in connection with the European arrest warrant, for example giving advice if competing warrants are issued by more than one member state (House of Lords European Union Committee, 2004: para 51). Three hundred cases were referred to Eurojust in 2003, around half involving drug trafficking and fraud. Other categories of cases were money laundering, terrorism and trafficking in human beings (House of Lords European Union Committee, 2004: para 12).

Future developments include the possibility that Eurojust may become the 'one-stop shop' for judicial cooperation between the EU and non-EU states (House of Lords European Union Committee, 2004: para 82).

Eurojust and Europol   A cooperation agreement between Europol (whose role is discussed in more detail below) and Eurojust was signed in 2004 and a communication link between the two organisations was set up in 2007, although shortcomings remain in Europol passing data to Eurojust (House of Lords European Union Committee, 2008: paras 178–180). The cooperation agreement was updated in 2008 with the adoption of five legal instruments: (1) the Framework Decision on racism and xenophobia; (2) the Framework Decision on data protection; (3) the Framework Decision on mutual recognition in probation matters; (4) the Framework Decision on terrorism; and (5) the Framework Decision on mutual recognition of judgments in criminal matters (Hillier, 2008).

In the longer term it is possible that Eurojust will be the supervisor of Europol, a development that is compatible with the situation in most EU countries, whereby police investigations in criminal matters are subject to some form of judicial or prosecutorial supervision (House of Lords European Union Committee, 2004: para 74).

The European arrest warrant

The European arrest warrant (EAW) was introduced in 2004 to speed up extradition procedures between member states and is based upon the principle of mutual recognition of member states' national criminal laws and procedures (House of Lords European Union Committee, 2003: para 2). It was implemented in the UK in 2004.

The practical impact of the warrant is to provide for the arrest and surrendering of a national of one EU member state for an action defined as a crime in another EU member state, in whose borders that crime was committed. Applications for extradition from the UK to another member state are processed by the Fugitives Unit of the Serious Organised Crime Agency (SOCA). Between January 2004 and August 2006 the Crown Prosecution Service issued a total of 307 EAWs in the UK on behalf of EU partners, which resulted in the arrest of 172 suspects. A summary of the data contained in the EAW is transmitted to EU countries via the Schengen Information System (SIS). The new version of SIS, SIS II, will enable the entire text of the EAW to be relayed in this fashion and it is anticipated that the UK's participation in SIS II will increase the workload of both the CPS and SOCA in connection with EAWs (House of Lords European Union Committee, 2007: para 77).

One criticism of this system is that the EAW focuses on enforcement while providing little protection to the rights of those who may be subject to this procedure (House of Lords European Union Committee, 2005a: para 41).

The European evidence warrant

The European evidence warrant would have created a common warrant for obtaining objects, documents and data in cases that reach beyond the boundaries of individual member states. However, the Third Pillar requirement of unanimous approval by all 27 member states impeded the adoption of this idea.

Situation Centre

Under the Second Pillar of the Maastricht Treaty, a Situation Centre (SitCen) was established under the sponsorship of the Council Secretariat to assess key issues affecting the EU's foreign policy. A counter-terrorism group (CTG) was set up within SitCen in January 2005. This brings together EU intelligence experts drawn from the external and internal security services of member states whose role is to assess the threat from terrorists both within and outside Europe. Their role does not extend to operational matters, although their advice is provided to member state Ministers of Justice who are charged with dealing with the terrorist threat.

The existence of SitCen has tended to legitimise the exclusion of Europol from direct liaison with member states' intelligence agencies, a situation which is based upon the formalised arrangements where liaison between Europol and a member state is constructed through a single national unit such as the UK's SOCA. Since 2007 (when the Danish Protocol amended the Europol Convention) it has been possible for member states to authorise direct contacts between Europol and other designated agencies, which include those such as MI5, that are responsible for intelligence gathering. However, the low level of security clearance by Europol officials may impede progress in this direction (House of Lords European Union Committee, 2008: paras 120–122).

Frontex

In 2004 a Council resolution established Frontex, which became operational in July 2005. This is an external borders agency (based in Warsaw) with a remit to secure the external borders of the EU, thus helping to respond to the problem of illegal immigration. In practical terms it seeks to promote coordination between member states, train border guards and perform risk assessments. Although the UK cooperates with Frontex and participates in some of its operations, it is excluded from membership, as this is restricted to states that are part of the Schengen group of countries.

Crisis management

In 2002 the EU member states adopted a joint response programme to chemical, biological, radiological or nuclear (CBRN) weapon attack, which sought to establish a common strategy to cope with such problems. It was followed by proposals put forward by the Commission and Council on practical steps to be taken in connection with issues of this nature. These included a European Programme for Critical Infrastructure Protection (termed EPCIP) and a crisis alert system called ARGUS that is designed to coordinate the crisis management programmes put forward by the EU Commission.

Cooperation between the EU and other nations

The activities mounted by the EU in connection with organised crime and terrorism have embraced arrangements concluded with nations not within the EU, thereby further extending the scope of criminal justice and police activity. EU policy with non-member states has been developed in the areas of asylum and migration. This approach has been criticised for being based on EU self-interest – to prevent refugees and asylum seekers from entering EU countries as opposed to seeking to strengthen the capacity of external countries to refugees in their regions of origin (House of Lords European Union Committee, 2005a: paras 66–68).

Following the terrorist attacks of September 2001, a cooperation agreement between the USA and Europol to combat all forms of serious international crime was concluded on 6 December 2001 and a supplementary agreement was signed on 20 December 2002 to expand the range of collaboration to include the exchange of personal data. Additionally, Europol set up a liaison office in Washington in 2002 as its point of contact regarding the transmission of information and criminal intelligence requests from Europol and EU member states to US law enforcement authorities. Further developments related to terrorism which have implications for global policing and criminal justice matters included the conclusion of an EU–USA extradition agreement in 2003 and an agreement that was reached in 2004 (and re-negotiated in 2007) regarding the transfer of passenger name record data (that is, data held in airlines' booking systems) between the EU and USA.

Agreements that are concluded at an international level to tackle global crime may pose civil liberties objections in some nations that are required to implement them. In the UK, the 2002 agreement relating to the transfer of personal data between Europol and the USA was criticised because it permitted the exchange of data to a wide range of American authorities for purposes that were beyond Europol's remit (House of Lords European Union Committee, 2003: paras 49–50, and 2005b: paras 76 and 78). Problems associated with the 2003 USA–EU extradition agreement included its vagueness on key issues such as the death penalty and whether it permitted the transfer of suspects to countries where there was a risk of torture or other forms of sinhumane treatment (ESSTRT Consortium, 2006: 20).

European policing arrangements

The need to combat crime and terrorism provides a rationale for the formation of police units whose remit goes beyond individual nation states. There are two developments affecting policing that can be pursued to tackle cross-border crime. The first of these is 'international police cooperation', where the police forces of individual nations work together on initiatives to combat crime while owing their authority and allegiance first and foremost to their own state. The other is 'transnational policing', which is characterised by law enforcement networks that are relatively autonomous of individual nation states or owe their authority and allegiance to other non-state polities or political communities, such as the European Union (Walker, 2003: 111).

This section examines the various mechanisms that have been developed to facilitate police cooperation between nation states to tackle cross-border crime and terrorism. Many, but not all, of these operate within the geographic confines of the EU.

The International Criminal Police Organisation (Interpol)

Interpol was established in 1923 to further assistance between police forces and related agencies that exist to combat international crime. Interpol's General Secretariat is housed in Lyon and liaises with the National Central Bureau of each member country, of which there are now 187 (House of Lords European Union Committee, 2008: para 28). Its broadening membership has moved it away from its original European orientation to that of a worldwide body, although Interpol has a liaison officer stationed at Europol and the two bodies signed a Joint Initiative in 2001.

Interpol primarily fulfils its responsibilities by collecting and circulating information about individuals. Information such as criminal names, fingerprints, DNA profiles, travel documents and stolen property (e.g. passports and vehicles) are stored on databases. A communications system referred to as I–24/7 provides direct access to these databases.

Interpol also provides emergency assistance to law enforcement agencies by despatching response teams to help deal with episodes such as major crime and disasters. For example, an Interpol team aided victim identification alter the Indian Ocean tsunami in 2004. A 24-hour Command and Coordination Centre, which monitors events around the world, has been set up within Interpol to respond to such requests for assistance. Its work overlaps with that performed by Europol in such areas as terrorism, drugs, organised crime and people trafficking. However, its orientation is on crime that has already occurred rather than Europol's concern to respond to its future manifestations (House of Lords European Union Committee, 2005b: para 69, and 2008: para 191).

Interpol is also involved in international responses to terrorism. In 2002, it set up the Fusion Task Force, whose main role was to identify members of criminal groups who were engaged in terrorist activity. Interpol's importance in this area of activity especially rests on the fact that it is the only police organisation with worldwide coverage (House of Lords European Union Committee, 2005b: paras 69 and 74).

The Trevi Group

The Trevi Group of the European Council of Ministers was formed in 1974. TREVI is an acronym for terrorism, radicalism, extremism and violence, and it comprises a forum for regular meetings of ministers responsible for internal affairs and for senior European police officers. Its main purpose is to provide a mechanism for the exchange of information. Its work was initially focused on terrorism, but it has subsequently developed into different areas covering serious crime and drug trafficking.

Trevi operates outside the formal structures of the EU although its senior officials liaise with the European Council. Much of the day-to-day work of this body is performed by working groups composed of police officers, civil servants and others with relevant expertise. It considers issues such as police training and technology, serious crime, public order and disaster prevention (Morgan and Newburn, 1997: 67).

The Maastricht Treaty's Third Pillar arrangements absorbed Trevi. Its work is now the responsibility of the Coordinating (or K4) Committee, established under the Maastricht Treaty. It was the forerunner of Europol, under whose auspices this organisation was initially established.

Schengen initiatives

The Schengen Agreement (1985) and Convention (1990) sought to further the objective of a single market by facilitating the freedom of movement of people, goods and transport within the EU. Schengen operates outside the institutional framework of the EU but has nonetheless been a source of pressure for the creation of a coordinated EU criminal justice process.

A number of arrangements have been concluded under Schengen. These include:

- Cooperation over drugs-related crime (especially in order to limit drug smuggling);
- Cooperation between police forces and legal authorities across national frontiers (which in some countries, such as Holland, resulted in police organisational reform);
- The development of standardised policies in connection with illegal immigration and visas;
- Simpler extradition rules between member countries;
- The establishment of a database, the Schengen Information System (SIS).

A key aspect of the Schengen Agreement was the abolition of the EU's internal frontier controls between member states, coupled with stringent immigration controls along the EU's external borders. The UK was, however, sceptical of this development, believing that while open EU frontiers were of benefit to law-abiding citizens, other groups, including criminals, terrorists and illegal refugees, could take advantage of this situation. Britain (and the Irish Republic) therefore remained outside the Schengen Agreement. However, the UK gained approval in 2000 to participate in those aspects of the Schengen *acquis* that related to criminal law and policing, and to participate in aspects of the Schengen Information System (SIS) (see Box 9.2).

BOX 9.2

THE SCHENGEN INFORMATION SYSTEM (SIS)

The Schengen Information System (SIS) is an EU-wide database for the collection and exchange of information relating to immigration, policing and criminal law for the purposes of law enforcement and immigration control (House of Lords European Union Committee, 2007: foreword). It was formally established by the 1990 Schengen Convention and became operational in 1995. It was a corollary of the relaxation of border controls in the 1985 Schengen Agreement since pooled information was required in order for law enforcement and immigration control officers (working at borders or elsewhere within their respective countries) to undertake a range of tasks that are specified in categories referred to as 'alerts'.

Alerts comprise lists of persons wanted in a Schengen state. They list non-EU citizens ('aliens') who should be denied entry, missing persons, persons wanted as witnesses or for the purposes of prosecution or the enforcement of sentences, persons or vehicles to be placed under surveillance and objects sought for the purposes of seizure or for

(Continued)

(Continued)

use in criminal proceedings (Schengen Convention 1990, cited in House of Lords European Union Committee, 2007: para 12).

The information stored on the SIS is relatively basic (including details such as names and aliases, sex and physical characteristics, date and place of birth, nationality and whether the person is violent). Member states hold supplementary information on persons who are the subject of its alerts in a separate database known as SIRENE (Supplementary Information Request at the National Entry), to which all member states may request access. Each member state has a SIRENE bureau that acts as a link between member states' police forces and the SIS.

The UK was granted permission to opt into the SIS in 2000. This participation was due to have commenced in January 2005 (House of Lords European Union Committee, 2007: para 18) but did not take place because of technical difficulties. Europol has also had access to some SIS alerts since 2006 but access has not been implemented immediately.

Limitations of the SIS (arising from the accession of new EU member states) and the desirability of including biometric data (such as photographs, fingerprints, DNA profiles and retina scans) resulted in the development of a second-generation SIS (called SIS II) (House of Lords European Union Committee, 2007: para 20). Biometric identifiers will be stored on SIS II. The new system will also provide links between the different alerts stored on the system. It is intended that SIS II will be fully deployed during 2011.

The UK intends to join SIS II, but since it is not a full member of the Schengen Convention (that is, it maintains its border controls with other member states) it will not have access to the immigration data stored on SIS II, although it will have access to other data concerned with policing and criminal cooperation (House of Lords European Union Committee, 2007: para 21). It is anticipated that the UK's membership will occur during 2011.

When the UK joins SIS II, checks made through the Police National Computer will automatically trigger a check on the SIS. If a match is made, the officer making the enquiry will be referred to SIRENE UK (housed by SOCA), which will then act as a link between the UK and the SIS (House of Lords European Union Committee, 2007: para 55).

The European Police Office (Europol)

Article K1(9) of the Maastricht Treaty (which came into force in 1993) created a European Police Office within the formal European structure to secure an enhanced degree of police cooperation in international matters such as terrorism and the drugs trade. Europol was established under the auspices of the Treaty's Third Pillar of Justice and Home Affairs, which is concerned with policing, immigration, asylum and legal cooperation. However, the Maastricht Tready did not

establish a European-wide police office, although a European Drugs Unit (which lacked a formal constitution or powers) was set up in 1993. In compliance with article K3(2) of the Maastricht Treaty, The Convention on the Establishment of a European Police Office was drawn up in July 1995 and Europol formally came into being towards the end of 1998. It became operational from its headquarters in The Hague in July 1999.

Europol is funded by the member states and has around 250 members drawn from these states (House of Lords European Union Committee, 2003: para 3). Its work is conducted by Europol Liaison Officers who are seconded to Europol Headquarters from the police organisations of member countries. The seconded officers are located in Europol's Liaison Bureau. Not all Europol officers are drawn from a police background. In 2009, of the 42 UK nationals working at Europol, only 11 had a law enforcement background (West, 2009). Europol was not devised as a European wide police force conducting criminal investigations. Its role was to act as an intelligence agency, facilitating the exchange of information among the national policing units of member states and to analyse information received from them in connection with transnational criminal activities – a function regarded as 'one of Europol's success stories' (Walker, 2003: 119; House of Lords European Union Committee, 2008: foreword).

The 1995 Convention gave Europol the role of improving:

> the effectiveness and cooperation of the competent authorities in the Member States in preventing and combating terrorism, unlawful drug trafficking and other serious forms of international crime where there are factual indications that an organised criminal structure is involved and two or more Member States are affected by the forms of crime in question in such a way as to require a common approach by the Member States owing to the scale, significance and consequence of the offences concerned. (1995 Convention Article 2 (1), quoted in House of Lords European Union Committee, 2003: para 2)

The specific crimes covered by Europol are:

- Unlawful drug trafficking;
- Trafficking in nuclear and radioactive substances;
- Illegal Immigrant smuggling;
- Trade in human beings;
- Motor vehicle crime;
- Crimes committed in the course of terrorist activities.

Other crimes listed in the Annex to the 1995 Convention are:

- Crimes against life, limb or personal freedom;
- Crimes against property or public goods including fraud;
- Illegal trading and harm to the environment (Article 2 of the 1995 Convention, cited in House of Lords European Union Committee, 2003: para 8).

The limitation imposed on Europol regarding the requirement of factual indications that an organised criminal structure is involved posed a number of difficulties, including the nebulous nature of this term, which was defined differently by different member states (House of Lords European Union Committee, 2008: paras 31–33), and the fact that serious transnational crimes, such as serial killings, occurring in more than one member country were not necessarily organised. It gave rise to suggestions, put forward during the Danish Presidency in 2002, that Europol's remit should be amended to the generic term 'serious international crime' (House of Lords European Union Committee, 2003: para 9). However, this term was also criticised for its vagueness (House of Lords European Union Committee, 2003: para 10) and was later abandoned.

The orientation of Europol is primarily forward-looking and is based on an intelligence-led model of policing implemented through Organised Crime Threat Assessments (OCTAs) rather than reacting to past events (House of Lords European Union Committee, 2008: paras 68–69). These were introduced in the wake of the 2004 Hague Programme, replacing the former Organised Crime Report. OCTAs are published by Europol on an annual basis and are designed to inform the Justice and Home Affairs Council of the main threats that face the EU, and to facilitate Europol-led responses to these threats by the member states (House of Lords European Union Committee, 2008: para 77).

In order to accomplish its functions, Europol utilises a computerised system of collected information which is discharged through two programmes – the Europol Information System (EIS) and the Overall Analysis System for Intelligence and Support (OASIS), whose work is stored in analysis work files (AWFs). Member states may participate in as many, or as few, AWFs as they wish. These two programmes are, however, 'separate and independent' (House of Lords European Union Committee, 2008: para 86). Europol has entered into data-sharing arrangements with a number of non-EU countries, including America and Australia, which have liaison officers stationed at Europol. It has also concluded strategic agreements with several other countries, such as the Russian Federation, that do not entail the transfer of data.

The future direction of Europol

A key difficulty faced by Europol was that it was established by a Convention between the member states rather than a Treaty. This situation has caused the organisation a number of problems since amendments to a Convention are slow and cumbersome. Changes need to be brought about by Protocols that require the ratification by all signatory members. This has impeded making progress in the role, powers and governance of Europol and has prompted moves, initiated by the Justice and Home Affairs Council in 2006, to establish Europol on the basis of a Council Decision (based on the Third Pillar of the Maastricht Treaty) rather than a Convention.

This was agreed in 2008 and the reform came into force in 2010, making Europol an EU agency. Europol's remit is still focused on organised crime. However, this term has been defined broadly to cover serious crimes that affect two or more member states and where the 'scale, significance and consequences' of the offences require member states to adopt a common approach (House of Lords European Union Committee, 2008: para 35).

Further changes may affect Europol. The 'Future Group' (created at an informal meeting of the Justice and Home Affairs Council at Dresden in 2007) seeks to improve the manner in which data is transferred between member states, perhaps through the use of automatic data transfer instruments. The 2009 Treaty of Lisbon abolished the Pillar structure of the Maastricht Treaty. It will set out the role of Europol and the manner in which the European Parliament and Council can determine its structure, operation, field of action and tasks, and the way in which European and national parliaments can scrutinise its work.

Although the main purpose of Europol is to 'pool and share data' (Occhipinti, 2003: 2), moves have been made to give it an operational role. The main mechanism to achieve this is Joint Investigative Teams (JITs). In 2002 Europol was empowered to initiate JITs by authorities within two or more member states in relation to a specific purpose and for a limited period. Such cooperation was, however, voluntarily entered into by the member states. This issue was considered further at a meeting of the EU Justice and Interior Ministers at Vienna in 2006, but progress could only take place if member states ratified protocols to advance this proposal. Should Europol eventually secure executive policing powers, it might in the long term assume a role in Europe akin to that of the FBI in America (Occhipinti, 2003: 2).

UK policing and international crime

The main development affecting UK policing and the European dimension of crime has been the creation of the Serious Organised Crime Agency (SOCA). In the early 1990s it was argued that a national British force would inevitably be required to respond to the increasingly international nature of serious crime (Condon, 1994), especially in the European context where there was a greater likelihood of cross-border crime. This sort of organisation was subsequently created with the establishment of SOCA by the 2005 Serious Organised Crime and Police Act.

SOCA is the sole unit through which Europol communicates with the UK. Although it has been argued that communications between SOCA and Europol are 'very effective' (House of Lords European Union Committee, 2008: para 256), a deficiency has been observed regarding the relationship between SOCA and the UK's 52 individual police forces, especially in relation to issues such as the communication of Europol documents. This has led some forces dealing with transnational criminal activity to prefer using Interpol rather than Europol (House of Lords European Union Committee, 2008: para 257). Also, SOCA does not have responsibility for counter-terrorism. This task is instead fulfilled by the Metropolitan Police Counter-terrorism Command (SO19), which seconds an officer to Europol's UK Liaison Bureau.

A further difficulty is that SOCA's remit extends only to serious organised crime, and it has been argued that there is also a need for a central mechanism to coordinate communications between the UK police and their EU counterparts on other forms of crime (Home Affairs Committee, 2007b: para 77). The government's view was that the newly-created Law Enforcement Forum would provide a platform for discussing and resolving such issues (Home Affairs Committee, 2007a: para 5).

Factors impeding international police cooperation: a case study of the EU

Measures that seek to enhance cross-border police cooperation in response to crime and terrorism are faced with a number of hurdles. The nature of these is discussed below in the EU context, although they could be encountered in any form of international approach to crime and terrorism.

Different political traditions

EU countries have different political systems and the difference between unitary systems (as in the UK) and federal systems (as in Germany) has implications for the ceding of power to supranational institutions. It has been noted, for example, that this has affected the powers of the German Member of the Eurojust College, since criminal law lies within the competence of the states (Länder) rather than the federal government. As a result, the German representative has been described as merely 'an information gate' (House of Lords European Union Committee, 2004: paras 37–38).

There are also significant differences within EU countries regarding political culture, and this influences practical policies to combat crime and terrorism when these impinge on civil and political liberties. The balance between security and liberty is defined differently within member countries, which affects issues such as the judicial oversight and democratic control over the implementation of EU-level measures in areas such as counter-terrorism policy. Here, 'some technologies, such as biometrics, camera surveillance, and radio frequency identification tags, arouse different levels of concern in EU member states' (ESSRT

Consortium, 2006: 4). The development of a Common European Asylum System is complicated by the different standards that apply towards asylum seekers in member countries.

Linguistic problems

Linguistic problems also arise, both in the storage of data by member states in their own language and also in the different meanings given by different states to technical terms. For example, terms such as 'intelligence' and 'information' lack differentiation in some European languages (House of Lords European Union Committee, 2008: para 242). Linguistic problems may also give rise to a lack of precision regarding issues such as legal terminology. This may affect the manner in which data is recorded and stored on computerised databases, making its retrieval of information more difficult (House of Lords European Union Committee, 2008: para 247).

Reluctance of agencies to cooperate

The reluctance of police and security agencies to share intelligence and other forms of information has traditionally hindered cooperation within member states. This arises from factors such as interdepartmental rivalries and concerns that include the need to protect sources and the need for the organisation that holds the information to be satisfied that the body requesting access to it is secure (House of Lords European Union Committee, 2005b: para 17).

Sharing information is even more problematic when extended to inter-state cooperation. The reluctance of some member states to supply their national Europol liaison officers with information that can be shared with member states is one problem of this nature. It is a difficulty attributed in part to concerns regarding the security of the Europol Information System, which was 'a disincentive for Member States imputing particularly sensitive data onto the system' (Home Affairs Committee, 2007b: para 6). The system needs to be trusted in two regards: member states need to trust the security of each other's intelligence services and they need to trust the technology of the data systems (House of Lords European Union Committee, 2008: 53). The reluctance of member states to use formal Europol mechanisms to share sensitive information, especially in the early stages of an investigation, is a manifestation of this problem (House of Lords European Union Committee, 2008: paras 60 and 218). One consequence of this has been that around four-fifths of information exchanged by liaison officers stationed at Europol is shared on an informal basis so that only those states directly concerned with a specific investigation or operation have access to it (House of Lords European Union Committee, 2008: para 50).

Different working practices

Cooperation between police forces across Europe is also impeded by their different working practices. This problem has served to limit the adoption of intelligence-led methods of policing by Europol. Some member states were 'unenthusiastic' towards it and there was no agreed definition of the concept (Home Affairs Committee, 2007a: para 71–72). A related problem has adversely affected the use made by member states of the Europol Information System (EIS) since the data systems used by police organisations within many individual member states do not enable automatic data loading on to the EIS (House of Lords European Union Committee, 2008: para 245).

Accountability

The mechanisms of accountability for a number of developments affecting European policing initiatives have long been regarded as inadequate (Hebenton and Thomas, 1995: 198-9). Eurojust, for example, is subject to very limited scrutiny by the European Parliament and is directly accountable to the Council of Ministers. The European Commission is responsible for proposing the budget of Eurojust, but exercises no control over its operation and decisions, and there are no formal mechanisms for its work to be scrutinised by national parliaments (House of Lords European Union Committee, 2004: paras 14 and 103).

This problem especially affects Europol, which has a complex structure of governance involving the Justice and Home Affairs Council Ministers of the European Parliament, the EU Commission (which became involved in Europol issues when the Treaty of Amsterdam came into force in 1999), the Europol Management Board (one member of which is appointed by each member state) and a Director (who is appointed on a fixed-term basis of four years by the Council and who is accountable to the Management Board for his activities). Traditionally, the role played by the European Parliament in connection with Europol's budget has been 'insignificant' (House of Lords European Union Committee, 2008: para 154), but this situation altered when Europol became an agency in 2010.

A particular problem concerns national parliaments whose remits extend only to budgetary issues (since Europol is funded by contributions from member states) but which lack the ability to define Europol's objectives or to scrutinise its work (Home Affairs Committee, 2007b: para 101; and House of Lords European Union Committee, 2008: para 169). One measure to improve Europol's accountability was the proposal of the European Commission in 2002 to set up a joint committee of the national parliaments and the European Parliament which would meet twice a year to scrutinise Europol's work. A smaller group of members nominated by the joint committee would maintain a closer degree of contact with Europol.

'The transformation of Europol into a European equivalent of the Federal Bureau of Investigation (FBI) in America is an inevitable development'. Discuss

To answer this question you should draw on the material contained in this chapter and consult the references that are cited. The main points you should address are:

- The nature and scale of cross-border crime in Europe that might justify extending the present role of Europol;
- The current role performed by Europol and how this differs from that of the FBI (in particular with regard to executive policing powers);
- Proposals that have been put forward to extend the role played by Europol in responding to cross-border crime;
- A consideration of the impediments that might prevent the future development of an organisation in the EU akin to that of the FBI;
- A conclusion in which you should assert whether such a development is likely or not based on an assessment of the arguments that you have put forward earlier in the discussion.

REFERENCES

Bowden, T. (1977) *Breakdown of Public Security: The Case of Ireland 1916–1921 and Palestine 1936–1939*. London: Sage.

Clinton, B. (2001) 'The Struggle for the Soul of the Twenty-first Century'. Dimbleby Lecture, BBC1, 16 December. [Online] www.australianpolitics.com/news/2001/01-12-14.shtml accessed 15 February 2009].

Condon, Sir P. (1994) 'Britain's Top Cop Sees National Police Force as Inevitable Step', *The Guardian*, 12 January.

ESSTRT Consortium (2006) *New European Approaches to Counter Terrorism*. [Online] www.cmi.fi/files/ESSTRT_final_report.pdf [accessed 16 March 2009].

European council (1997) *Action Plan to Combat Organised Crime*. OJC 251, 15 August.

van de Bunt, H. and van der Schoot, C. (2003) *Prevention of Organised Crime: A Situational Approach*. Amsterdam: Boom Iuridische Uitgevers, distributed by Willan Publishing.

Hebenton, B. and Thomas, T. (1995) *Policing Europe: Cooperation, Conflict and Control*. New York: St Martins Press.

Hillier, M. (2008) Speech in the House of Commons, 4 December, HC Debs, Vol 485, Col 10WS.

Home Affairs Committee (2007a) *Government's Response to the Committee's Third Report: Justice and Home Affairs Issues at European Union Level*. First Special Report, Session 2006–07. House of Commons Paper 1021. London: TSO.

Home Affairs Committee (2007b) *Justice and Home Affairs Issues at European Union Level*. Third Report, Session 2006–07. House of Commons Paper 76–1. London: TSO.

House of Lords European Union Committee (2003) *Europol's Role in Fighting Crime*. Fifth Report, Session 2002–03. House of Lords Paper 43. London: TSO.

House of Lords European Union Committee (2004) *Judicial Cooperation in the EU: The Role of Eurojust*, Twenty-thrid Report, Session 2003–04. House of Lords Paper 138. London: TSO.

House of Lords European Union Committee (2005a) *The Hague Programme: A Five-year Agenda for EU Justice and Home Affairs*. Tenth Report, Session 2005–06. House of Lords Paper 84. London: TSO.

House of Lords European Union Committee (2005b) *After Madrid: The EU's Response to Terrorism*. Fifth Report Session 2004–05. House of Lords Paper 53. London: TSO.

House of Lords European Union Committee (2007) *Schengen Information System, II (SIS II)*. Ninth Report, Session 2006-07. House of Lords Paper 49. London: TSO.

House of Lords European Union Committee (2008) *Europol: Coordinating the Fight against Serious and Organised Crime*. Twenty-ninth Report, Session 2007–08. House of Lords Paper 183. London: TSO.

Morgan, R. and Newburn, T. (1997) *The Future of Policing*. Oxford: Clarendon Press.

Occhipinti, J. (2003) *The Politics of EU Police Cooperation: Towards a European FBI?* Boulder, CO: Lynne Reinner.

Walker, N. (2003) 'The Pattern of Transnational Policing', in T. Newburn (ed.), *Handbook of Policing*. Cullompton, Devon: Willan Publishing.

West, Lord (2009) Speech in the House of Lords, 12 January, HL Debs, Vol 706, Col WA102.

10

The future direction of policing in a time of financial restraint

> ### CHAPTER AIMS
>
> The aims of this chapter are:
>
> - To evaluate the present funding arrangements of the police service;
> - To consider the impact of future cuts in public expenditure on the police service;
> - To analyse developments affecting police force amalgamations and the modernisation of police working practices in the context of financial stringency.

Police funding

It is inevitable that public spending will be reduced following the 2010 general election. This concluding chapter considers what impact future financial restraints may impose on policing.

The government spending for police authorities is set for a three-year period within the context of the Comprehensive Spending Review. Total government grants to the police increased by 19% in real terms between 1997/98 and 2008/09 (Home Affairs Committee, 2008: para 65). The most recent Comprehensive Spending Review (CSR), announced in December 2007, increased central grants made to police forces by 2.9% in 2008/09, 2.9% in 2009/10 and 2.7% in 2010/11. The total provision for police revenue grants in 2009/10 was £9,428 million (Coaker, 2009).

Although figures produced at the beginning of 2010 suggested that the UK was slowly emerging from the 2008/09 recession, it is inevitable that the police service will be required to operate in a 'much tighter fiscal environment' over the coming five years (Home Office, 2009: 7). It must therefore be anticipated that the next CSR will incorporate reductions on a par with those to be imposed elsewhere on the public sector following the 2010 election.

Future reductions must be placed in the context of views that the current CSR settlement is inadequate to sustain the contemporary demands placed on the police service. The Association of Police Authorities (APA) informed the Home Affairs Committee in 2008 that this settlement would result in shortfalls that were roughly in line with the earlier ACPO/APA predictions contained in their joint submission, *Sustainable Policing* (Association of Chief Police Officers and Association of Police Authorities, 2006). This argued that the service required annual net resource increases of between 5% and 7% to stand still (Home Affairs Committee, 2007: para 36) and anticipated that under the CSR that was announced in 2007 for the period 2008/09–2010/11 the service would suffer shortfalls rising from £391 million in 2007/08 to £966 million in 2010/11 (Home Affairs Committee, 2008: para 65).

Issues regarding the inadequacy of the global funding of the police service were augmented by additional problems affecting the financial aspects of individual forces.

The distribution of the general grant to police authorities is determined by a complex calculation based on a number of components. The most important of these is the needs-based formula. The main determinant in the formula is the projected resident population, but cost adjustments are built in for the socio-economic and demographic factors that may impact on crime levels – for example, numbers of long-term unemployed and population sparsity (Ruffley, 2009). A particular problem with the projected resident population is that it is based on data collected in the past. This meant, for example, that the allocation of money in 2008–11 was based upon population data collected in 2004, which thus failed to take into account migration and the disproportionate impact this has had on some parts of the country (Coaker, 2009).

Further difficulties with the formula include the principle that averaged out the differences between the crime and disorder partnership areas within each police authority. This principle tended to reward 'areas of uniformity in population distribution, density and relative wealth'. Police authorities characterised by strong contrasts, containing areas of high and low areas of density, tended to lose out (Brain, 2008: 18).

However, the formula has never been fully applied and this poses further problems for some forces. Its application has been subject to a process of floors and ceilings: some police authorities receive more than they are entitled to on a strict application of the formula whereas other forces receive less. At the extreme ends, this meant that the West Midlands force received nearly 11%, or £48 million, less than the funding formula would have allocated in 2007/08 if applied correctly, whereas Northumbria Police received over 12%, or £29 million, more. Sir Ronnie Flanagan recommended that the Home Office should move towards a fuller application of the formula in future Spending Reviews so that funding is allocated on objective need (Home Affairs Committee, 2008: para 69). This would mean that areas that currently received less than their allocation would benefit, but those that currently receive more would lose out (Home Affairs Committee, 2008: para 70). The adoption of this recommendation would have significant repercussions on the financial viability of the latter category of police forces.

Local funding

In addition to money provided by the Home Office, police forces receive funding from their local Council Tax payers through a precept that is collected by local government. This is an important, and increasing, source of funding for police forces. It has risen from a global figure of 13% of total police funding in 1997/08 to 21.5% in 2006/07 (Home Affairs Committee, 2007: para 41). There are wide disparities affecting the police authority precept collected in Council Tax. The average proportion of police force funding derived from this source in England and Wales was 26.9%, but there were significant differences between the shires (average 31.7%) and the six metropolitan forces (average 16.4%). There was also considerable variation in the shires (ranging from 46.1% in Surrey to 22.1% in Cleveland) (McNulty, 2008).

The structure and organisation of police forces

One way through which the police service might adapt to financial restraints is to make adjustments to its organisation. This could be achieved by mergers, which would reduce the current number of police forces in England and Wales, or though enhanced collaboration, affecting some of the activities they perform.

Amalgamations

An important justification for amalgamating police forces was that this reform would save money: it was estimated that merger savings might amount to £70 million a year and that the Net Present Value of merger savings and productivity gains could amount to £2,250 million over 10 years (HMIC, 2005: 11).

Although the compulsory programme of amalgamations was abandoned in 2006 and are unlikely to be resurrected, voluntary mergers remain on the police policy agenda. Sir Ronnie Flanagan's evidence to the Home Affairs Committee on 26 February 2008 stated that if Her Majesty's Inspectorate of Constabulary (HMIC) concluded that collaboration was not succeeding in 'closing the gap' relating to the provision of the protective services, the whole question of mergers could be back on the agenda at some stage in the future. Subsequently, it was stated that the government would encourage voluntary mergers 'where this would be in the public interest' (Home Office, 2009: 10).

These arguments suggest that financial considerations may underpin the future organisation of police forces. Although larger forces might be able to weather constraints imposed by the current CSR financial settlement, and any further cuts required by the subsequent one, others are in a weaker position. There are two categories of police forces in this latter situation. Some would lose out if the current needs-based funding formula was fully implemented in its present form. One estimate suggested that Cumbria would lose around 20% of its grant (the equivalent of 303 officers), Northumbria 13% (803 officers) and the Metropolitan Police Service (MPS) would lose the equivalent of 1,113 officers. In total, 19 forces would lose the equivalent of 4,164 officers (Brain, 2008: 18–19). This might lead to 'amalgamations of smaller, weaker forces with more powerful neighbours' (Brain, 2008: 18).

The second category of police forces which might seek voluntary amalgamations are those that have become heavily reliant on local sources of funding. Further reductions in central funding to these police authorities may act as an incentive for mergers where police authorities cannot make up any shortfall in central funding by further increasing the Council Tax precept. They would effectively be 'starved into submission' and forced to amalgamate with their neighbours in order to survive.

Collaboration

As a consequence of the financial imperative, collaboration has been put forward as the alternative to enforced police force amalgamations. It 'has great potential for producing efficiency gains and cost-saving initiatives' (Loveday et al., 2007: 17). It is particularly significant in a period in which 'managing a tighter settlement' (Home Affairs Committee, 2007: para 55) becomes a key aim of police forces. It might be anticipated, therefore, that financial restraints will ensure that this approach is pursued with more vigour in the future since, thus far, progress in advancing it has been disjointed (Loveday et al., 2007: 21).

An added justification for collaboration is that it makes police forces more resilient, in their ability to detect, prevent and respond to any challenges they may face. This resilience has been threatened by changes affecting the mix of the workforce, arising from a modernisation agenda whereby the number of police officers with designated powers has declined, due to the employment of civilians to perform jobs that were formally carried out by attested police officers. Collaboration provides a way to secure additional attested police forces who would be able to respond to a sudden emergency.

In 2008, forces and authorities were required to prepare Protective Service Improvement Plans (PSIPs), which set out their protective services priorities. HMIC performed an important role in providing feedback on these plans. The feedback formed the basis of police authority proposals to make significant improvements in 'high need' areas of protective services (that is, areas where there were significant gaps) by 2009. Subsequently, all forces would be required to meet ACPO minimum standards in all protective service areas by 2011.

However, HMIC has expressed concern at the adequacy of the PSIPs produced by police forces to improve the delivery of the protective services (HMIC, 2009: 4). The key explanation given was the disparate approaches that individual forces applied to the way in which they planned for and delivered the protective services (HMIC, 2009: 4). The solution was the creation of 'a new, universal protective services planning language' (HMIC, 2009: 4). It was suggested that the NPIA should consider developing templates for action plans, protective service improvement plans and externally focused partnership plans which would enable the government and potential collaboration partners to more easily 'read across' what individual forces were doing (HMIC, 2009: 6).

In the meantime, Home Office aid has been provided to 13 collaboration demonstrator sites, involving 31 forces, with the aim of sharing good practice and disseminating the lessons learned to the service. It was stated that 'our vision is for collaborative solutions to be undertaken as part of mainstream policing, complementing and adding value to national and local structures, forming a key part of how policing is delivered in the 21st Century' (Home Office, 2008: 72). These proposals were advanced in the 2009 Policing and Crime Act that gave the Home Secretary the power to give guidance and directions on which forces should collaborate and how this should be achieved. In addition, 10 regional intelligence units, which are concerned with countering level 2 criminal activities, were established in 2008 by ACPO, police forces and local authorities. Some Home Office funding was made available to establish these units.

Administrative collaboration

Shared support services may also be used to achieve economies of scale and therefore save money. This means forces pooling what are termed 'back-office functions', such as payroll and pensions, and human resources management. Collaboration of this sort has been developed in the East Midlands in areas of operations that include resource management, demand management and workforce modernisation. However, the Home Affairs Committee noted that there was room for considerable improvements to be made in administrative collaboration (Home Affairs Committee, 2008: paras 210–21). The Home Office has the power to mandate shared services, but has not thus far exercised it.

Value for money

In order to accommodate financial restraints, police forces will be required to enhance initiatives designed to ensure that the very best value for money is obtained from what resources are made available. One important incentive to securing the best use of resources was introduced in 1999 when the Home Office introduced efficiency savings targets for police authorities. The current target is 3%, of which 1.5% should be a cashable gain (Loveday et al., 2007: 15). In addition, activity-based costing (which calculates the costs of different police activities at BCU level) became a mandatory requirement in the 2003/04 National Policing Plan (Home Affairs Committee, 2007: para 21).

The term 'workforce modernisation' refers to developments that seek to improve performance, efficiency and productivity on the frontline of policing that are sustainable in the long term. The NPIA's National Improvement Strategy for Policing (NISP), which sets out a 10-year programme for securing improvements across policing, is at the heart of this strategy (Home Office, 2009).

The delivery of policing

There is considerable pressure to ensure that police officers are able to devote increased amounts of time to providing a visible presence within communities and to engage in 'frontline' policing tasks, embracing core functions that include patrol, response to 999 calls and the work performed by Criminal Investigation Departments (CIDs) and other specialist tasks. In 2003/04, 62.1% of officers' time in England was spent on these functions, rising to 64.2% in 2006/07 (McNulty, 2007). Reforms affecting the delivery of policing will be required in order to sustain these services in a time of financial stringency.

Reducing bureaucracy and paperwork

Contemporary police work entails a considerable amount of form-filling and paperwork. This has become an important aspect of police performance management and also ensures that officers can be held properly accountable for their actions. However, paperwork and bureaucracy eat into the time that officers are able to devote to frontline policing functions. In 2002, 52 'change proposals' were put forward to address this issue and increase the police presence in communities (O'Dowd, 2002). Subsequently, Sir Ronnie Flanagan argued that the service could save 'not less than 5–7 million hours … equivalent to 2,500–3,500 officers' across the service by reducing bureaucracy (Flanagan, 2008: para 5.64). There are a number of ways this might be achieved.

BOX 10.1

THE USE OF POLICE TIME

The bureaucracy that officers are required to perform as part of their daily duties is a key reason for removing them from the streets. This issue was examined in a detailed study of the tasks performed by officers on a 'typical' shift. It was found that officers were spending a similar amount of their time in a police station (43%) as they were outside it (57%) and that approximately only 17% of an officer's time was spent on patrol, the great bulk of which was on mobile rather than foot patrol (Singer, 2001: 27–28). Of the total time spent in the station, 41% was devoted to paperwork (Singer, 2001: 9–12).

It was argued that the time taken to process prisoners and prepare prosecutions was especially time-consuming and that the full range of activities involved occupied an officer for just under three hours (Singer, 2001: 12). Other paperwork that officers were required to complete included crime reports, intelligence reports, forms to log recovered property, missing person details, information required for special force initiatives and paperwork connected with the shift administration and the officer in question (Singer, 2001: vi).

A bureaucracy champion One initiative to reduce bureaucracy has been the appointment of a bureaucracy 'champion' to ensure the delivery of the proposals contained in the Flanagan Review (Flanagan, 2008) and the Government's Green Paper on policing (Home Office, 2008). This official (termed the 'Independent Reducing Bureaucracy Advocate') is Jan Berry, who chairs a frontline practitioner group to test proposals relating to the police, government and the criminal justice system for their impact on the frontline, and who also works with ACPO, the NPIA and the government to identify the top ten most frequently pursued processes in policing in order to design a standard process for each.

It was argued that the objective of reducing bureaucracy should be put forward within the context of a broader approach to sustainable business improvement and cultural change. It urged the adoption of a common business improvement model across policing – 'a systems approach that understands and reflects customer and stakeholder demand, encourages proactive leadership, incorporates front-line experience and removes over-working and duplication' (Berry, 2009: 8). Improvement programmes of this nature have been adopted in policing. One such is Quest, which has contributed towards reducing unnecessary deployment, increasing the detection of offences, improving response times and delivering a more proportionate response to incidents by those forces that have participated in it (Berry, 2009: 9).

Crime recording and case-file building Sir Ronnie Flanagan's review of policing recommended the adoption of a two-tiered approach to crime and incident recording, with serious offences, which would account for 20% of recorded crime, recorded fully, and local offences, which would account for 80%, recorded more concisely (Flanagan, 2008: para 5.32). This approach was piloted in Staffordshire, Leicestershire, Surrey and the West Midlands, and support for more proportionate forms of crime recording, enabling officers to exercise their independent judgement, was given subsequently by the Home Office (2009: 80).

A similar approach could be adopted towards case-file building for minor cases, typically those heard in a magistrates' court. Here the emphasis is not upon a less strenuous investigation but on a reduced amount of documentation completed after the investigation has taken place. The volume of paperwork is also increased by the need to obtain authority from the Crown Prosecution Service to charge suspects. This could be reduced if police charging powers were used to their full extent and were additionally extended to cover all summary offences and other categories of offence too (Home Affairs Committee, 2008: para 174).

A related reform was the Speedy Summary Justice Programme. This aimed to slash the paperwork on case-file preparation where a guilty plea was likely and saw the introduction of more integrated prosecution teams of co-located police and CPS lawyers. It has also been argued (Home Office, 2009: 80) that alternative resolutions to minor criminal actions which do not require a court appearance can be another way to reduce police bureaucracy, although this may not necessarily save a police officer's time.

Stop and account documentation   The documentation associated with stop and account procedures has been regarded as a major cause of bureaucratic burdens placed upon police officers. The Home Affairs Committee stated that 'a manually-recorded system of Stop and Account now takes on average seven minutes per individual encounter, not including time spent logging, checking and countersigning' (Home Affairs Committee, 2008: para 178). Sir Ronnie Flanagan concluded that 'the process has become bureaucratic rather than focusing on what I believe is most important in the one to one interactions between the police and members of the public – courtesy, respect and accountability' (Flanagan, 2008: para 5.58). He proposed to reform the stop and account procedure, so that officers record the details digitally rather than manually, and give the member of the public a record card denoting officer identity, place and time.

The key difficulty with this reform concerns the danger that this power may henceforth be exercised without adequate accountability, thus increasing the risk of alienating communities who perceive themselves to be on the receiving end of an 'over-policed society'. Nonetheless, the government proceeded with it, arguing that the scrapping of the 'over-lengthy' stop and account form saved the equivalent of 690,000 hours of police time and that this saving would be further increased by streamlining the recording of stop and searches (Home Office, 2009: 81).

The use of technology   Home Office funding has been made available towards the costs of Personal Digital Assistants (PDAs) (hand-held computers) which are designed to reduce the amount of time spent by officers at police stations, thus enabling them to devote more time to visible patrol and responding to incidents. These devices enable officers to access police national computers and databases while out on the streets and no longer require data gathered on the streets to be transferred on to a computer on the officer's return to the station as this is now done automatically. There should be 30,000 of these devices in use by frontline officers by April 2010 (Coaker, 2009).

There are, however, difficulties with this sort of technology. The Home Affairs Committee noted that some police officers were sceptical of their value, especially if software problems corrupted electronic notes that then had to be re-entered (Home Affairs Committee, 2008: para 186). Concern was also expressed about entering data into PDAs rather than notebooks when dealing with confrontational situations because of the degree of concentration that was required to enter the data electronically.

A further problem relates to different forces adopting different IT systems. This would mean that force data systems were not linked up, resulting in the duplication of data entry. The Home Affairs Committee referred to a figure of 70% of information being entered into police data systems more than once (Home Affairs Committee, 2008: para 196). To remedy this problem, the Home Affairs Committee recommended that the National Policing Improvement Agency should take the lead in negotiating the purchase of PDAs and their supporting infrastructure on a uniform basis, in order to reduce costs and remove contractual burdens from individual forces (Home Affairs Committee, 2008: para 206).

The police workforce

A crucial aspect of workforce modernisation is to use police staff to carry out tasks traditionally undertaken by sworn officers in order to provide 'a genuine around the clock service that properly supports the operational police officer' both within and outside the police station (Singer, 2001: 24–25). It has been argued that scope remains for forces and police authorities to improve value for money in the use of their resources (Audit Commission, 2007: 15).

This aspect of workforce modernisation is not new and emerged as part of the imposition of the principles of new public management on the police service in the early 1980s. It was initially referred to as 'civilianisation' and sought to free up police officers for operational duties. Between 1960 and 1986 the total number of civilians in the police service increased from 8,933 to 43,675, and totalled 53,011 in 1997 compared to 127,158 police officers (HMIC, 1998: 48). In 1995/06 expenditure of civilian salaries amounted to £1.02 billion compared with £3.95 billion for police salaries (HMIC, 1998: 40). Initially the bulk of civilian posts consisted of manual and clerical appointments whose work had previously been performed by police officers drawn the lower ranks of the service, but later some civilians were brought in at a higher level to perform more technical work.

One difficulty with the initial progress of the policy of civilianisation was the grant system used in England until 1994. Whereas increases in the establishment for police forces (if approved by the Home Office) were incorporated into grants received from central government, increases in the number of civilians employed by police forces did not attract this form of financial support. This increased the burden placed upon local sources of finance and provided an incentive for police authorities to seek increases in the number of police officers employed. It was concluded that 'pressure to civilianise would clearly be stronger if the aims of HMIC and the incentives delivered by the grant mechanism reinforces one another, rather than pulling in different directions' (Audit Commission, 1990: 8).

Sir Ronnie Flanagan proposed to push civilianisation further when he argued that support staff might undertake a greater number of tasks, such as taking statements, in order to release police officers for front line policing duties (Flanagan, 2008: para 4.8). The 2008 Green Paper made reference to the 2002 Police Reform Act, establishing investigation, detention and escort officers in order to free up police time. It was noted that the take-up of this provision was not as widespread as the government had hoped and the government urged forces to make greater use of these designated posts (Home Office, 2008: 48).

A related development would be for the police service to make greater use of the private sector through the mechanism of public–private partnerships. A police function could be provided by a private sector body that was contracted to deliver this service. This procedure is sometimes referred to as 'outsourcing' and would enable forces to focus on their core responsibilities by offloading activities that private companies might perform more cost effectively (Loveday et al., 2007: 35).

There are a number of advantages to these approaches, such as financial savings and improved services when these are provided by a bespoke service provider. But there are problems too. In particular, it is necessary to ensure that developments that entail the increased use of non-sworn police staff and private sector organisations to deliver police services do not undermine resilience to the extent that a police force cannot effectively respond to adverse situations that arise unexpectedly (see Loveday et al., 2007: 23–25).

A further development that is needed to advance the modernisation of the police workforce is to enhance the autonomy of BCU commanders to fashion their workforces in the manner they deem to be most appropriate to the needs of the locality. However, initiatives at this level are subject to veto by force headquarters since staffing levels are determined at force level. This has had a particularly detrimental effect on the ability of BCU commanders to attain workforce modernisation, in particular through the innovative use of the extended police family to deliver police functions (HMIC, 2004: 136–169).

The rationalisation of police support staff

A further aspect of workforce modernisation relates to the employment of police support staff. There is a wide disparity in the use of police support services by individual forces (Home Office, 2009: 87–88) and savings could be made by standardising the approach (perhaps by providing for common services across BCUs). It has been argued that 'if every force were to reduce the proportion of its workforce in business support to below 7% this would save at least £75 million per annum by 2013/14' (Home Office, 2009: 89).

Procurement of goods and services

Financial savings affecting the delivery of policing could also be secured by changing the way in which goods and services are purchased. The 43 police forces in England and Wales spend around £3.3 billion each year on the purchase of goods and services, of which £2.8 billion are spent by police authorities (Home Office, 2009: 82).

It has been pointed out that one central body could make savings by exercising its greater purchasing power and to achieve this the government proposed to introduce a national procurement framework which police authorities would be required to use. In line with the NPIA's Wave Plan, this would initially embrace the purchasing of vehicles (entailing the use of a standard beat car), body armour and e-forensic services, and a national police uniform will be introduced in 2012. It was argued that a national approach to procurement, coupled with the NPIA's Information System Improvement Strategy (ISIS) (which relates to the development, procurement and implementation of a national police IT structure), would secure savings of £400 million by 2014 (Home Office, 2009: 86).

Monitoring the attainment of value for money

The need for the police service to provide better value for money must not undermine the overall standards of policing. Police authorities will be required to insert a value for money statement into their local policing plans commencing in 2010/11. The NPIA will exercise a wide role in assisting the service to improve its efficiency and inspections conducted by HMIC and Audit Commission will focus on value for money. This will be an important aspect of the 2010 HMIC Workforce Inspection, which will focus on the costs and performance of police forces and authorities. It has also been suggested that incentives to secure effectiveness and efficiency might be included alongside the needs element in the next Comprehensive Spending Review (Home Office, 2009: 91).

Additional recommendations have been made concerning bureaucracy. It has been argued that police authorities should be required to provide details of their progress in developing a systems approach in their annual business plans, and that HMIC should include the progress made by forces in adopting sustainable business improvement principles as part of its inspection criteria (Berry, 2009: 12).

Coalition government police reforms

A Conservative–Liberal Democrat Coalition government took office following the May 2010 general election whose policies will shape the future policing agenda.

Public spending cuts were immediately put forward to address the large budget deficit inherited by the government. The reduction affecting policing was put forward on 14 July when the House of Commons approved an amendment to the police grant, the effect of which was to cut around £135 million from the 2010/2011 police budget. The Minister, Nick Herbert, argued that this constituted a reduction equivalent to 1.46% of the core funding which each force received from central Government (Herbert, 2010).

This measure, however, will form the prelude to a more significant cut that will emerge from the next Comprehensive Spending Review which the Home Secretary warned the Service would 'be big' and 'tough to achieve' (May 2010a). One estimate based on public spending projections from the Institute of Fiscal Studies suggested that the worst case scenario would be a reduction of 60,000 police, PCSO and civilian posts by 2015 (Brain, 2010).

A number of other measures affecting policing were immediately introduced by the Coalition government. By the end of 2010, the stop and account form will be stopped in its entirety and changes will be introduced designed to reduce the bureaucratic burden placed on officers by existing stop and search documentation. Charging decisions relating to a range of minor offences will be returned to the police from the CPS on a phased roll-out programme. Centralised targets and the Policing Pledge were abolished by the Home Secretary 'with immediate effect' (May 2010a) and a promise was also made to dismantle Key Performance Indicators which were branded 'targets in disguise' (May, 2010b).

The government's main proposals affecting policing will be incorporated in a Police Reform and Social Responsibility measure to be presented to the first Session of the new Parliament towards the end of 2010. A key underpinning of this legislation will be measures to reduce the extent of central direction over policing in favour of transferring power to localities and restoring discretion to the criminal justice practitioners who work within them. The legislation will include proposals to replace police authorities with 'a directly-elected individual at force level' who will be responsible for 'setting the force budget, agreeing the local strategic plan, playing a role in wider questions of community strategy and appointing – and if necessary removing – the local chief constable' (May, 2010a). Safeguards would be included to protect police operational independence. The measure may also include reforms to police terms and conditions (perhaps amending the present situation whereby police officers cannot be made redundant). The legislation is also likely to create a border Police force as part of a re-focused SOCA (May, 2010a).

Identify approaches that the police service in England and Wales might adopt to cope with an era of financial stringency.

To answer this question you should:

- Identify the chief ways through which the police service is currently financed;
- Consider the adequacy of existing funding arrangements;
- Analyse the additional problems that police forces might face in being subjected to spending cuts following the 2010 general election;
- Evaluate the key measures that might be adopted to cope with these problems, including changes to the structure and organisation of policing and the way in which police work is delivered.

REFERENCES

Association of Chief Police Officers and Association of Police Authorities (2006) *Sustainable Policing: the case for Resourcing the Police Service from 2008/9 to 2020/11*. London: Police Expenditure Group.

Audit Commission (1990) *Footing the Bill: Financing Provincial Police Forces* Police. Paper Number 6. London: Audit Commission.

Audit Commission (2007) *Police Use of Resources 2006/7*. London: Audit Commission.

Berry, J. (2009) *Reducing Bureaucracy in Policing*. Final Report. Produced by the Central Office of Information (COI), London, on behalf of the Independent Reducing Bureaucracy Advocate.

Brain, T. (2008) 'A Whiter Shade of Green', *Policing Today*, 14 (5). 17–19.

Brain, T. (2010) quoted in 'Budget Cuts "Threaten 60,000 Police Jobs"', BBC News UK [Online] http://www.bbc.co.uk/news/uk-10639938 [Accessed 12 July 2010]

Coaker, V. (2009) Speech in the House of Commons, 4 February, HC Debs, Vol 487, Cols 850–857.

Flanagan, Sir R. (2008) *The Review of Policing Final Report*. London: Review of Policing.

Herbert (2010) Speech in the House of Commons, 14 July, HC Debs, Vol 513, Col 957.

Her Majesty's Inspectorate of Constabulary (HMIC) (1998) *What Price Policing? A Study of Efficiency and Value for Money in the Police Service*. London: HMIC.

Her Majesty's Inspectorate of Constabulary (HMIC) (2004) *Modernising the Police Service: A Thematic Inspection of Workforce Modernisation – the Role, Management and Deployment of Police Staff in England and Wales*. London: Home Office.

Her Majesty's Inspectorate of Constabulary (HMIC) (2005) *Closing the Gap: A Review of the 'Fitness for Purpose' of the Current Structure of Policing in England and Wales*. London: HMIC.

Her Majesty's Inspectorate of Constabulary (HMIC) (2009) *Get Smart: Planning to Protect. Protective Service Review 2009*. London: HMIC.

Home Affairs Committee (2007) *Police Funding.* Fourth Report, Session 2006–07. House of Commons Paper 553. London: TSO.

Home Affairs Committee (2008) *Policing in the Twenty-first Century.* Seventh Report, Session 2007–08. House of Commons Paper 364. London: TSO.

Home Office (2008) *From the Neighbourhood to the National: Policing our Communities Together.* Cm 7448. London: Home Office.

Home Office (2009) *Protecting the Public: Supporting the Police to Succeed.* Cm 7749. London: TSO.

Loveday, B., McClory, J. and Lockhart, G. (2007) *Footing the Bill.* London: The Policy Exchange.

May (2010a) Speech to the ACPO Conference, Manchester, 29 June. http://www.ukpoliceonline. co.uk/index.php?/topic/42596-theresa-mays-acpo-speech-in-full-money-red-tape-and-the-future/ [Accessed 12 July 2010]

May (2010b) Speech to the Police Federation Annual Conference, 19 May. www.polfed.org/ Home_Secretary__2010.pdf [Accessed 12 July 2010]

McNulty, T. (2007) House of Commons, 10 December, HC Debs, Vol 469, Col 90–92W.

McNulty, T. (2008) House of Commons, 21 January, HC Debs, Vol 470, Col 1777–1780W.

O'Dowd, Sir D. (2002) *Change Proposals to Increase the Presence of Police in Communities.* London: Policing Bureaucracy Task Force.

Ruffley, D. (2009) Speech in the House of Commons, 4 February, HC Debs, Vol 487, Col 858–864.

Singer, L. (2001) *Diary of a Police Officer.* Police Research Series Paper 149. London: Home Office Policing and Reducing Crime Unit Research, Development and Statistics Directorate.

Index